SURRENDER AND TRUST

A DEVOTIONAL JOURNEY
BOOK TWO

SURRENDER AND TRUST

A DEVOTIONAL JOURNEY
BOOK TWO

By DAVID THURMAN
with Pastor Daniel Martin

Printed by KDP Publishing, an Amazon.com company

Available on Amazon.com and other online stores

© 2021 W. David Thurman

All rights reserved. No part of this book may be reproduced in any form without the express written consent of the author.

ISBN-13: 978-0-9990492-5-9

THE CALL Logo and cover contribution by Mary Thurman

Cover Photograph: "Pensacola Morning" by David Thurman

"Unless otherwise noted, all Scripture quotations are from The ESV® Bible (The Holy Bible, English Standard Version®), copyright © 2001 by Crossway, a publishing ministry of Good News Publishers. Used by permission. All rights reserved."

Author's Note: Although a few illustrations may be allegorical, most of the stories in this book are true. Pseudonyms have been used for some persons in order to protect their privacy.

DEDICATION

"Behold, I make all things new" (Rev. 21:5)

TABLE OF CONTENTS

Further Matters For Your Devotional Journey . . . i
    Time With God xiii
    Ten Tips for Devotional Time . . . xiv
    Daily Examination xv
    I Surrender All *by Pastor Daniel Martin* . . xvi

SECTION III – TRUST

Week One: Contrition 3
Week Two: Sources of Pride 13
Week Three: The Shema 25
Week Four: Control 36
Week Five: Submission 47
Week Six: Love One Another 58
Week Seven: Judgment 71
Week Eight: Consolation and Desolation . . . 81
Week Nine: Offense 92
Week Ten: Power of Confession 104
Week Eleven: Power of Forgiveness . . . 117
Week Twelve: Goodness of God . . . 129
Week Thirteen: Practicum - Stillness . . . 139

SECTION IV – POWER AND GLORY

Week One: Power 149
Week Two: The Cup 159
Week Three: Weakness 171
Week Four: Triumph 181
Week Five: Refiner's Fire 192

Week Six: Leadership	203
Week Seven: Fear of Man	216
Week Eight: The Cave	227
Week Nine: Generational Thinking	239
Week Ten: Restoration	251
Week Eleven: Glory	261
Week Twelve: The Bride	271
Week Thirteen: Practicum – My People	279
Appendix A – Discernment: A Process for Making Godly Decisions	293
Appendix B – Meme's Keys to Restore Wounded Souls.	297
Appendix C – Engaging With Christ in Everyday Life - A Template *by Steve Parker*	299
Appendix D – List of Idols	307
Appendix E – Full Index of Devotions	308
Appendix F – Index of Scripture Passages	315
Appendix G – Bibliography	319

FURTHER MATTERS FOR YOUR DEVOTIONAL JOURNEY

(Please read this instructional section before you begin the devotions)

I. REVIEW

Book Two of *Surrender and Trust* contains *Section III – Trust* and *Section IV – Power and Glory* of the devotional journey. Because the devotions are written in a progression, I highly recommend that you go through the devotions in Book One before you begin Book Two.

Book One contained an instructional section for the devotions, **Preliminary Matters For Your Devotional Journey**. In this second instructional section, we are trying to build on **Preliminary Matters**. So this instructional section will repeat some of the instructions from Book One and add to them. Please read ALL of this instructional section before you proceed to the devotions.

From the outset, I need to be clear that these devotions are Christian devotions. My personal beliefs arise from orthodox doctrine (such as the Apostles' Creed) and are Trinitarian in confession – that the one true God is Triune existing in the Persons of the Father, the Son, and Holy Spirit. These devotions reflect these beliefs which define references to God or to the Lord.

II. REASONS TO ENGAGE IN A DEVOTIONAL LIFE

The reasons for a daily personal devotional time are so numerous, they cannot all be listed. But here are a few compelling reasons for devotions:

A. <u>INTIMACY</u>. In life, we enter into intimacy through cultivated relationship. I get to know you; we spend time together; we share our experiences, our thoughts, and our history; we do things together; and we have disagreements and resolve them. As we do these things, our relationship moves to deeper and deeper levels until it reaches a point of intimacy. There is intentionality to it.

A daily devotional time cultivates my relationship with the Lord. Through faithfulness in devotion, I develop depth of relationship unto intimacy.

B. <u>HEART MONITOR</u>. My heart is not static. As I go through each day, my heart moves closer to the Lord and my heart moves further away from Him. A daily devotional time monitors the state of my heart each day and helps to adjust my heart to the right place to start the day. It is a form of "attitude adjustment."

A mature Christian has an awareness of God in everyday living. This awareness grows as the thoughts and intents of my heart are reviewed often.

C. <u>TRANSFORMATION</u>. God's plan is that I change, grow, and mature unto fullness in Him. Through my devotional time, God changes me.

During my time with God, He shows me sin, shame, dysfunctions, and other challenges in my life. I don't know they exist until I take time to seek Him and to expose myself to Him. He then lovingly helps me to address them and to grow in holiness and in knowledge of Him.

God also shows me gifts and strengths that He has given me. He helps me to apply them in my life and in the lives of others. Through devotion, God reveals myself to me.

D. <u>ILLUMINATION AND REVELATION</u>. In my devotional time, God illuminates scripture to my heart. He makes a path from my head to my heart through which I don't just know scripture but it becomes a part of me. God instills wisdom inside of me.

God also gives me guidance which is direction from God that is specific to me or to others. In devotions, I seek God for His will and He answers in ways that I otherwise miss if I were not spending the time with Him.

E. **OTHER REASONS**. There are many other reasons for devotions – worship, peace, joy, encouragement, conviction, repentance, discipline, resource, seeking, waiting, knowledge, and creativity. But my existence is wrapped up in God. Devotions are fundamentally about Him and not about myself.

See *Time With God* which follows this section for more reasons for a devotional life.

III. THREE MAJOR KEYS

As you enter into this journey, there are three major keys that facilitate the journey and enhance the impact of the journey. Please attend to these keys now because they will prove to be immensely helpful to you as you enter in.

A. <u>TIME</u>. The first key is to reserve time each day for your devotion. I call it "dedicated time." To reserve time, you need to rework your schedule and routine. Dedicated time needs to be a priority! You will get out of these devotions what you put into them. The primary devotion in devotions is the dedication of time to the Lord.

Many of the devotions in this book incorporate the personal devotions of Pastor Daniel Martin, who is a pastor in Selma, Alabama. In 2011, God put it on Pastor Martin's heart to set aside an hour each day for prayer, seeking, and worship. As you read Pastor Martin's devotions, you realize the incredible impact on his life of his commitment to dedicate time to the Lord.

The recommended time for daily devotions is an hour a day. But that can be a goal if you are starting a devotional life. You can build toward it. A strong recommendation though is a <u>minimum</u> of 30 minutes a day. If you treat this devotional book as a "5 minute boost" then you will get 5 minutes of value from it. This devotional book is written for meaningful dedicated time.

B. <u>COMPANION</u>. The Biblical mandate for a spiritual journey is to take a companion – a coworker. A companion provides direction, accountability, protection, and encouragement. God did not intend for us to journey alone. In the kingdom of God, persons who function alone ("lone wolves") are actually vulnerable sheep and are prime targets for slaughter.

Going on this devotional journey with a similarly committed companion is the second key to this journey and it is a <u>strong</u> recommendation. Each person has individual devotional time each day, then meets with the companion regularly (recommendation: weekly if possible) to discuss the devotions, thoughts and experiences, issues, and insights, and to pray together.

If possible, please find a mentor or spiritual director who will journey through the devotions with you. As part of The Call ministry residency for which this devotional was written, each resident is assigned a mentor who serves as a guide, a teacher, a resource, and a coworker. If you do not have a mentor (or a spiritual director) who can journey alongside you, then find a friend or a peer whom you trust as a devotional partner. But a mentor or spiritual director that can give you guidance and insight is recommended.

It is also possible to go through this journey together with a small group. Because intimacy and vulnerability are encouraged though, the group needs to be close, trustworthy, and accountable to one another. An atmosphere of freedom, grace, and acceptance is essential.

C. <u>JOURNAL</u>. The third key to this devotional journey is to keep a daily journal of your devotional time. A journal assists in defining thoughts, recording experiences, and remembering important principles and applications. A regular review of the journal is a good reminder of things I have learned, seen, and applied.

This book has some places for notes and for thoughts. But these places are not intended to serve as a journal. My primary recommendation is to maintain a computer journal in a word processing file. A computer journal is in one place and it can be easily revised, expanded, or printed.

The personal devotions of Pastor Martin were written on a computer. Pastor Martin revisited his devotions regularly as a personal reminder to himself and to add to them. He reviewed his devotions monthly, and then often revisited them a year later. Many times he added to them. Sometimes he wrote summaries of a week or a month to remind himself to practice their applications. If the Lord was dealing with him in a certain area of his life, he came back to the same journal entry day after day. Pastor Martin's wonderful devotions are available to us today because he faithfully kept a journal of them on his computer.

Some people prefer to write rather than to type. That also is fine. But please keep a daily journal whether it is in digital form or in written form.

IV. <u>DEVELOPING A DEVOTIONAL TRACK</u>

Time dedicated to the Lord is a spiritual discipline. We want devotion to become a daily habit that is woven into our journey so finely that it becomes part of our fabric.

A devotional track is a regular pattern or course that is used for daily devotions. A devotional track is a guide to assist you in growing in this discipline. Developing a regular devotional track can encourage consistency and can increase the benefit from the time dedicated to the Lord.

The suggested track below has five phases:

A. OPENING.

B. READING EXERCISE.

C. MEDITATION.

D. JOURNAL.

E. CLOSING.

Because you are using *Surrender and Trust* as a devotional, you already are doing the middle three phases – Reading Exercise, Meditation, and Journal. To complete the devotional track, add an Opening and a Closing. In fact, you may already be doing them instinctively.

So the suggested track is relatively easy with *Surrender and Trust*. Here is a more detailed description of the suggested devotional track:

A. <u>OPENING</u>.

The opening transitions me from the busyness of my life to a focus on God and His kingdom. The opening prepares me for an experience of God and of His love. The purpose of the opening is to turn from the busyness of my life and to close down the thoughts, feelings, and attitudes that it engenders; and to turn toward God and focus my heart, mind, and soul on Him.

Eliminate distractions. Find a place of privacy and quiet for your time with God. You are alone with Him. Turn off cell phones, televisions, or other devices that distract you. Dedicated time is <u>uninterrupted</u> time with God.

My suggested opening: (1) Surrender > (2) Worship > (3) Presence.

1. <u>Surrender</u>. Surrender is yielding every part of my being to Jesus. I try to submit my mind, heart, body, and whole being to God. I verbalize to God that I surrender myself fully to Him. Then I search myself to see whether there is an area in which I am not surrendered.

I appeal to you therefore, brothers, by the mercies of God, to present your bodies as a living sacrifice, holy and acceptable to God, which is your spiritual worship.

Do not be conformed to this world, but be transformed by the renewal of your mind, that by testing you may discern what is the will of God, what is good and acceptable and perfect. **Rom 12:1-2**

Did you hear what Paul just said? Surrender is a key to discerning the will of God in your life – by testing and discerning. Surrender is a key to being who I am in God. That is one reason the devotional is named *Surrender and Trust*.

2. <u>Worship</u>. Worship is an acknowledgement of God and of Who He is – in song, in spoken word, in meditation, or in physical action. Worship changes my focus from myself and puts it on the Lord. Worship changes my perspective and helps me let go of my cares and burdens, and to give them to the Lord.

Worship is a good method to center myself (some call it "recollection"). Center helps eliminate outside distractions, cares, and issues, and looks inward to God's dwelling. Worship invites God into my outlook and adjusts my self-perception to put me in right standing with God and with other humans.

As I come before God, worship also encourages me to acknowledge and confess my sins to God. I may need to repent and to receive forgiveness.

3. <u>Presence</u>. In presence, I ask the Holy Spirit to be present – in me and around me. Presence invites God into my heart, mind and body. Presence asks the Lord to envelope me in His Spirit so that I can abide in Him in a tangible and transformative way. I want His Presence to last through the day.

Other possible elements for the Opening can be found in Possible Devotional Elements (Section V) below, including Examination, Confession, Desired Grace, and Thanksgiving.

B. <u>READING EXERCISE</u>.

In *Surrender and Trust*, the reading exercise is the heading, scripture, theme, illustration, and application in the daily devotion.

1. <u>Headings</u>. Each devotion has a heading which shows the section, the week and day, and the topic of the week. *Surrender and Trust* at the time of

publication has four major sections of 13 weeks each (52 weeks total). The sections are:

BOOK ONE

Section I – Faith, Hope, and Love

Section II – Surrender

BOOK TWO

Section III – Trust

Section IV – Power and Glory

Each week has a different topic that is covered. The topic for the week is shown in the heading.

Please note that the date in the heading of each devotion is blank. The date is blank so that the reader can begin the devotional journey at any point in the year. Some devotional books start with January 1, but our residency programs begin at different times of the year. So your journey can begin when you are ready. Please write the date of each daily devotion in this blank when you do the devotion.

2. Scripture. Below the heading of each devotion is the scripture for the day. Every person reads scripture differently, but the primary goal is to incorporate the scripture in such a way that it becomes reality in your heart and in your life.

Please read the scripture carefully and slowly. Some people like to read the scripture quickly, and then go back and read it slowly. That is fine. Other people like to read repetitively – reading the scripture multiple times to allow it to sink in. The manner in which you read scripture is fine as long as you allow time for the Holy Spirit to speak through the scripture or to highlight certain portions of it to you.

Note your feelings as you read the scripture. Sometimes I am drawn toward the scripture in a positive way. Other times I don't feel good about what the scripture says. Attraction or repulsion toward scripture is important for discernment. It may say something about my heart or about my thought process. Try to discern the reason for these movements if they occur.

Other times you may be struck by, or drawn toward, a certain theme, phrase, or even a word in the scripture. If that occurs, take time to dwell on it. Allow the Holy Spirit to quicken that portion to you and to illuminate it divinely to your heart.

3. Theme and Illustration. In most devotions, a one line theme will appear

below the scripture passage followed by an illustration (in bold) such as a story, a quote, or most often, a personal devotion of Pastor Martin. Pay attention to the theme and illustration as they provide guidance for the devotion. But you are not bound by them. If the Holy Spirit prompts you to focus on a different theme or aspect from the scripture, that is fine.

4. Application. The body of the devotion is the application. The application is one or more points about the theme for the day. Carefully consider these points as you read them.

C. MEDITATION. The end of the devotion is a suggested meditation. The focus and method of the meditation will vary. Setting aside a block of time (at least 10-15 minutes) each day for the meditation is recommended. Use the meditation for a time of quiet and of listening to the Holy Spirit.

Other possible elements for a Meditation can be found in Possible Devotional Elements (Section V) below, including Waiting, Contemplation, Imagination, and Love. Most of these elements are incorporated into one or more of the Meditations in Book Two.

D. JOURNAL.

Write in your journal thoughts, insights, questions, movements, or applications that you received during the devotion. Although your feelings are not your guidepost, your feelings can be instructive so record your feelings during the devotion.

Review of my journal helps me recall areas of movement or of desire. A regular review – weekly and then monthly – allows me to see ways in which God has worked in me or spoken to me through my time with Him.

Every seventh day is a review day. This day is a chance to go back over the past week and review what the Lord has been doing over the course of the week. Keeping your journal faithfully is very important for this review. Take time to review your journal entries over the past week and note any prominent themes, patterns, or applications. The seventh day affords the opportunity to explore an area over the past week in more detail.

I keep a journal on the computer. In my review, when I note something important, I put an asterisk by the entry. That way, I can easily go back and explore it further.

E. CLOSING.

Closing usually involves a prayer that arises from the daily devotion and then looks forward to prepare me for the day. Some people, though, prefer a formalized prayer like the Lord's Prayer or portions of The Shema (See III.Week Three for The Shema). You then end your time of devotion and look forward to the day, keeping the devotional theme in mind to apply.

V. POSSIBLE DEVOTIONAL ELEMENTS.

Below is a list of spiritual exercises or practices that you may want to try or to incorporate into your devotional track. I recommend that you review them and determine which, if any, may be helpful to you as your journey continues. Books on some elements are listed that give much more detail.

1. Surrender. Surrender is actively yielding every part of my being to God – every thought, every desire, every organ, and every cell (Rom 12:1-2).

2. Center (or Recollection). Center helps eliminate outside distractions, cares, and issues, and looks inward as God's dwelling place. Center tries to put me in right standing with God and man by concentration on the Holy Spirit in my core. Center changes my focus from this world and puts it on the Lord.

3. Worship. Worship is an acknowledgement of God and Who He is – in song, in spoken word, in meditation, or in physical action. In worship, I exalt, praise, and lift Him up (Psa 22:3).

4. Examination. A regular examination reviews and discerns my words, my actions, my heart, and my desires. Examination can lead to other elements such as joy, confession, repentance, or seeking (2 Cor 13:5). Many devotional practitioners use a daily examination to monitor movements of the heart and spirit. (In his *Spiritual Exercises*, St. Ignatius described steps in a General Examination of Conscience ("Examen") – an examination of my life generally, and a Particular Examination of Conscience – steps to examination of a particular area of focus or emphasis. See *Daily Examination* after this section for suggested steps in a daily examination of awareness.)

5. Confession. Confession acknowledges and discloses my sins to God. During confession, I seek and receive forgiveness, and I repent with a commitment to change so that I do not repeat my sin (James 5:16).

6. Desired Grace. A desired grace is something that I am seeking from God for my life, for the day, or for my journey such as a special touch, a virtue, or a blessing.

7. Presence. Presence invites God into my heart, mind, body, and soul. Presence asks the Lord to wrap me in His Spirit so that I abide in Him in a tangible and transformative way. God is around me all the time. Presence is simply a recognition of His company. See *Present Perfect* by Gregory A. Boyd.

8. Reading. Reading includes scripture or other inspirational material that I want to understand and to instill in my life. Repetitive reading is a good way to make it part of me and to plant it in my heart. (For a method of reading and applying scripture that has existed for centuries, research and explore

Lectio Divina - "divine reading.")

9. <u>Meditation</u>. Meditation focuses the mind and heart on a specific thought. The thought can be a word, an image, a scripture, or a person.

10. <u>Listening</u>. Listening is quieting my own prayer and asking for God's direction, guidance, or insight. Through listening, I seek illumination, revelation, or prompting.

11. <u>Love</u>. Love focuses on the relationship of love between me and God. During the time of love, I receive God's love for me and I love God with all my heart, mind, soul, and strength. See *Practicing the Presence of God* by Brother Lawrence.

12. <u>Imagination</u>. Asking the Holy Spirit to direct my mind, imagination explores a story in the Bible, an event, or a desired outcome. You can imagine the thoughts and feelings of the characters involved. See *Journey With Jesus* by Larry Warner (based on *The Spiritual Exercises of St. Ignatius*).

12. <u>Contemplation</u>. In contemplation, I "blank" my mind, emotions, and physical feelings so that I can experience God in my soul and in my spirit. I eliminate any sensory or mental stimulation so the Holy Spirit can move without interference from my flesh, my mind, or my imagination. See *The Ascent of Mount Carmel* by St. John of the Cross.

13. <u>Journal</u>. In my journal, I write down what God shows me each day. Journal helps me define what I am feeling, thinking and experiencing, and also helps me remember it.

14. <u>Waiting</u>. Waiting is setting aside time to wait on the Lord. That time can be dedicated to worship or to service. But fundamentally, I wait on the Lord to speak, to move, or to act (Isa 40:30-31).

15. <u>Seek My Face</u>. The Lord often encourages His followers to seek His face (or countenance) (Psa 27:8). Seeking the Lord is not only seeking His Presence and His Being through a deep desire for Him, but it also seeks His favor on my life.

16. <u>Thanksgiving</u>. A time dedicated to give thanks and to express gratitude to God (Psalm 136).

17. <u>Hymnology</u>. The study and use of hymns and their words to inspire worship and glory. See *Amazing Grace – 366 Inspiring Hymn Stories for Daily Devotions* by Kenneth W. Osbeck. Pastor Martin uses hymns in his devotions often. A good example is *I Surrender All* by Pastor Martin which follows this instructional section.

18. <u>Physical Expression</u>. Devotional elements such as worship, meditation, or

seeking can be enhanced through physical or artistic expression. Dance, physical positions, drawing, or other tangible expression can add meaning or depth to other devotional elements.

19. <u>Memorization</u>. Memorization of scripture or of prayers can provide a basis for meditation, reflection, or application. Memorization, and then repetition, helps to make scripture a part of you and helps you apply it to your life. Some Christians even chant scripture or prayer, or use portions of them as a meditative mantra.

20. <u>Aids</u>. Use of aids such as worship music, devotional videos, or inspirational talks can be useful for devotional time. Feel free to sing along or to speak portions of the content.

21. <u>Mentor</u>. Meeting regularly with a mentor or a spiritual director is a valuable practice. Wisdom, insight, direction, and correction are some of the benefits from this relationship. A healthy mentoring relationship can make a huge difference in the life of a believer.

VI. <u>FREEDOM</u>

There is freedom in developing a track and there is freedom to change the content some, little, or none. Each person is fearfully and wonderfully made. Part of that wonder (and fear) is that each person is different. You should cultivate time dedicated to the Lord that suits your life and your journey.

If you are thriving from what you are presently doing, then don't make any changes. You have freedom! My suggestion is to consider the devotional track that is described above. You can try it and then change it if you wish, or try other devotional elements listed above and weave them into your devotional time. Be careful to dedicate time to the Lord daily, but also walk in freedom in doing it.

One important freedom is that you can stay on the same devotion for more than one day – especially if you sense changes are being made in your heart, your life, your lifestyle, or your disciplines. If you want to take time to explore the devotion topic and its application more thoroughly, then spend two or three days on it. Because the devotional dates are blank, you can pick up the next devotion when you have explored the prior devotion fully. Book One and Book Two contain a total of 365 devotions. But take the time you need to absorb the devotion. You are *in no way* limited to a year to complete this devotional.

But there is a danger to freedom. Let me encourage you not to use freedom as an excuse to neglect your daily devotional time or to stop your personal devotions. Devotional time is vital to your journey with the Lord. Be faithful and consistent in it.

VII. EXPECTATIONS

In Book Two of *Surrender and Trust*, some Meditations focus more on meditative, contemplative, or listening elements of devotion. During these times, spend time silently alone with God.

Every person has a different devotional experience. One trend though that many devotional writers have noted as the devotional life develops is a trend from active effort to passive waiting. Initially, the devotional life requires effort in quieting your thoughts and emotions as you grow in the discipline of focus on the Lord or on the meditation. This effort is an active engagement.

As you grow in the discipline though, you learn to relax, let go of control, and allow God to move within you as He desires. This absence of mental stimulation or emotional effort is more passive and contemplative. Many devotional writers assert that the deeper experiences occur as we learn to be more passive – to the point of almost a blank or "empty" of everything except the Lord.

During your Meditations, God may move dramatically or inspiringly. Or he may move softly and gently. Or there may just be silence. But He is present. Allow Him to be present with you and to move as He wants. Allow Him to be God and see yourself as His faithful servant fully surrendered to His ways and His plan for your life and your soul.

Try to diminish expectation that God move in a certain way. The point is to wait and to be mindful of His Presence, and to live in His Presence. It is almost paradoxical. Sometimes we worship Him and bow before Him because He is God. But He also is our constant companion. So other times we need to be still, acknowledge His companionship, and simply BE with Him.

VIII. A FINAL WORD

The final word is to give yourself grace in growing in your devotional life. During this journey over time, you will experience ups and downs. You will have moments of inspiration and of joy. At other times, you may feel nothing or may get discouraged. Persevere!

Also, my mind wanders. I have been doing devotions for many years, and my mind still wanders. If your mind wanders during your devotional time, it is okay. Do not beat yourself up over it. When you catch it, simply bring yourself back to the devotion. If you can pick up where you left off, then do so. If you need to start the devotion over, then do that. Give yourself grace in the devotional discipline. The Lord knows your heart in it.

Don't allow the devotion to minister condemnation to you. If the Holy Spirit convicts your heart, then be convicted and address the conviction appropriately with repentance and a commitment to change. But the purpose of this journey is to avail yourself of grace. God gives grace – abundant grace. Give yourself grace as well. [1]

Let's continue with our devotions!

---

[1] Many thanks to Eileen Crusan, Spiritual Director/Supervisor, with the Emmaus Center for Spirituality, Charlotte, NC (www.emmauscenterforspirituality.com) for her generous review and input on this instructional section.

TIME WITH GOD

Time with God daily is necessary for me to:

1. Discern the movements of my heart.
2. Increase in my knowledge of Him.
3. Live daily in the presence of the Lord.
4. Hear His word for the season of my life.
5. Correct my fluctuating attitudes and emotions.
6. Yield myself fully to Him.
7. Bring me back into right standing before Him.
8. Find direction and purpose for my life.
9. Reveal my own heart to yourself.
10. Be instructed in God's ways.
11. Renew my mind.
12. Reorient me to God and to His thoughts.
13. Walk with God as the king of my heart.
14. Allow God's love to infuse me so I can likewise love other people.
15. Sense the times that the Holy Spirit gives me a gentle nudge instead of using the baseball bat that I normally require.[2]

---

[2] Unless otherwise attributed, stories and material are by the author.

TEN TIPS FOR DEVOTIONAL TIME

1. Be honest with yourself and with God. God knows the thoughts and intentions of your heart anyway so be as honest with God and with yourself as you can. Don't try to "hide" from God.

2. Eliminate all distractions during devotional time. No TV; cell phone and computer off; be alone in a place of quiet.

3. If your mind wanders during your devotional time, don't beat yourself up. Receive grace and just come back to where you were in your devotion.

4. You may need to slow down your mind or emotions to enter into the devotional time. You can use imagery or relaxation exercises to take your mind off of worldly matters.

5. Don't focus on time. Allow the devotion to flow naturally. Sometimes most of the devotional time is preparation of your heart. Other times it is spent on the scripture. Other times it is worship and meditation. Allow yourself to be led by the Holy Spirit in your time.

6. Reference the devotional instructions above often for guidance.

7. Give your devotional life time to develop. If you feel lost or overwhelmed, then take comfort in the normalcy of that. Give yourself time to grow in your devotional life.

8. Ask for revelation of the root cause of sin or problems in your life. Part of surrender is vulnerability. Be prepared to be exposed or even torn apart as the Holy Spirit works in your heart to address issues, to heal your heart, and to pour Himself into it.

9. Just listening. Abide in His presence and listen. God moves all around us. He is always working in our lives. We need to develop sensitivity to those movements. There are interior movements (such as whispers to our mind or a tug on our heart) and exterior movements (such as circumstances of our life). We need quiet reflection and patient alertness to detect God's movements. Pay attention to the movements of your heart and your mind. Important things are often soft and gentle. Jesus is gentle with us and He is patient.

10. Grace, grace, and more grace.

DAILY EXAMINATION

(An examination used daily, or even multiple times daily, can assist in discerning the movements of your heart and spirit, and can develop spiritual sensitivity to areas of challenge and struggle. The examination can help you to walk closer to the Lord each day, and enhance experiences of awareness, repentance, grace, forgiveness, and reconciliation.)

Step #1. Ask the Holy Spirit to show you the joys and blessings of the last 24 hour period. Give thanks to God for the grace He has given to you and for favor that He has shown you. Offer a heart of thanksgiving!

Step #2. Ask the Holy Spirit for the grace of wisdom, of discernment, and of insight about your life in the last 24 hour period. Ask Him to "shine a light" on your heart and your life.

Step #3. As you explore the last 24 hours, ask the Holy Spirit for the grace to see times and places in which you have been aligned with God and have acted out of love for Him. Then ask to see times and places in which you moved away from God or failed to act out of a love for Him. First, examine your thoughts; second, examine your words; finally, examine your actions. You are taking account of what you thought, what you said, and what you did.

Step #4. Based on what you notice in Step #3, ask the Holy Spirit to help you see honestly and without condemnation, what causes you to stray from God's love and friendship. With deep sincerity, ask for forgiveness from God and for help to overcome the causes of your straying.

Step #5. As you look to the next 24 hour period, ask the Holy Spirit for help to keep you aligned with God and with God's desire for you. Ask for grace for needed change of your thoughts, words, and actions, and that you might notice, with honesty and humility, where you fall short of His will for you.

End the examination with the Lord's Prayer.[3]

---

[3] Source Material: *The Spiritual Exercises of St. Ignatius*, §24-43 pp. 15-23 (Translated by Louis J. Puhl, S.J.)(Loyola Press 1951). For further material on spiritual discernment and decision making, see Appendix A - *Discernment: A Process for Making Godly Decisions*.

I SURRENDER ALL

By Pastor Daniel Martin

During this time (11/23/20-11/26/20), I gave much thought to the battles fought by Abraham before he started toward Mt. Moriah, and by Jesus in Gethsemane. Two very related events.

1 All to Jesus I surrender,
All to Him I freely give;
I will ever love and trust Him,
In His presence daily live.[4]

O Savior, please come and open up my life. Open it up to Yourself, so that You and You alone are Master of this life, this body, this soul!

Open it up so that You have full Control, so that I have NO control.

O when I surrender to what You want, to Nothing that I want, at that point real LIFE can begin to flow. Until I reach that point my flesh is always waiting in the wings to undercut, undermine all the glorious, powerful, LIFE-GIVING things You have in store for me and my world.

I do not want my flesh to be in that position.

I want what You want to be the first priority – the Only priority in my life.

O Bring me to this place! Then Keep me in this place!

Yes, I know it will require a one time, full commitment of All the kingdoms, areas, desires of my life! But it will then require a Daily, Hourly commitment of the same.

This death, the cross, will have pain come with it.

But O, the much higher pain, loss, regret, fears, and deep negative clouds which overhang a life of partial commitment, surrender, yielding—which is really No SURRENDER except to myself.

O the freedom and glory which come with a full Self Sacrifice!!

O I want this Freedom, this Sacrifice, this Sacrifice of ALL, ALL, ALL!!!

Refrain:
I surrender all, I surrender all;
All to Thee, my blessed Savior,
I surrender all.

I surrender all to THEE.

O the glory of going from "I" to "THEE"!

It seems almost I can hear this conversation going on inside me—

---

[4] *I Surrender All* by Judson W. Van De Venter (Public Domain 1896).

Flesh: "But what about ME??!!"

My spirit: "Shut up, flesh! You are stupid! You care nothing for "me," the eternal me, the me who was saved by the total surrender of the Son of God! The "me" who is my Soul!

"You care nothing for the future, only the present, fleeting, fading, tiny thrill you give me as it robs me of all the valuables in my life, leaving me empty and full of loss, pain, regret, and fears—all so you can momentarily get what you want—which doesn't ever satisfy you in the long run.

"And besides, flesh, My Choice to Surrender ALL To Jesus, will be what is best for you, what eventually blesses, pleases, delights and releases glory to you in the long run.

"Surrender in the short haul requires giving up trinkets, trifles, empties, to gain the Eternal Treasures (also "here and now") which come from Giving ALL, resulting in down the road, gaining ALL!

"So flesh, cool it! You are not going to get your way.

"I want my Lord, the One Who really cares about me, really wants the Best for me, to have Full Control, while you, flesh, have No Control.

"With You in control, I am a wreck waiting to happen, led by flimsy, stupid, ignorant, desires which end in great loss, pain, disaster, even to you, flesh!

"The only sane way to travel in this life, is in total surrender to the One Who really cares about me!"

O Jesus, come and assist me to all day long today surrender ALL to You. Do it in bite sizes.

All I have to surrender is this Hour, this Time, and its Choices to You!

2 All to Jesus I surrender,
Humbly at His feet I bow;
Worldly pleasures all forsaken,
Take me, Jesus, take me now!

O the power of these words!! ALL - it is not surrender until it is ALL! But that is okay, the only things which are Safe in my life are those which are Totally in Your Hands. What I keep in my hands is in great danger of being marred, spoiled, ruined, Lost!

O help me to Humbly Bow, (there is no way to truly bow, except Humbly). All other bowing is not really bowing. Humbly bowing is releasing TOTAL control of my life to You and Your plans.

A recognition of who is the sheep, and Who is Lord, the Good Shepherd! A sheep who is totally ignorant, totally weak, totally not able to steer this life correctly.

O the key of this line:

Worldly Pleasures ALL Forsaken. Worldly Pleasures All FORSAKEN!

Forsaken WHY?
- So they will not ruin, wreck, mess up my life.

- So they will not have the control over me which keeps me from rising into all God has for me!
- So they will not be lord.
- So Jesus, the One who really cares about everything in my life, can be in Total Control!

O, Take Me, Jesus! Take me Now! Come in and take me, Come in and Take Over!

Ending this morning (11/23/20) with this thought:

Surrender is Not surrender, until Surrendering is Happening!

Not just the thought of it, but the DOING OF IT!

3 All to Jesus I surrender,
Lord, I give myself to Thee;
Fill me with Thy love and power,
Let Thy blessing fall on me. [Refrain]

ALL to You I surrender. What is left out of the word "ALL"? Nothing. When I surrender ALL, that means everything!

There are some things I may have the title to, some things I can quickly claim again as my own. But Not if I am Surrendering ALL!

If I Am Surrendering ALL... there is nothing I can claim, if You call for it.
- Nothing I Have.
- Nothing I Am.
- Nothing I Want.
- Nothing I Own.

Even my Desires, Ambitions, Aims, Plans, Hopes, Dreams! All must be surrendered to You.

ALL of My Time! ALL of my Choices!

HOW can He claim it all? I tell Him He can! Otherwise there is no surrender!

How dangerous is this? Very Dangerous to all that I want to cling to, to claim as my own, that my flesh feels is absolutely necessary!

Then WHY should I Surrender ALL?
- Because Jesus first surrendered ALL for me!
- Because He is FOR me in the strongest sense of this word!
- Because ALL He calls for is for My Good in the long run—the only run which really counts.
- Because whatever I hold onto, I lose, whatever I freely give I get to keep in the long run.
- Because the opposite of surrender to You is so horrible, so destructive, so evil.

To not surrender to You is to Rebel against You, the only One Who gave up all for my good!

Yes, there are "dangers" in surrendering, unknowns, fears about what might happen to my flesh. But there are even greater unknowns, greater fears, regrets, anguishes, etc. in NOT Surrendering.

After all, when I say NO to You,
- I am on my own.
- I have to take care of myself from that point.
- I, who can do Nothing, now am responsible for Everything! Impossible!!

When I say NO to You, from that point on, all glory begins to leave my life. I am miserable, discontented, dissatisfied, and groaning within over what I am losing. And I took over so I would NOT lose. Living unsurrendered is always losing!

Those who refuse to surrender to You, ALWAYS Lose! (Ask Balaam, the rich young ruler, etc).

Those who endure the pain and loss of surrendering, ALWAYS Win!! (Ask Abraham and Isaac).

So, I, TODAY, must begin making up my mind that I will surrender to whatever You put Your finger on TODAY!!

Today is the only day I can surrender.

I can't surrender yesterday—whatever it is, it is in the books.

But I can surrender today, what I failed to surrender yesterday. And I Must!

I can't surrender tomorrow, it is not here.

I can surrender all TODAY!

Please shepherd me, whatever that requires, into FULL Surrender to You, This Day, blessed Savior and Friend!

Lord, I give myself to Thee; O Jesus, I declare this. I proclaim it. I want it to be SO!

But saying it is not the same as DOING it!

I must DO it!

I must do it in the PRESENT, in the NOW! Until that happens there is NO Surrender!

Yesterday's surrender will not cover today.

O Jesus, please show me exactly HOW from where I am, I need to Surrender in every issue, every detail, every part of my life!!

As the second verse said,

"Take me, Jesus. Take me NOW!"

Fill me with Thy love and power. O Yes! Please fill me with Your Love!

Could this be one of the keys to being able to surrender, when it is very difficult? Being Filled with Your LOVE!!??

Absolutely! Yes! It is a key!

When my mind is filled with a knowledge and depth, experiencing and taking in Your LOVE, that lifts me. I am no longer focusing on what the surrender costs. (That always cripples surrender, makes me weak and futile in all attempts at surrender!)

But when my focus is on...
- Your love for me.
- All You surrendered for me.
- How Much You are FOR me.
- How much You CARE for me.
- How blessed and pleased it makes You when I surrender...

Suddenly the grind of the surrender becomes lost in the Glory and Splendor which always accompanies surrender!

Let Thy blessing fall on me. O Savior, please let Your Blessing fall on me!

SIGHT!

Being able to see that the above words about Your love and its ability to birth DESIRE to surrender in me.

Being able to SEE the Glory, Delight, and Future that surrender always opens up to me.

FREEDOM!!

Freedom to shed the cloaks of fear, worry, regret, and anguish over surrendering!

There comes a time when I must just DO it!

O help me to Know that there is GLORY ahead, no matter how far out in the future it is, no matter what the temporary pain of the loss of what I surrendered, that GLORY is just ahead.

O the instant glory of the fact that the act is now done, that I have surrendered, even though there may be, will be loss and pain involved.

Always where there is surrender there is also a deep understanding of the GLORY of the loss of:
- Anguish
- Anxiety
- Fear
- Dread
- Regret of Not Surrendering, fearing the future because where there is no surrender, the future is very fearful on my own, when I can do Nothing without You!

JOY!!!

O the Glory of the JOY and PEACE which flood when the surrender is done, and all is well.

The truth came to me that Abraham, walked to Mt. Moriah with JOY, because he at that point had fought whatever battles he had to fight to say "Yes" to what You told him.

Once they were on their way, and the issue was totally settled with him about what he was going to do, there was a JOY in the Journey, not because of what he was going to have to do, but in knowing it was going to happen, and that it was going to End Well!

O for the JOY, FREEDOM, and SIGHT I need to actually accomplish the surrender!!

4 *All to Jesus I surrender,*
Make me, Savior, wholly Thine;
May Thy Holy Spirit fill me,
May I know Thy power divine.

O Blessed Redeemer, You who fought the battle of surrender over and over again. Leaving Heaven. Coming to earth. Enduring all You endured as You walked this earth, able to cancel the program at any time, but You didn't come to fail in surrender.

You came to succeed in TOTAL surrender! (This is the power behind the Philippian truth that caused You to be given a name which is above ALL names, to which ALL things must bow!!)

You fought the battle in Gethsemane! O what a Fight this was! A Real fight!

Surrender Your Holiness, Righteousness, Purity---LOSE all of that and take on the full weight of all the evil, ugly, foul, wicked, unholy, unrighteous things I and my world have done, just so we, those who were in so much opposition to You, could come to You, live in Your Presence forever, be known as Yours?!!

Gethsemane is "surrender battle ground."

The place most battles are fought are not on the battle field, but on the Battleground of SURRENDER before the other battle begins.

When the surrender battle is won, before the "real" battle is fought, the "real" battle has also been won, although not on the visible field!

O the GLORY of the battles which are won on our knees, before the "real" battle ever shows up.

Help me JESUS to TOTALLY Surrender ALL to You, so that the battle which has not yet been waged, has actually already been won, on the field of SURRENDER!!

There is a sense that Abraham was already winning, had already accomplished the victory in his surrender before he left home. It appeared to have been won on the top of the mountain, but it was really won in the deep valley of coming to the place of Surrendering, before he ever left home.

O help me to increasingly win the battle between my ears, the battle of the mind, the battle of the Struggle!

O help me to remember that the SOONER I simply give in, give up, Surrender to You, the sooner the trauma, the angst, the fear, the dread totally leave.

O the GLORY of Surrender! Even in the "losing" stages!

Where surrender to You takes place, there is always GLORY, LIFE, PEACE, no matter how much or what conflict is caused by the surrender. (And there is often great conflict, loss, cost involved in Surrender.)

But the GLORY of surrender begins to show up even when the glorious results are not seen at all. There is great glory and victory in the surrender itself, even though the flesh may be screaming and yelling.

There is no other feeling like the feeling of peace which comes when the process has taken longer than it should, when the inner struggle has been fierce, when the "not my will, but Thine" has been difficult and postponed too many times—and then at the point of full surrender, there is an "Ahhhh" even though the outer turmoil created by the surrender is raging.

5 All to Jesus I surrender,
Make me Jesus wholly Thine,
Fill me with Thy Holy Spirit,
Truly know that Thou art mine.

O the GLORY of Your Presence, that Presence which floods at the point of surrender.

Come, Spirit of God, and help me, work in me that TOTAL Surrender whose fullness cannot be described.

Bring me to that place where I truly Know that You are Mine, which was preceded by me saying to You that I am totally Yours! I want it!

I want to Embrace it, knowing that the sooner I embrace it, the Sooner its glory begins to flow and take over in me!

O God, help me to SURRENDER ALL to You!!

O how I must have this in my life.

Without it, I fall apart, my world falls apart, my growth in You not only stops, it is stunted, cannot do anything but sag.

Show Me Please exactly what You want me to SURRENDER this New day, hour by hour.

Give me mind and will to DO it, regardless of how Small or how Large! They are ALL important.   -Pastor Daniel Martin, 11/23/20-11/26/20

SECTION III – TRUST

Week One: Contrition

Week Two: Sources of Pride

Week Three: The Shema

Week Four: Control

Week Five: Submission

Week Six: Love One Another

Week Seven: Judgment

Week Eight: Consolation and Desolation

Week Nine: Offense

Week Ten: Power of Confession

Week Eleven: Power of Forgiveness

Week Twelve: Goodness of God

Week Thirteen: Practicum – Stillness

STOP!
Please read instructions in Further Matters before you begin these devotions. The guidelines are important!

NOTES:

SECTION III – TRUST: WEEK ONE

III.Week One, Day 1 (Date:)   **CONTRITION**

> Enter into the rock and hide in the dust from before the terror of the LORD, and from the splendor of his majesty.
> The haughty looks of man shall be brought low, and the lofty pride of men shall be humbled, and the LORD alone will be exalted in that day.
> For the LORD of hosts has a day against all that is proud and lofty, against all that is lifted up—and it shall be brought low;
> against all the cedars of Lebanon, lofty and lifted up; and against all the oaks of Bashan;
> against all the lofty mountains, and against all the uplifted hills;
> against every high tower, and against every fortified wall;
> against all the ships of Tarshish, and against all the beautiful craft.
> And the haughtiness of man shall be humbled, and the lofty pride of men shall be brought low, and the LORD alone will be exalted in that day. **Isa 2:10-17**

The Lord alone shall be exalted in that day.

The second Temptation of Jesus occurred at the pinnacle of the Temple. The temptation was to jump so that Jesus' power and status could be put on display when the angels protected Him from harm. It was a temptation to put on a show – a little demonstration to the faithful at the Temple of just Who Jesus was.

The second Temptation appealed to the pride of life. The pride of life takes many forms: self glory, self promotion, self exaltation, reputation, status, superiority, self congratulation, self adoration, self reliance, self determination beauty, or vanity. The devil appealed to Jesus' sense of identity in relationship to his fellow humans.

But Jesus didn't react based on humans, the impact on humans, what humans thought, or how humans would respond. His answer focused not on humans, but on God: "*You shall not put the Lord your God to the test*" (Matt. 4:7). Jesus judged His actions based on His relationship with God, not based on how people would perceive Him.

Jesus understood that to the Lord alone belong glory, exaltation, reputation, congratulation, and praise. Jesus was devoid of self exaltation and of the aspects of pride that accompany it. Jesus did not pursue vainglory.

Meditation: We spent a week at the end of Section II seeking the Lord for the flow of the Holy Spirit. Over the next two weeks, we will be seeking the Lord for the grace of a deeper revelation of Himself – a "desired grace."

Today is a day of exaltation of the Lord. Seek an attitude void of pride. Write in your journal about the glory, splendor, majesty, reputation, and beauty of God. Then eliminate distractions and spend time in exaltation of the Lord. Lift up Him alone.

☦   ☦   ☦   ☦   ☦   ☦   ☦

NOTES:_____

III. Week One, Day 2 (Date:)   **CONTRITION**

> Thus says the LORD: "Let not the wise man boast in his wisdom, let not the mighty man boast in his might, let not the rich man boast in his riches, but let him who boasts boast in this, that he understands and knows me, that I am the LORD who practices steadfast love, justice, and righteousness in the earth. For in these things I delight, declares the LORD." **Jer 9:23-24**

To worship God in truth is to acknowledge Him to be what He is,
and to acknowledge ourselves to be what we are.

To worship God in truth is to acknowledge Him to be what he is, and to acknowledge ourselves to be what we are. To worship Him in truth is to acknowledge with heartfelt sincerity what God truly is: infinitely perfect, worthy of infinite adoration, infinitely removed from any sin, and so on, for all the divine attributes. The man who does not employ all powers to render to this great God the worship that is due Him is not being guided by reason.[5]

The deeper the revelation of God and of His attributes - His power, His strength, His splendor, His glory, His beauty, and His love - the less there is of self, of pride, of vainglory, and of reason to boast. A person who has even a slight comprehension of God fears Him alone and does not have any regard for himself or herself. My humility increases as my true knowledge of the Holy One increases.

Meditation: Write down the names of God that come to mind such as "The Almighty," "The Alpha and the Omega," "The God Who Is Near," or "I Am That I Am."

After you have made your list, meditate on those names and on what they mean. Journal about what those names mean to you and about what those names reveal to you about Him.

✠   ✠   ✠   ✠   ✠   ✠   ✠

> Please remember to journal regularly as part of your devotional discipline. A journal helps define your thoughts and keeps a record for later use and sharing.

---

[5] Thomas a Kempis, *The Imitation of Christ*, p. 66 (Moody 1958).

III. Week One, Day 3 (Date:)   **CONTRITION**

> "Woe is me! For I am lost; for I am a man of unclean lips..." **Isa 6:5a**
> And when I saw it, I fell on my face... **Eze 1:28b**
> "I had heard of you by the hearing of the ear, but now my eye sees you; therefore I despise myself, and repent in dust and ashes." **Job 42:5-6a**
> "Depart from me, for I am a sinful man, O Lord." **Luke 5:8b**
> When I saw him, I fell at his feet as though dead. **Rev 1:17a**

Therefore I despise myself, and repent in dust and ashes.

These reactions came from men who received a deep and glorious revelation of God. These are all great men of God – Isaiah, Ezekiel, Job, Peter, and John. They already had knowledge of the Lord. But when confronted with the awesome power, glorious splendor, holiness, and magnificent majesty of The Almighty, they were awestruck, dumbfounded, penitent, and groveling. They all had a contrite reaction.

Revelation of the divine not only reveals God to me, but revelation of the divine reveals me to myself. I need to see God properly in order to see myself properly. It is like a reflection. Revelation of God exposes me for who I am – my flesh as but dust and my heart as sinful and impure. Revelation of the divine compels me to contrition. That revelation leaves no room for pride or self glory.

> **Meditation:** Today is a day of humbling yourself before the Lord. Pray for the Lord to reveal Himself to you, and to reveal yourself to you. Then kneel, bow, or prostrate yourself before Him. Spend time before the great, awesome, and holy majesty of our God.

> Remember grace as you seek humility and contrition. The revelation of God reveals our fallen nature, but the revelation of God also reveals His love and His grace. The Holy Spirit can minister powerful conviction, but He does not minister condemnation to those persons who are in Christ Jesus.

III. Week One, Day 4 (Date:)　　　　　　　　　　　　**CONTRITION**

> The fear of the LORD is instruction in wisdom, and humility comes before honor. **Pro 15:33**

Fear of You and humility.

Proverbs 15:33 - Fear of the Lord teaches wisdom; humility precedes honor.

O God, let these 2 become big and growing in me—

FEAR OF YOU and HUMILITY!!

How I NEED these two!! Come and teach me, show me, lead me, in the development of them both. Show me things I do, say, think, and meditate that hinder their growth, work contrary to them, etc. I need these two active and alive in me. Come and have Your way with them in my life!!

Help me to CHOOSE the fear of You and humility at every point!

Deliver me from pride and the fear of man. I have dwelt with them and encouraged them, embraced them and delighted in them for far too long. Deliver me from their strangle holds and give me the Godly, life-giving ways of fearing You and living in deep humility! I NEED YOU MORE...!!!

Remove all corrupting fears from me.

Place within me all fear of You that is so clean, pure, and empowering!! (Strange, that fearing You actually EMPOWERS me!! But it is true!)　　　–Pastor Daniel Martin, 12/12/15

Today we revisit the counsels of St. John of the Cross on how to enter a deeper walk with the Lord.

> Endeavor to be inclined always:
> Not to the easiest, but to the most difficult;
> Not to the most delightful, but to the most distasteful;
> Not to the most gratifying, but to the less pleasant;
> Not to what means rest for you, but to hard work;
> Not to the consoling, but to the unconsoling;
> Not to the most, but to the least;
> Not to the highest and most precious, but to the lowest and most despised;
> Not to wanting something, but to wanting nothing.
> ...for Christ, desire to enter into complete nakedness, emptiness, and poverty in everything in the world.[6]

---

[6] St. John of the Cross, *The Ascent of Mount Carmel*, I.13.6 (From *The Collected Works of St. John of the Cross*, Kavanaugh and Rodriguez (ICS Publications 1991)).

St. John of the Cross counsels me to seek not to the most, but to the least; not to the highest and most precious, but to the lowest and most despised. These counsels are based not upon self condemnation, but upon a revelation of the Lord and the manner in which it also reveals myself to me.

> **Meditation:** Spend time with these counsels and discern how they apply to you and your life. Write in your journal how these counsels can find application in your life. Then surrender your life to the Lord and ask for His grace in walking with Him.

☩ ☩ ☩ ☩ ☩ ☩ ☩

NOTES:_____

_____

_____

_____

_____

_____

_____

_____

_____

_____

_____

III. Week One, Day 5 (Date:)   CONTRITION

> The saying is trustworthy and deserving of full acceptance, that Christ Jesus came into the world to save sinners, of whom I am the foremost. But I received mercy for this reason, that in me, as the foremost, Jesus Christ might display his perfect patience as an example to those who were to believe in him for eternal life. **1 Tim 1:15-16**

I am the foremost of sinners.

This testimony comes from Paul, the great apostle. Paul had a wonderful revelation of Jesus. And he also had a deep revelation of himself and the amazing grace which he received.

St. John of the Cross offers further guidance to the believer who desires a closer walk with the Lord.

But, to insure that we give abundant enough counsel, here is another exercise that teaches mortification of concupiscence [lust] of the flesh, concupiscence of the eyes, and pride of life, which, as St. John says, reign in the world and give rise to all the other appetites (1 Jn. 2:16).

First, try to act with contempt for yourself and desire that all others do likewise.

Second, endeavor to speak in contempt of yourself and desire all others to do so.

Third, try to think lowly and contemptuously of yourself and desire that all others do the same.[7]

This guidance requires caution in its application. But it does make sense – if the believer has the self awareness to view himself as the foremost of sinners.

Not long after I read this guidance, I represented an adoption agency in a hotly contested case about termination of parental rights. When an attorney for the other side rose to deliver her closing argument, that attorney argued the facts of the case. Then, she turned and began to attack me. Some questions I had asked during the trial concerned her. In these modern times, what constituted a family, and the contexts of parenting a child, had expanded. My views were obviously old-fashioned, antiquated, and wrong.

As I sat there being castigated, I thought "Wow, Lord! You are helping me apply this guidance from St. John of the Cross quickly, aren't You?"[8]

---

[7] *The Ascent of Mount Carmel*, I.13.9.

[8] Unless otherwise noted, stories and illustrations are by the author.

Meditation: *"Love does not boast."* Spend time with the guidance from of St. John of the Cross above. Think about how it might apply to you. Journal about it. As you go through the next few days, keep this guidance in mind and try to find contexts in which you can apply it.

☦ ☦ ☦ ☦ ☦ ☦ ☦

NOTES:_____

_____

_____

_____

_____

_____

_____

_____

_____

_____

_____

_____

_____

III. Week One, Day 6 (Date:)   **CONTRITION**

> Live in harmony with one another. Do not be haughty, but associate with the lowly. Never be wise in your own sight. **Rom 12:16**

Associate with the lowly.

God protects the humble and delivers him (James 4:6; Job 5:11). He loves and comforts the humble; unto the humble man He inclines Himself; unto the humble He gives great grace; and after his humiliation He raises him to glory. Unto the humble He reveals His secrets (Matt. 11:25), and sweetly draws and invites him unto Himself. The humble man, though he suffer confusion, is yet perfectly in peace; for he rests on God and not on this world.

Do not think that you have made any progress, unless you esteem yourself inferior to all.[9]

The heart of the Lord is close to the poor and broken. The heart of the Lord is close to the humble and lowly. To draw closer to the Lord, I need to humble myself. To receive revelation of the Lord, I need to humble myself.

> **Meditation:** Read the quote above slowly. Underline each time it conveys the concept that God draws close to the humble person. What does it say about the heart of God that He draws close to the humble person?
>
> Next, meditate on the last sentence of the quote. Consider how you view yourself in relationship to other persons. Write down what the Lord shows you in your journal.

✠   ✠   ✠   ✠   ✠   ✠   ✠

> If you have not already identified a mentor, spiritual director, or devotional partner, please work on it now. It is important to go through this devotional with another believer who can give you input and guidance. Wisdom commands it and humility desires it.

---

[9] *The Imitation of Christ*, p. 67.

III. Week One, Day 7 (Date:) **CONTRITION**

> And Mary said, "My soul magnifies the Lord,
> and my spirit rejoices in God my Savior,
> for he has looked on the humble estate of his servant. For behold, from now on all generations will call me blessed;
> for he who is mighty has done great things for me, and holy is his name.
> And his mercy is for those who fear him from generation to generation.
> He has shown strength with his arm; he has scattered the proud in the thoughts of their hearts;
> he has brought down the mighty from their thrones and exalted those of humble estate;
> he has filled the hungry with good things, and the rich he has sent away empty.
> He has helped his servant Israel, in remembrance of his mercy,
> as he spoke to our fathers, to Abraham and to his offspring forever."
> **Luke 1:46-55**

Today is a review day. Read back over your journal for this week.

Meditation: Today meditate on the prayer of Mary, *blessed among women* (Luke 1:42). This prayer is called the Magnificat of Mary. As you slowly read it, note how the might and magnificence of the Lord parallel the humility of His creation. Then join with this prayer in magnifying the Lord.

☩ ☩ ☩ ☩ ☩ ☩ ☩

NOTES:_____

_____

_____

_____

SECTION III – TRUST: WEEK TWO

III.Week Two, Day 1 (Date:)   **SOURCES OF PRIDE**

> For Adam was formed first, then Eve; and Adam was not deceived, but the woman was deceived and became a transgressor. **1 Tim 2:13-14**

Adam was not deceived.

O God, You just had the word "humility" to come across my consciousness. Help me to humble myself before You, to diligently go for humility in every area of my life. O how much I need Humility.

As I go for humility several things happen:

- Pride loses more of its grip on me.
- You give grace to me.
- I understand and see more clearly. (Pride BLINDS me so horribly, causing me to see what is not there, and to not see what IS there!)
- I feel Your presence and pleasure more.
- I become freed from things that have bound me so horribly in the past.
- I have a clearer view of You.
- I can move forward unencumbered with all the weights that pride place on me! –Pastor Daniel Martin, 7/26/13

This scripture describes the Fall of Man. It is a difficult passage because it states that Eve was deceived but Adam was not deceived. Yet Adam still sinned.

My interpretation is that Eve was beguiled in such a way that she was not consciously aware that her transgression was wrong. Adam, on the other hand, knew perfectly well it was wrong, but he partook anyway. The source of Adam's sin was pride which resulted in disobedience and rebellion. Adam wanted to be like God so he obeyed his will instead of God's will.

Any time that I engage in self glory, self promotion, self exaltation, self congratulation, vanity, or vainglory, I become a thief. All glory, praise, exaltation, and adoration belong to God. When I try to appropriate those things for myself, I seek to grasp something that belongs only to God. This is one reason why pride is so repulsive to God that He keeps His distance. *For though the LORD is high, he regards the lowly, but the haughty he knows from afar* (Psa 138:6). My pride is fundamentally rebellion against God.

Meditation: Today we continue to seek the Lord for a deeper revelation of Himself in humility. Think back over the last few days for any thoughts or acts of pride or self promotion. Repent of them. Seek the Lord for the grace of humility. Tell the Lord: "I want to know You. My seeking You is grounded in humility before You."

☦ ☦ ☦ ☦ ☦ ☦ ☦

NOTES:_____

_____

_____

_____

_____

_____

_____

_____

_____

_____

_____

_____

_____

III. Week Two, Day 2 (Date:)　　　　　　　　　　**SOURCES OF PRIDE**

> "There was a rich man who was clothed in purple and fine linen and who feasted sumptuously every day. And at his gate was laid a poor man named Lazarus, covered with sores, who desired to be fed with what fell from the rich man's table. Moreover, even the dogs came and licked his sores.
> The poor man died and was carried by the angels to Abraham's side. The rich man also died and was buried, and in Hades, being in torment, he lifted up his eyes and saw Abraham far off and Lazarus at his side. And he called out, 'Father Abraham, have mercy on me, and send Lazarus to dip the end of his finger in water and cool my tongue, for I am in anguish in this flame.'
> But Abraham said, 'Child, remember that you in your lifetime received your good things, and Lazarus in like manner bad things; but now he is comforted here, and you are in anguish. And besides all this, between us and you a great chasm has been fixed, in order that those who would pass from here to you may not be able, and none may cross from there to us.'
> And he said, 'Then I beg you, father, to send him to my father's house—for I have five brothers—so that he may warn them, lest they also come into this place of torment.'
> But Abraham said, 'They have Moses and the Prophets; let them hear them.'
> And he said, 'No, father Abraham, but if someone goes to them from the dead, they will repent.'
> He said to him, 'If they do not hear Moses and the Prophets, neither will they be convinced if someone should rise from the dead.'" **Luke 16:19-31**

You in your lifetime received your good things.

Wealth and the social status that accompanies wealth are sources of pride. Because of wealth, many live on estates, the "right" neighborhoods, or in gated communities to keep out the "undesirable elements." Our cities and communities wall off the poor, just as the rich man in this parable kept out Lazarus who sat at his gate. The rich man spurned Lazarus and used his wealth for his own pleasure.

It is hard to love the Lord when I love my possessions and my social status.

I tend to view my possessions as my own, to do with and to use as I see fit. This view is wrong and deceptive. There is a common myth – the myth of the "self made" man. When I "succeed" in life and acquire things, I believe that I am their source and cause. In fact, many people such as parents, mentors, teachers, and associates have contributed to my "success." That is one reason why possessions should be used for the good of the community, not just for the individual (Acts 2:44-45).

The truth is that I do not own anything. All possessions, just like all glory and adoration, belong to the Lord. Even more, I take pride when I decide to give a small portion of my possessions to the Lord. That also is false pride.

"Who has first given to me, that I should repay him? Whatever is under the whole heaven is mine" (Job 41:11).

> **Meditation:** Identify five things that you own that you deem precious. Write them down in your journal and write the reason why each thing is precious to you.
>
> Next, surrender those possessions to the Lord. For each possession, tell the Lord that He owns that possession and He can do with that possession whatever He pleases. Take special note of your thoughts and feelings as you tell Him that. How much pride do you take in each possession?
>
> Finally, consider Lazarus, who received bad things in this life, but in death was carried by the angels to Abraham's side. How do you identify with Lazarus?

☦ ☦ ☦ ☦ ☦ ☦ ☦

NOTES:_____

_____

_____

_____

_____

_____

_____

_____

III. Week Two, Day 3 (Date:)   **SOURCES OF PRIDE**

> "Therefore, O king, let my counsel be acceptable to you: break off your sins by practicing righteousness, and your iniquities by showing mercy to the oppressed, that there may perhaps be a lengthening of your prosperity."
> All this came upon King Nebuchadnezzar.
> At the end of twelve months he was walking on the roof of the royal palace of Babylon, and the king answered and said, "Is not this great Babylon, which I have built by my mighty power as a royal residence and for the glory of my majesty?"
> While the words were still in the king's mouth, there fell a voice from heaven, "O King Nebuchadnezzar, to you it is spoken: The kingdom has departed from you, and you shall be driven from among men, and your dwelling shall be with the beasts of the field. And you shall be made to eat grass like an ox, and seven periods of time shall pass over you, until you know that the Most High rules the kingdom of men and gives it to whom he will."
> Immediately the word was fulfilled against Nebuchadnezzar. He was driven from among men and ate grass like an ox, and his body was wet with the dew of heaven till his hair grew as long as eagles' feathers, and his nails were like birds' claws.
> At the end of the days I, Nebuchadnezzar, lifted my eyes to heaven, and my reason returned to me, and I blessed the Most High, and praised and honored him who lives forever, for his dominion is an everlasting dominion, and his kingdom endures from generation to generation; all the inhabitants of the earth are accounted as nothing, and he does according to his will among the host of heaven and among the inhabitants of the earth; and none can stay his hand or say to him, "What have you done?"
> At the same time my reason returned to me, and for the glory of my kingdom, my majesty and splendor returned to me. My counselors and my lords sought me, and I was established in my kingdom, and still more greatness was added to me.
> Now I, Nebuchadnezzar, praise and extol and honor the King of heaven, for all his works are right and his ways are just; and those who walk in pride he is able to humble. **Dan 4:27-37**

Those who walk in pride He is able to humble.

Sincerity is nothing but humility and you acquire humility only by accepting humiliations. All that has been said about humility is not enough to teach you humility. All that you have read about humility is not enough to teach you humility. You learn

humility only by accepting humiliations. And you will meet humiliation all through your lives. The greatest humiliation is to know that you are nothing. This you come to know when you face God in prayer. When you come face to face with God, you cannot but know that you are nothing, that you have nothing. In the silence of the heart God speaks. If you face God in prayer and silence, God will speak to you. Then you will know that you are nothing. It is only when you realize your nothingness, your emptiness, that God can fill you with himself.[10]

Power is an endless source of pride. Because of my power, I garner admiration, adulation, and flattery for myself...not that I seek them. With power, I not only bend the truth, I create reality and twist "facts" to make my own truth it as it suits my ends.

Through power, I manipulate others. They serve me, my selfish interests, and my desires.

Power makes me feel as if I am immune from the rules that apply to others. One of my business partners had walked in places of great political power. He used to tell me "Power is the greatest aphrodisiac there is!"

Power, even power in a church, has a corrupting influence on human morals and human perception. In this story, Nebuchadnezzar was warned of his fall in a dream which Daniel interpreted. Nebuchadnezzar was given an opportunity to repent and to change. Daniel exhorted the king to practice righteousness and to show mercy to the oppressed as countermeasures to his pride. But the king still stumbled.

Meditation: Think of a time in your life when you experienced power or popularity with the people around you. Now consider the impact that power or popularity had on you. How did the situation go? What happened? Write in your journal about it.

Next, ask God to reveal His power to you. Seek Him for revelation of His power, might, strength, and dominion. Discern your status before an Almighty God.

Remember to eliminate all distractions as you engage with the devotions. This time is dedicated to God. Part of that dedication is to set aside the time and to focus only on Him – His will, His desires, His work.

[10] Mother Teresa, *Total Surrender* p. 111 (Servant 1985).

III. Week Two, Day 4 (Date:) **SOURCES OF PRIDE**

> For the word of the cross is folly to those who are perishing, but to us who are being saved it is the power of God. For it is written, "I will destroy the wisdom of the wise, and the discernment of the discerning I will thwart."
> Where is the one who is wise? Where is the scribe? Where is the debater of this age? Has not God made foolish the wisdom of the world? For since, in the wisdom of God, the world did not know God through wisdom, it pleased God through the folly of what we preach to save those who believe.
> For Jews demand signs and Greeks seek wisdom, but we preach Christ crucified, a stumbling block to Jews and folly to Gentiles, but to those who are called, both Jews and Greeks, Christ the power of God and the wisdom of God.
> For the foolishness of God is wiser than men, and the weakness of God is stronger than men. **1 Cor 1:18-25**

The foolishness of God is wiser than men.

As for me, since I am poor and needy, let the Lord keep me in His thoughts. Help me to have the humility today to know and recognize my weaknesses and needs.

<u>**Help me to know just how little I know and just how little I can do without You!**</u>

Then help me to know that You are all I need in the middle of my weaknesses and needs, that You are more than enough to make up for my lack.

O what a wonderful and rich store of salvation, wisdom, knowledge, strength, guidance, and life are in You!! Help me to draw all day long from this rich store, ABIDING in You hour by hour and letting WHO/WHAT You are, be enough for me.

Thank You for my helplessness that makes me cling to You, love You, and depend on You. I love You, Lord!!   –Pastor Daniel Martin, 1/5/13

My intellect is important. I use it to consider, to analyze, and to reason. My intellect is one thing that distinguishes me from animals. It makes me superior.

But intellect is a source of great pride. At institutions of higher learning, there is an occasional display of elitism, disdain, snobbery, and superiority that brilliance breeds. My belief that I am smarter than another person is a source of personal comfort and of self congratulation.

Knowledge and pride are bedfellows. *This "knowledge" puffs up, but love builds up* (1 Cor 8:1). Reason can feed my pride, and is in return corrupted by the pride in my heart. In fact, pride's deception prevents me from realization of how much the pride in my heart influences my reason. So the Cross becomes foolishness to the mind of humans and its sacrificial nature becomes weakness to humans.

But I do not know God through wisdom alone. Acquisition of knowledge does not equate to faith. Wisdom can point me to God, but one believes "with the heart" (Rom 10:10). At some point, pride and intellect must join with the heart. At that point, the word of the Cross becomes the power of God.

> **Meditation:** Today, as part of your desire to receive a deeper revelation of God, surrender your intellect to Him. Take your mind, your thoughts, your imagination, and your creativity, and give them over to God. Yield them completely to Him.
>
> Then spend time in silence and emptiness of mind before Him. If you need a focus, focus on the Holy Spirit within you. But spend time in communion with God, void of a thought life (unless you are certain the thought was implanted by Him). If your mind wanders, don't fret. Just bring it back. Try it for a block of time (15-30 minutes to start).
>
> This exercise is difficult for many, but it is similar to what many call contemplative prayer. Trust Him in the emptiness.

Those who want to reach union with God should advance neither by understanding, nor by the support of their own experience, nor by feeling or imagination, but by belief in God's being. For God's being cannot be grasped by the intellect, appetite, imagination, or any other sense; nor can it be known in this life.[11]

╬ ╬ ╬ ╬ ╬ ╬ ╬

NOTES:_____

_____

_____

_____

_____

_____

---

[11] *The Ascent of Mount Carmel* II.4.4, p. 160.

III. Week Two, Day 5 (Date:)   SOURCES OF PRIDE

> I have written something to the church, but Diotrephes, who likes to put himself first, does not acknowledge our authority. **3 Jn 1:9**

He likes to put himself first.

The description of Diotrephes uses a Greek word that only appears here in the Bible. Some translations say "loves to have the preeminence" (MKJV). But the Greek word means "loves (or fond) of being first."

Preeminent status and reputation feed my ego. But competitiveness can also feed my flesh and push me to be on top. It is easy to fall into the trap of focusing on my standing among men rather than remaining mindful of my ongoing need of grace before God.

A. W. Tozer says:

It [the veil] is woven of the fine threads of the self-life, the hyphenated sins of the human spirit. They are not something we do, they are something we are, and therein lies their subtlety and their power.

To be specific, the self-sins are self-righteousness, self-pity, self-confidence, self-sufficiency, self-admiration, self-love and a host of others like them. They dwell too deep within us and are too much a part of our natures to come to our attention till the light of God is focused on them. The grosser manifestations of these sins - egotism, exhibitionism, self-promotion - are strangely tolerated in Christian leaders, even in circles of impeccable orthodoxy.[12]

> **Meditation:** Begin your meditation by asking God to focus His light on your heart. Review the self-sins listed by Tozer one by one. Write in your journal what God shows you about each one.
>
> Then ask God about your competitiveness. Consider times that a competitive spirit has caused you to disrespect another person, to trash talk, or to act like a jerk. Spend time loving God and receiving His love as you submit your competitive pride to Him.

✟   ✟   ✟   ✟   ✟   ✟   ✟

> Be assured that God is working in your heart as you seek Him and dedicate time to Him. He will operate with perfect love.

---

[12] A. W. Tozer, *The Pursuit of God* p. 29 (N/P 1948).

III. Week Two, Day 6 (Date:)   SOURCES OF PRIDE

> "And I pleaded with the LORD at that time, saying,
> 'O Lord GOD, you have only begun to show your servant your greatness and your mighty hand. For what god is there in heaven or on earth who can do such works and mighty acts as yours? Please let me go over and see the good land beyond the Jordan, that good hill country and Lebanon.'
> But the LORD was angry with me because of you and would not listen to me. And the LORD said to me, 'Enough from you; do not speak to me of this matter again. Go up to the top of Pisgah and lift up your eyes westward and northward and southward and eastward, and look at it with your eyes, for you shall not go over this Jordan.'"
> **Deut 3:23-27**

This story hurts my heart.

In the book of Numbers, the congregation of Israel moved from one rebellion to another (Num 11, 12, 14, and 16). Then, Moses' beloved sister, Miriam, died (Num 20:1). Immediately after Miriam's death, the people rose up against Moses and Aaron due to the lack of water (Num 20:2).

The glory of the Lord appeared and God instructed Moses to speak to the rock and it would yield water. Moses no doubt was an emotional wreck. Instead of strictly obeying and speaking to the rock, Moses struck the rock twice with his rod (the symbol of God's authority), and cried "Listen now, you rebels; shall *we* bring forth water for you out of this rock?" (Num 20:10-11). At that moment, he and God both knew that Moses had failed to honor God before the people and in his own heart (Num 20:12).

The consequences of this one act were dire. Because they did not honor Him as holy before the people, God informed Moses and Aaron that they would not be permitted to enter the Promised Land (Num 20:12). Understand the impact of this sentence upon Moses. His whole life consisted of preparation and fulfillment of a call - a call that would culminate by leading the people of Israel into the Promised Land. Moses was devastated. He begged God to relent and to allow him enter the Promised Land. It was the desire of his heart. But the Lord would not heed Moses' pleas and He finally told Moses, "Enough from you! Do not speak to Me about this matter again" (Deut 3:26).

Why was the Lord's discipline on Moses so harsh? Why did He hold Moses to such a high standard? The greater the authority granted to a disciple, the greater the responsibility upon that disciple (Luke 12:48). The greater the revelation of the glory of God, the more honor to God is required. God held Moses to a standard commensurate with his authority and revelation.[13]

---

[13] Excerpt from *The Call – Book Two (Progressive Fivefold Function)* (by the author).

My ministry can be a source of great pride. My spiritual gifts; my position or standing in the body; my intimacy with the Lord; or my influence among the saints – any of these areas can lead to self-congratulation or smugness, especially if the Lord has given me a special anointing or a powerful platform.

Pride is so subtle. We can engage in it and have no realization that it is enveloping us. We seek recognition and praise. We love it when other people tell us how godly we are, or what good things we have done. It makes us feel good about ourselves. One minute we are focused on God and His glory. The next minute we are focused on our own recognition.

There is no room in my ministry for pride or self glory. The deeper the revelation of the Lord to His servants, the stricter is His standard regarding pride or self glory.

> **Meditation:** "Oh God, my prayer is that my ministry glorify You and You alone. Please keep me from self glory, self promotion, and self exaltation. Let all that I do point to You and to You alone. Help me, O God, for I am flawed. I like the idea of standing out and of being special. Please keep me from these faults, O God. Keep me mindful of You and You alone – not of myself and not of my status or of my power. All glory, praise, honor, and power belong to You."

╬ ╬ ╬ ╬ ╬ ╬ ╬

NOTES:_____

_____

_____

_____

_____

_____

_____

_____

III. Week Two, Day 7 (Date:)   **SOURCES OF PRIDE**

Review your journal entries over the past two weeks.

> **Meditation:** Focus on areas of your life that the Lord has exposed that you need to change. How does each area relate to deeper revelation and knowledge of the Lord?
>
> Then focus on Him and the revelations of Himself that He has shown you. Dwell on these areas and give thanks to Him for His goodness in sharing Himself with you.

☩ ☩ ☩ ☩ ☩ ☩ ☩

NOTES:

SECTION III – TRUST: WEEK THREE

III.Week Three, Day 1 (Date:)   **THE SHEMA**

> "Hear, O Israel: The LORD our God, the LORD is one.
> You shall love the LORD your God with all your heart and with all your soul and with all your might. And these words that I command you today shall be on your heart.
> You shall teach them diligently to your children, and shall talk of them when you sit in your house, and when you walk by the way, and when you lie down, and when you rise.
> You shall bind them as a sign on your hand, and they shall be as frontlets between your eyes.
> You shall write them on the doorposts of your house and on your gates." **Deut 6:4-9**

Hear, O Israel!

Help me to OBEY what I hear You say!

Lord, help me to go beyond listening, to harkening—harkening defined as listening with the full intention of obeying and doing whatever I heard requires me to do. I see from Men's Fraternity that this is a great weakness in my life—getting excited about what can be from what I have heard, but never acting on it to see the life coming from it. – Pastor Daniel Martin, 1/27/11

This scripture is the seminal passage of The Shema (along with Deut 11:13-21 and Num 15:37-41) – a prayer historically recited by devout Jews daily.[14]

The word "Shema" is translated "Hear!" But that word meant more than that. It also meant to heed, to harken, being obedient, and doing it. In fact, many times in our English translations, the word "Shema" is actually translated "obey."[15]

Obedience may be why Jesus called it a "commandment" when He quoted from the Shema (Matt 22:35-40). Loving God is something that commands attention – the type of attention that is bound as a sign on our hands, as frontlets between our eyes, and written on the doorposts of our houses and on our gates.

---

[14] Gerhard Kittel (Editor), *The Theological Dictionary of the New Testament* Vol. I pp.218-219 (Eerdmans 2006).

[15] Source: http://norwayave.org/bill-mcdowell/2015/12/14/the-called-it-the-shema.

Devotion to God is a matter of obedience – an obedience that can wound our selfishness and our pride.

> **Meditation:** Make Deut 6:4-9 your prayer today. Recite it over and over. Ask the Holy Spirit to write it on your heart.

☦ ☦ ☦ ☦ ☦ ☦ ☦

NOTES:

III. Week Three, Day 2 (Date:)　　　　　　　　**THE SHEMA**

> And one of the scribes came up and heard them disputing with one another, and seeing that he answered them well, asked him, "Which commandment is the most important of all?"
> Jesus answered, "The most important is, 'Hear, O Israel: The Lord our God, the Lord is one.
> And you shall love the Lord your God with all your heart and with all your soul and with all your mind and with all your strength.'
> The second is this: 'You shall love your neighbor as yourself.' There is no other commandment greater than these."
> And the scribe said to him, "You are right, Teacher. You have truly said that he is one, and there is no other besides him.
> And to love him with all the heart and with all the understanding and with all the strength, and to love one's neighbor as oneself, is much more than all whole burnt offerings and sacrifices."
> And when Jesus saw that he answered wisely, he said to him, "You are not far from the kingdom of God." And after that no one dared to ask him any more questions. **Mark 12:28-34**

With all of your mind.

My son, trust not to your present feeling; it shall be quickly changed into another...

But he who is wise and well-instructed in the Spirit stands above all these changeful things, not heeding what he feels in himself or which way the wind of instability blows; but the whole intention of his mind makes progress to the due and desired end. For thus he will be able to continue throughout one and the selfsame and unshaken; in the midst of so many various issues the single eye of his intention being directed unceasingly toward Me.[16]

Jesus added something. In response to the question from the scribe (no doubt a learned man), he recited part of the Shema. But to loving with all of your heart, soul, and strength, He added "with all of your mind." Dr. Scot McKnight says that, as a good Jew, Jesus would have recited the Shema daily.[17] If Jesus recited the Shema daily, He knew its content. Why did Jesus add to it?

Part of the answer may be the Hebrew understanding of the heart. To a Hebrew, the heart was not only the source of emotion and feeling as some

---

[16] *The Imitation of Christ*, p. 159 (emphasis added).

[17] Scot McKnight, *The Jesus Creed* p. 8 (Paraclete Press 2009).

would think of it today; the heart was also the seat of desires, and of choices of the will. All human intellectual activity took place in the "heart."[18] This concept is not foreign to our experience. The heart commands the mind. In many rationalizations, the mind simply follows the heart and its desires (See II.Week Ten, Day 3).

In essence, the heart to the Hebrew was the core of all parts of human existence – all of the "inner man." We are commanded to love God with all of our inner being – our will, our intellect, and our emotion; the conscious and, to the extent we are able, the subconscious.

Thus, the Hebrew concepts in the Shema (both heart and soul) conveyed the idea "with all of your mind." So Jesus added something to the Shema. Or did He just clarify it for all of the persons who were not ancient Hebrews?

> **Meditation:** What does "all of your heart" mean to you? Write it down in your journal.
>
> What does "all of your mind" mean to you? Write it down as well.
>
> Then ask the Holy Spirit to show areas of your heart and mind that need change or repair in order to love God with all of your heart and with all of your mind.

☩ ☩ ☩ ☩ ☩ ☩ ☩

NOTES:_____

_____

_____

_____

_____

_____

_____

_____

_____

---

[18] Source: https://bibleproject.com/explore/shema-listen/.

III. Week Three, Day 3 (Date:)   **THE SHEMA**

> For whoever would save his life will lose it, but whoever loses his life for my sake and the gospel's will save it. For what does it profit a man to gain the whole world and forfeit his soul?
> For what can a man give in return for his soul? **Mark 8:35-37**

A loud cry in the ears of God.

For it is a loud cry in the ears of God, that ardent affection of the soul, when it says: "My God, object of my love, Thou art all mine, and I am all Thine."

Enlarge me in love, that with the inward palate of my heart I may learn to taste how sweet it is to love, and in love to be dissolved and to bathe myself. Let me be bound by love, mounting above myself, through excessive fervor and wonder. Let me sing the song of love, let me follow Thee, my Beloved, on high; let my soul spend itself in Thy praise, rejoicing through love. Let me love Thee more than myself, nor love myself but for Thee; and in Thee all that truly love Thee, as the law of love commands, shining out from Thyself.[19]

Many of Jesus' teachings focus on the soul and its relative worth. In those teachings, Jesus distinguishes between the relative value of life in this world - fleshly gratification, temporal existence, this mortal coil – and the inestimable value of the soul.

The Hebrew word translated "soul" can have a number of different meanings depending on context. But in the Shema, your "soul" is your entire being, your whole person, your essence, and the person that God created (See Comment on "soul" in I.Week Twelve, Day 7). The implication is that we love God with all and with everything – wholly, completely, and fully.

Meditation: Read the quote from *The Imitation of Christ* in the illustration above. Now, make this quote a prayer. You can change the prayer to make it your own. Then offer your prayer to God.

☊   ☊   ☊   ☊   ☊   ☊   ☊

> Spend the time that you need to explore and even to expand each devotion. These devotions are designed so you can spend more than one day on a devotion if God is moving.

---

[19] *The Imitation of Christ*, p. 105.

III. Week Three, Day 4 (Date:)   **THE SHEMA**

> "For you are a people holy to the LORD your God. The LORD your God has chosen you to be a people for his treasured possession, out of all the peoples who are on the face of the earth.
> It was not because you were more in number than any other people that the LORD set his love on you and chose you, for you were the fewest of all peoples,
> but it is because the LORD loves you and is keeping the oath that he swore to your fathers, that the LORD has brought you out with a mighty hand and redeemed you from the house of slavery, from the hand of Pharaoh king of Egypt." **Deut 7:6-8**

The Lord has brought you out with a mighty hand.

That caused me this morning to remember a song with the words:

Wonderful love! Wonderful love!
Wonderful love of Jesus!
Wonderful love! Wonderful love!
Wonderful love of Jesus![20]

Looked it up and was even further blessed and excited about the Powerful things I have because of the WONDERFUL LOVE OF JESUS!!

In vain in high and holy lays,
(Can't make the sense of "lays". Could be a meadow, a station/position, etc.)
My soul her grateful voice would raise;
For who can sing the worthy praise
Of the wonderful love of Jesus!

In whatever place, position, situation I find myself, no matter Why, no matter Where...My soul will raise a very grateful voice because of the WONDERFUL LOVE OF JESUS! You could have responded to us in our messes according to the filth, evil, ugliness in us, "our GUILT."

But that is not Your nature. Your nature is NOT to respond to us on the basis of our unworthiness, vile, evil, guilt...Your nature, LOVE, is to respond to us in LOVE, giving us, Placing on us, Worth and Value (John 3:16).

My soul, my entire being sings because of the depth I now see in Your love that I never saw before!

My heart Sings of the wealth, the massiveness of Your great LOVE for me this morning!

O, Jesus, Your love IS WONDERFUL!! WONDERFUL!!! WONDERFUL!!!!

---

[20] E. S. Lorenz, *Wonderful Love of Jesus* (Public Domain 1883).

*Wonderful love! Wonderful love!
Wonderful love of Jesus!
Wonderful love! Wonderful love!
Wonderful love of Jesus!*

O the Glory of the list of the things Your LOVE IS!

A *joy* by day,
a *peace* by night;
In storms a *calm*,
in darkness *light*;
In pain a *balm*,
in weakness *might*,
Is the wonderful love of Jesus!

And there is More! There is no limit to the Glory and Wonderful applications of this amazing LOVE, WONDERFUL LOVE, LIFE-GIVING LOVE!! It is also:

*My hope for pardon when I call,
My trust for lifting when I fall;
In life, in death, my all in all,
Is the wonderful love of Jesus!* -Pastor Daniel Martin, 11/28/20

When the Shema says "with all of your might (or strength)," the word for "might" is actually not a noun. It is an adverb that intensifies the meaning of other words. It means "very," "much," or "extremely." So in the Shema, it implies with muchness or with every effort. The Bible Project tells us that it means to love God with every possibility, with every opportunity, and with every capacity.[21] The ways of loving God have no limits.

God commands His people to love Him without limits – in every way. Consider what this means about the love that God has for us! His love for us is very, much, and extremely. His love for us involves every possibility, every opportunity, and every capacity. It is unlimited and it is wonderful!

We are His treasured possession.

> **Meditation:** Spend time with the devotion of Pastor Martin above. Allow God to show you every possibility, every opportunity, and every capacity of loving Him in your life.

☩   ☩   ☩   ☩   ☩   ☩   ☩

> This devotion contains another example of use of a hymn or song to enter into worship and meditation. Consider use of this practice.

---

[21] Source: *https://bibleproject.com/explore/shema-listen/*.

III. Week Three, Day 5 (Date:)   **THE SHEMA**

> If I have made gold my trust or called fine gold my confidence,
> if I have rejoiced because my wealth was abundant or because my hand had found much,
> if I have looked at the sun when it shone, or the moon moving in splendor, and my heart has been secretly enticed, and my mouth has kissed my hand,
> this also would be an iniquity to be punished by the judges, for I would have been false to God above. **Job 31:24-28**

I would have been false to God above.

The Shema is fundamentally about love, and Jesus emphasized that focus. But there was a related focus for the children of Israel. Israel was surrounded by religions that recognized many gods – polytheistic worship. If one god didn't work for you and give you what you wanted, then you could try another god – careful, of course, not to offend the gods that you had already adopted.

So when the Shema proclaimed *"The Lord your God, the Lord is one,"* it was a call to loyalty, to faithfulness, to allegiance, and to covenant. Don't go god-hopping! Don't be false to God above!

The ancient gods were "resources" to their polytheistic worshippers – one god controlled agriculture, another wealth, another power, and another love. You worshipped a god because you desired something from that god.

These same idols still exist today. They just take a different form. People still serve gods of power, gods of wealth, gods of control, gods of status, and gods of pleasure because their hearts desire those things. These gods rule in the heart, which is intended as the temple of the One True God, rather than in the manmade temples, shrines, and altars of the past.

Loving God completely and wholeheartedly means that no other gods have a place in my heart – a place that belongs only to Him.

Meditation: Meditate on loving God in terms of loyalty, faithfulness, allegiance, and covenant. Identify any areas of your heart that may vary or waiver from these virtues. Tell the Lord you want your heart to be fully devoted to Him in love. Ask Him how your heart can be fully devoted to Him.

III. Week Three, Day 6 (Date:) **THE SHEMA**

> But if we have food and clothing, with these we will be content.
> But those who desire to be rich fall into temptation, into a snare, into many senseless and harmful desires that plunge people into ruin and destruction. For the love of money is a root of all kinds of evils. It is through this craving that some have wandered away from the faith and pierced themselves with many pangs.
> But as for you, O man of God, flee these things. Pursue righteousness, godliness, faith, love, steadfastness, gentleness.
> Fight the good fight of the faith. Take hold of the eternal life to which you were called and about which you made the good confession in the presence of many witnesses. **1 Tim 6:8-12**

For the love of money is a root of all kinds of evils.

In his Spiritual Exercises, St. Ignatius imagines two standards (or banners) – the banner of Christ and the banner of Satan – and the respective hosts gathered thereunder. When Satan sends out his minions to draw people to his camp, Satan uses wealth, honor, and pride as his snares.

"First, they [Satan's minions] are to tempt them [people] to covet riches (as Satan himself is accustomed to do in most cases) that they may the more easily attain the empty honors of this world, and then come to overweening pride. The first step, then, will be riches, the second honor, the third pride. From these three steps, the evil one leads to all other vices."[22]

The progression that St. Ignatius describes is helpful because often the issues in our life occur due to progressions that a root cause generates. A love of money is a root cause that leads to honor which leads to pride.

Many other progressions also exist. One friend has described a personal need for affirmation stemming from lack of self esteem. The need for affirmation led to a fear of man which led to participation in a community of acceptance that engaged in unhealthy lifestyles.

Another friend has described a need for control due to a fear of failure. The need for control led to an inordinate desire for situations in which he was dominant and worshipped which led to a fantasy life filled with pornography.

But there is another impact of all of these temptations. Yielding to them can prevent you from loving God fully, completely, and wholly. Jesus focused many of His teachings on the snares of the world. Jesus did not want any hindrance to keep His disciple from fulfilling the Shema.

---

[22] *The Spiritual Exercises of St. Ignatius* §142, p. 61.

> **Meditation:** Consider the temptations with which you struggle. Identify sins on the surface, and then ask the Holy Spirit to reveal the attitudes of your heart that cause them. What are the root causes of temptation in your life? How can you uncover what leads to temptation and to sin?
>
> As the Holy Spirit reveals, write down the root causes and their progressions. Then seek the Lord about removal of them from your life. How can you keep your heart on track? Cry out for help. Tell Him you desire to love Him and Him alone.

✟ ✟ ✟ ✟ ✟ ✟ ✟

NOTES:_____

_____

_____

_____

_____

_____

_____

_____

_____

_____

_____

III. Week Three, Day 7 (Date:)　　　　　**THE SHEMA**

"Hear, O Israel: The Lord our God, the Lord is one. And you shall love the Lord your God with all your heart and with all your soul and with all your mind and with all your strength.
"The second is this: 'You shall love your neighbor as yourself.' There is no other commandment greater than these." **Mark 12:29b-31**

Today is a day to review the past week of devotions.

Meditation: Memorize the commandments from Jesus quoted above. Consider whether you want to repeat these words as a part of your devotional life – either daily or at least regularly. Note in your journal what you decide.

☦　☦　☦　☦　☦　☦　☦

NOTES:_____

_____

_____

_____

_____

_____

_____

_____

_____

SECTION III – TRUST: WEEK FOUR

III.Week Four, Day 1 (Date:)   **CONTROL**

> For by him all things were created, in heaven and on earth, visible and invisible, whether thrones or dominions or rulers or authorities—all things were created through him and for him. And he is before all things, and in him all things hold together. And he is the head of the body, the church. He is the beginning, the firstborn from the dead, that in everything he might be preeminent. **Col 1:16-18**

I believe in You, O Lord, Maker of the heavens and the earth.

I once asked a very wise mentor "What is authority?" He said "Authority comes from the word 'author.'" If you are the source of something, you have authority over it. The inventor of the car engine has authority over that engine. He made it. He can repair it if it breaks because he knows what makes it go. God is the creator of the universe. He has authority over it.

Authority is the power to govern, manage, or judge a person, place or thing. That is why pride and power go hand in hand. Pride seeks control and power is the means to obtain that control.

God has absolute authority. He possesses all power in the universe. The authority of His Word is supreme and unquestioned. He has control over the universe and in fact, in Him alone all things are held together. The first lifeline – "I believe in You, O Lord, Maker of the heavens and the earth" – is a statement of faith. But it is also a recognition of the authority of God as the Creator of all things.

The authority of God provides the foundation for my trust in Him. He created me and He knows me intimately. He understands what is best for me and for my soul. His power over heaven and earth means security, support, and stability for my life, because He is my hiding place (Psa 32:7).

The fundamental question is whether I will allow Him the control over my life which His authority warrants.

> **Meditation:** First focus on God as Creator – the maker of everything in the universe. Next, focus on God, His power, and His authority in the universe. Journal your thoughts about these attributes of God as God has revealed them to you.
>
> Next, focus on yourself and your standing in relationship to the Creator. How much control of you does the authority of God warrant? Now review the last few days of your life. How much control of your life do you allow God to have… on a daily basis? …on an hourly basis? …on a momentary basis?

III. Week Four, Day 2 (Date:)   **CONTROL**

> Now a centurion had a servant who was sick and at the point of death, who was highly valued by him. When the centurion heard about Jesus, he sent to him elders of the Jews, asking him to come and heal his servant.
> And when they came to Jesus, they pleaded with him earnestly, saying, "He is worthy to have you do this for him, for he loves our nation, and he is the one who built us our synagogue."
> And Jesus went with them. When he was not far from the house, the centurion sent friends, saying to him, "Lord, do not trouble yourself, for I am not worthy to have you come under my roof. Therefore I did not presume to come to you. But say the word, and let my servant be healed. For I too am a man set under authority, with soldiers under me: and I say to one, 'Go,' and he goes; and to another, 'Come,' and he comes; and to my servant, 'Do this,' and he does it."
> When Jesus heard these things, he marveled at him, and turning to the crowd that followed him, said, "I tell you, not even in Israel have I found such faith."
> And when those who had been sent returned to the house, they found the servant well. Luke 7:2-10

I too am a man set under authority.

O, I want my life to honor You! Thank You for bringing me to the place where I:

- **Recognize that I am not bringing honor to You in all my ways;**
- **Really WANT to honor You;**
- **See more and more the devastation that comes from not honoring You;**
- **See more and more the life and glory that flow from honoring You; and**
- **See the delight, peace, and wholesomeness that come from honoring You.**

Help me more and more, day by day to Grow in this matter of Honoring You! You are so WORTHY of it! Father, come and impact me more with the Declaration and cry coming from my heart, that I will HONOR You!

You Are worthy of this honor, worthy of full surrender to You! O Help me to HONOR You more and more all day long today! Help me in all my choices, my Words, my meditations, my actions, my motives to HONOR You! Show me the details of where I am not honoring You, and then grace me with the desire, will, power, and anointing to change and honor You.

Show me where I am knowingly or unknowingly honoring Satan, people, myself, things—instead of honoring You!

I want my life to be lived honoring You and only You! I want my life to bring honor and glory to You!!

Show me the specifics of where I am not making the grade, am missing the mark in honoring You. Show me anywhere that my meditations, marriage, preaching, studying, choices, time decisions, etc. don't honor You. I want to increasingly today honor You in all I am about!

Come and show me where I am needing to change in this, O my God and King!
- Pastor Daniel Martin, 9/14/14

The centurion in this story applies an understanding of authority and obedience that arose from his experience as a soldier and as a commander. His servant has a deadly illness. But the centurion believes that Jesus has authority over the illness. So the centurion submits himself to that authority and demonstrates a deep respect and submission to that authority.

But Jesus doesn't just point to the centurion's respect and obedience. He points to the faith of the centurion that undergirds them. My faith in God's authority is evident when I honor God and submit to His control.

> **Meditation:** Spend time meditating on the connection between authority and faith. Why did Jesus make that connection in this story?
>
> Now spend time meditating on rebellion against authority. In your meditation, write about a time of rebellion in your life. Explore the dynamics of what occurred, what caused the rebellion, and the fruits of the rebellion. What did rebellion against authority demonstrate? What part did a need to control play in it?

> Remember to meet with your mentor or devotional partner regularly. We like control in our lives. But God may have great benefit for you through submitting to the authority of the wisdom, insight, and gifts of another believer. If you are not meeting with a mentor or spiritual director regularly, explore the reasons why. Seek the Lord about meeting frequently with a wise believer.

III. Week Four, Day 3 (Date:)   **CONTROL**

> And when David and his men came to the city, they found it burned with fire, and their wives and sons and daughters taken captive.
> Then David and the people who were with him raised their voices and wept until they had no more strength to weep...
> And David was greatly distressed, for the people spoke of stoning him, because all the people were bitter in soul, each for his sons and daughters. But David strengthened himself in the LORD his God.
> 1 Sam 30:3-4, 6

In the very next second of my life, I am in need of You.

It is life-giving and healthy for me to admit how poor and needy I am! Even when I take in Your great love, strength, power, and victory, I, in myself am still just as poor, needy, and poverty stricken as ever—I just have You to more than make up for it—as long as I don't get the idea that I am no longer needy!

I am ALWAYS needy—I need You!

But with my constant need there is always a constant flow of You into my life, more than making up for my neediness—IF I will recognize my need and the vast supply of Your Help and Salvation!

<u>**O how subtle and devastating, depleting and destructive, are the thoughts that now because I have You, I am no longer needy!**</u> **I am still just as in need as before—I just now have the One who meets the needs of the present—BUT in the very next second of my life, I am in deep need of You!**

I always have had this need, I always do have this need, I always will have this need! And this is a very GOOD thing, because it constantly draws me to You and constantly causes me to lean and depend on YOU!   –Pastor Daniel Martin, 4/21/15

Helplessness is a state that we often resist. We don't like the idea that we can't do anything about the situation. But our helplessness is the source of some of the Lord's best work.

In this story, David has reached bottom. He and his men are refugees, and have lost all of their families and all of their possessions. They are distraught. But David strengthened himself in the Lord and sought God's will. What David does not know is that, within four days, he and his men will recover all of their families and possessions, Saul and Jonathan will die in battle, and David will have the crown of Israel hand delivered to him by David's enemy.

Humility arises from a correct awareness of my condition and of my reality. I am in continuous and desperate need of Him. Pastor Martin makes a good point. The moment that I feel that I am functioning well…that my relationships are solid…that I have things under control – that moment is a dangerous place. The point that I have "taken back" control of my life is an invitation to disaster. I always need help from Him. That need is a deep and intense need that should prevent me from trying to take control.

No sanctity is there therefore, if Thou, O Lord, withdraw Thine hand. No wisdom availeth, if Thou cease to guide. No courage helpeth, if Thou cease to guide...For left of ourselves, we sink and perish; but being visited of Thee, we are raised up and live. Unstable truly are we, but through Thee we are strengthened; we wax lukewarm, but by Thee we are inflamed.[23]

> **Meditation:** Today consider how you feel about helplessness in your life. Is it actually a blessing? Invite the Holy Spirit to come and to control your heart, mind, feelings, and spirit. Set your own control mechanisms aside. Allow Him to control every part of you. Then ask Him to help you yield control to Him throughout the day.

☩ ☩ ☩ ☩ ☩ ☩ ☩

NOTES:_____

_____

_____

_____

_____

_____

_____

_____

_____

_____

[23] *The Imitation of Christ*, p.123.

III. Week Four, Day 4 (Date:)   **CONTROL**

> We destroy arguments and every lofty opinion raised against the knowledge of God, and take every thought captive to obey Christ, being ready to punish every disobedience, when your obedience is complete.
> Look at what is before your eyes. If anyone is confident that he is Christ's, let him remind himself that just as he is Christ's, so also are we. **2 Cor 10:5-7**

We take every thought captive to obey Christ.

Be careful how you think. Your life is SHAPED by your thoughts. Do not entertain, allow, play with, or welcome any thoughts that are evil or empty of honoring God!

Do not let them run loose inside. Take all thoughts captive to the filter of whether or not they glorify God!

Give no place/ground to the devil! He will take whatever ground is given to him, and from that place start lobbing grenades and tentacles into other parts/ground/places in me. Do not be overcome of evil, but overcome evil with good. Respond to all inner workings of the enemy with "It is written!"

Let Philippians 4:8 be an active filter in my thoughts, actions, motives, and words! Whatsoever things are True, Honest, Just, Righteous, Pure, Lovely, Virtuous, Of good report, Praise worthy, Worthy of God, Clean, Honorable, Right, Excellent, Full of humility!!

O God come and deliver me from all that come to me or is now in me that does not match this filter! I want to be more like You! I want to be filled with all You are—not what the enemy is!

Come and change me, change me, and change me!   -Pastor Daniel Martin, 8/27/14

The Lord wants control of my mind. My mind is Christ's just as I am Christ's. Every thought is captive to obey Him. My mind is an area of control that belongs to the Lord.

Meditation: Today, the prayer is a "prayer of recollection" which is described next. Eliminate distractions and purify yourself – the temple of the Holy Spirit (1 Cor 6:19). Then, in your meditation time, relinquish control of your mind to the Lord. Try to empty your mind. Then ask the Holy Spirit to come within you and to take control of your mind. Spend a defined period of time (suggested time: 20 minutes) under His control.

The prayer of recollection consists in the realization of this great truth: God is in me, my soul is His temple. I recollect myself in the intimacy of this temple to adore Him, love Him, and unite myself with Him.[24]

╬ ╬ ╬ ╬ ╬ ╬ ╬

NOTES:_____

_____

_____

_____

_____

_____

_____

_____

_____

_____

_____

_____

_____

---

[24] Source: ***www.carmelitesofBoston.org*** (2014).

III. Week Four, Day 5 (Date:)　　　　　　　　　　**CONTROL**

> All things have been handed over to me by my Father, and no one knows the Son except the Father, and no one knows the Father except the Son and anyone to whom the Son chooses to reveal him. Come to me, all who labor and are heavy laden, and I will give you rest. Take my yoke upon you, and learn from me, for I am gentle and lowly in heart, and you will find rest for your souls.
> For my yoke is easy, and my burden is light. **Matt 11:27-29**

Take My yoke upon you.

This passage is a good one for the person that is burdened, anxious, and under stress. I memorized the last three verses of this passage many years ago and repeat them to myself when I am in a place of high stress.

This passage is an invitation to the yoke. The yoke is a symbol of control. The yoke is put onto oxen so that the labor of the oxen can be controlled and can be coordinated. The yoke means control of action.

The first verse is also important. That verse is a statement of authority: *All things have been handed over to Me by My Father.* "Because I have this authority, I have the ability - and the right, to control. But because of my gentleness and humility, my control is easy and I will lead you to rest."

> **Meditation:** Imagine you are submitting yourself to the yoke of Jesus. Ask Jesus to come to put His yoke upon you. Look at the face of Jesus as He brings His yoke and as He places you in it. Submit yourself to Him in worship as He attaches it. You may even want to sketch what it looks like in a drawing or in a word picture.
>
> Then as you go through the day, remember the yoke that you wear. Allow that yoke to guide your actions as you give Him control of your day situation by situation.

> Be sensitive to movements, nudges, or impressions during your devotional time. Subtle movements may be important. Record movements in your journal and allow time for changes to take hold. God is building a core foundation within you through which He will do many powerful and impactful things!

III. Week Four, Day 6 (Date:)   **CONTROL**

> And the Father who sent me has himself borne witness about me. His voice you have never heard, his form you have never seen, and you do not have his word abiding in you, for you do not believe the one whom he has sent.
> You search the Scriptures because you think that in them you have eternal life; and it is they that bear witness about me, yet you refuse to come to me that you may have life. **John 5:37-40**

The Father Who sent Me has Himself borne witness about Me.

Oh, how humbly and meanly ought I to think of myself! How ought I to esteem it as nothing, if I should seem to have aught of good! With what profound humility ought I to submit myself to Thy unfathomable judgments, O Lord; where I find myself to be nothing else than nothing, and still nothing! O weight unmeasurable! O sea that cannot be passed over, where I discover nothing of myself save only and wholly nothing![25]

Consider the (seemingly) outrageous statements that Jesus made about Himself.

"Truly, truly, I say to you, before Abraham was, I am" (John 8:58).

"I and the Father are one" (John 10:30).

"[D]o you say of him whom the Father consecrated and sent into the world, 'You are blaspheming,' because I said, 'I am the Son of God'?" (John 10:36).

Jesus was the model of humility and submission. But these statements don't appear to show much humility. In fact, in response to each of these statements, the outraged Jews tried either to stone Him or to arrest Him.

Humility is an attitude based on true recognition of reality – a reality that is dictated by God. If it were I, I would cringe to make these statements and I probably would refuse to do so out of false humility. But Jesus, in His true humility, allowed God to control His narrative. He spoke exactly what God told Him. His narrative arose out of the witness of the Father.

My humility arises from recognition of my status as nothing before God.

Yet by His grace, my humility also declares what the Father has witnessed. I am a child of God. I am saved, redeemed, delivered, and sealed. I am fully, wholly, and completely loved by the God of the universe.

Further, I am exactly what God has called me to be. In his humility, Paul did

---

[25] *The Imitation of Christ*, p.123.

not shrink from declaring exactly what God had called him to be – an apostle of God. *For I am the least of the apostles, unworthy to be called an apostle, because I persecuted the church of God. But by the grace of God I am what I am, and his grace toward me was not in vain* (1 Cor 15:9-10a).

God controls my narrative. I submit it to Him and allow Him to tell me who I am. He gives me my identity and He imprints it on my soul. By the grace of God, I am what I am.[26]

> **Meditation:** *"Love rejoices with the truth."* Start your meditation time by giving God control over your being. Then seek Him about who you are in Him. Allow Him to control your narrative. As He reveals it to you, write down in your journal His narrative of you and of your life.

☩   ☩   ☩   ☩   ☩   ☩   ☩

NOTES:_____

_____

_____

_____

_____

_____

_____

_____

_____

_____

---

[26] Writing a life narrative or a spiritual life history can be a very productive and informative exercise, especially if you allow a mentor or spiritual director to read it and to discuss it with you. For a prompt and direction on writing a life narrative, go to *www.surenderandtrust.net*.

III. Week Four, Day 7 (Date:)   **CONTROL**

Today is a day of praise.

> **Meditation:** Look back over your journal over the past week. Identify items or areas about which you can praise God. Then, find an active manner to praise God. It can be through music, art, physical expression, or a craft. Set aside a block of time (suggestion: 30 minutes) and engage in an active worship of our great, awesome, and powerful God.

☨   ☨   ☨   ☨   ☨   ☨   ☨

NOTES:_____

_____

_____

_____

_____

_____

_____

_____

_____

_____

_____

SECTION III – TRUST: WEEK FIVE

III.Week Five, Day 1 (Date:)   **SUBMISSION**

> Let every person be subject to the governing authorities. For there is no authority except from God, and those that exist have been instituted by God. Therefore whoever resists the authorities resists what God has appointed, and those who resist will incur judgment.
> Therefore one must be in subjection, not only to avoid God's wrath but also for the sake of conscience. **Rom 13:1-2, 5**

God shares His authority with people.

God shares His authority with people. He allows people to possess some of the power that He has – people like parents, teachers, legislators, police officers, pastors, judges, referees, employers, coaches, and presidents. Human authority exists in every context of life and that authority impacts every person.

When God shares His authority, He delegates it to a person. I call it "delegated authority." God can grant the authority at any time and He can take it away at any time because it really belongs to Him. Since the authority still belongs to God, Paul says we should be in subjection to delegated authority. Resisting authority resists God's appointment. Paul lists no general exceptions. It is an area in which we need to trust God's sovereign plan.

So what is the appropriate reaction to delegated authority? Am I obliged to obey it like I obey God's absolute authority? Because I understand that all authority comes from God, I have an attitude that respects and wants to obey delegated authority. That is my default mode: submission and obedience to all authority.

But there are exceptional times when I cannot obey delegated authority despite my desire to do so. One exception is when obedience to earthly authority would conflict with my obedience to God. In Acts 4, the supreme Jewish council instructed Peter and John to refrain from speaking or teaching in the name of Jesus. *But Peter and John answered them, "Whether it is right in the sight of God to listen to you rather than to God, you must judge, for we cannot but speak of what we have seen and heard"* (Acts 4:19-20). Peter and John refused to obey this august body because its edict conflicted with God's command to them.

Another exception occurs when obedience of the authority is unduly detrimental or destructive to me. Situations in which persons with authority are physically or mentally abusive may necessitate flight, opposition, or even defiance. That decision must be made soberly on a case by case basis –

mindful that scripture says one who suffers unjustly out of respect for God and His authority finds grace with God (1 Pet 2:19-20).

> **Meditation:** Identify areas of authority that impact your life. What authority has God ordained that impacts you? For each area of authority, discern your attitude toward it and the level of honor and respect that you feel toward it.
>
> Next, identify areas of authority or power that God has given you. For each area of authority or power, discern the level of honor and respect that you desire those under your authority show toward your authority. Write about these areas in your journal.

☩ ☩ ☩ ☩ ☩ ☩ ☩

NOTES:_____

_____

_____

_____

_____

_____

_____

_____

_____

_____

_____

III. Week Five, Day 2 (Date:)   SUBMISSION

> And he came to the sheepfolds by the way, where there was a cave, and Saul went in to relieve himself. Now David and his men were sitting in the innermost parts of the cave. And the men of David said to him, "Here is the day of which the LORD said to you, 'Behold, I will give your enemy into your hand, and you shall do to him as it shall seem good to you.'" Then David arose and stealthily cut off a corner of Saul's robe.
> And afterward David's heart struck him, because he had cut off a corner of Saul's robe. He said to his men, "The LORD forbid that I should do this thing to my lord, the LORD's anointed, to put out my hand against him, seeing he is the LORD's anointed."
> So David persuaded his men with these words and did not permit them to attack Saul. And Saul rose up and left the cave and went on his way. **1 Sam 24:3-7**

"The Lord forbid that I should do this thing to my lord, the Lord's anointed."

Self-defense is an absolute defense. If you shoot an unarmed man, it is murder. But if that man is armed and trying to kill you, you can shoot back. No one will hold you responsible for that man's life. That killing is justified.

And what if that man has tried to kill you a number of times before? He has hunted you "like a dog" and has told everyone around him that he wants to kill you.

Even more, the man trying to kill you has something that is rightfully yours. God told you that you would be king. God's prophet anointed you as king, and clearly proclaimed that you are the rightful king. God confirmed that anointing with a mighty presence of His Holy Spirit. And now the man who wants to remain as king and who is trying to kill you, is within your grasp.[27]

The man that God found after His own heart was a remarkable man. David was remarkable for his understanding of, and respect for, authority. David had every justification to take out Saul and seize the kingdom for himself. Not only had Saul tried to kill David, Saul even had murdered God's priests who had assisted David. This crime was so heinous that Saul's own servants would not obey Saul's order to carry out the execution (1 Sam 22:11-19).

David had two occasions where he had Saul's life in his hands. On one occasion, Saul was using the bathroom in a cave (1 Sam 24). On the other, Saul was asleep (1 Sam 26). One thrust of David's sword would have ended

---

[27] *The Call: Book Two – Foundational (Progressive Fivefold Function)*, pp.45-46.

it all. David's companions urged him to do it! (1 Sam 26:8; 24:4). But David understood principles of authority. He had such respect for the authority of the Lord that he refused to touch Saul. David's respect for authority was so great that he even felt pangs of conscience when he cut off the edge of Saul's robe in the cave (1 Sam 24:5).

David respected the Lord and His authority. He was willing to wait until God established his call in God's strength.

We, on the other hand, often do not hesitate to criticize, berate, or ridicule a leader in authority. Politicians are public figures and that seems to give greater license to show our judgment and disdain for people in power.

Peter gives a simple instruction: *Honor the emperor* (1 Pet 2:17b). The last time I checked, history does not describe the emperor at the time that instruction was written as a particularly honorable person. But the instruction is based upon respect for God and His authority, not upon the respectability of the emperor.

God sometimes wants us to do things that we don't understand. He may call us to submit to authorities with whom we disagree. That seems so unjust! But in those situations, we learn humility. God is teaching our hearts through submission.

> **Meditation:** Consider your own thoughts and words toward Presidents and other governmental leaders. Do those words bespeak an attitude of honor? What can you do to show an attitude of honor toward those persons in authority?

Take your time reading the scripture in each devotion. Read each scripture multiple times as you allow it to soak in and to become a part of you. We want the word of Christ to dwell in us richly so we are able to apply it to our lives each day. The scripture is a treasure that we desire to store in our hearts so that we can fulfill it and we can allow it to flow out of us in due season to bless others.

III. Week Five, Day 3 (Date:)   **SUBMISSION**

> And looking intently at the council, Paul said, "Brothers, I have lived my life before God in all good conscience up to this day."
> And the high priest Ananias commanded those who stood by him to strike him on the mouth.
> Then Paul said to him, "God is going to strike you, you whitewashed wall! Are you sitting to judge me according to the law, and yet contrary to the law you order me to be struck?"
> Those who stood by said, "Would you revile God's high priest?"
> And Paul said, "I did not know, brothers, that he was the high priest, for it is written, 'You shall not speak evil of a ruler of your people.'"
> **Acts 23:1-5**

"I did not know, brothers."

My son, he who endeavors to withdraw himself from obedience withdraws himself from grace; and he who seeks for himself private benefits (Matt 16:24) loses those that are common.

He who does not cheerfully and freely submit himself to his superior reveals that his flesh is not as yet perfectly obedient to him, but oftentimes kicks and murmurs against him. Learn therefore quickly to submit yourself to your superior, if you desire to keep your own flesh under the yoke.[28]

Paul has suffered an injustice. His rights have been violated and he has suffered violence. So Paul responds to the blow forcefully and credibly.

But when Paul is informed of the authority of the priest, as unjustly and abusively as it has been exercised, Paul immediately backtracks. Paul's respect for authority - even authority intent on evil, causes him to recant.

God establishes governmental authority; and God establishes spiritual authority. He places authority in the church as He sees fit. Honor is due to that authority – whether or not I agree with the authority and whether or not I agree with the manner in which that authority is exercised. My trust in the establishment of authority by God is required for my benefit. I need to trust God in the manner that He has delegated authority to other persons.

---

[28] *The Imitation of Christ*, p.121.

Meditation: Explore the tensions in this Bible story. Paul is treated unjustly but when he is informed of the position of his tormentor, he seems to recant. What situations have you experienced in which you were unjustly treated or unjustly accused? What role did authority play in those situations? How do you feel about the idea of respecting authority even if it acts unjustly or abusively?

Next, consider what God is doing in Paul's life. God granted the authority to the high priest. How is God working through the actions of the high priest, as abusive as they are, to instruct and to benefit Paul in this situation? What is Paul learning about submission and humility, and about his own flesh?

☦ ☦ ☦ ☦ ☦ ☦ ☦

NOTES:_____

III. Week Five, Day 4 (Date:)   **SUBMISSION**

> Remember your leaders, those who spoke to you the word of God. Consider the outcome of their way of life, and imitate their faith.
> Obey your leaders and submit to them, for they are keeping watch over your souls, as those who will have to give an account. Let them do this with joy and not with groaning, for that would be of no advantage to you. **Heb 13:7, 17**

Obey your leaders and submit to them.

In this scripture, believers are instructed to obey and to submit to their spiritual leaders. There is an implicit problem here: I need to have spiritual leaders in order to submit to them. How can I submit to them if I am not connected to them?

Every Christian should be subject to proper spiritual authority. That subjection is demonstrated initially by active membership in a church – a proper connection to the body of Christ. It is a part of the accountability that the writer of Hebrews directs. A church has authority to judge the lives of its members (Matt 18:17). Besides the obedience to scriptural mandate, there are many benefits that are gained by proper connection. It is a part of healthy soul care.

Conversely, there are many benefits that are lost by refusing to belong to a church. Yet many believers live in self-imposed, spiritual solitary confinement. It is "just me and Jesus" or "just me, my friends, and Jesus" as if somehow God had placed the mantle of spiritual authority on a lone wolf because of some special dispensation.

In his book *The Insanity of God*, Nik Ripken details lessons learned through experiences and interactions with members of the persecuted church all over the world. Mr. Ripken tells about Dmitri who was imprisoned and tortured for his faith. Because Dmitri clung to his faith, he was confined in isolation in a solitary cell for years. He was underfed, lived in freezing conditions, and subjected to regular beatings as his tormentors tried to break him. Here is what Dmitri told Mr. Ripken about his many years in prison: **His isolation from the body of Christ was more difficult than even the physical torture.**[29]

---

[29] Nik Ripken, *The Insanity of God*, p.155 (B&H 2013).

Meditation: *"Love does not envy."* Reread this devotional. Spend time in prayer about your attitude toward your spiritual leaders. Explore your feelings toward them as frail and fallible humans, and your feelings toward them as persons with authority.

If you don't have a connection with a church, consider the reasons why. Seek the Lord for guidance about bringing yourself into submission to spiritual authority.

☩ ☩ ☩ ☩ ☩ ☩ ☩

NOTES:_____

_____

_____

_____

_____

_____

_____

_____

_____

_____

_____

_____

III. Week Five, Day 5 (Date:)   **SUBMISSION**

> Then after fourteen years I went up again to Jerusalem with Barnabas, taking Titus along with me. I went up because of a revelation and set before them (though privately before those who seemed influential) the gospel that I proclaim among the Gentiles, in order to make sure I was not running or had not run in vain. **Gal 2:1-2**

In order to make sure I was not running or had not run in vain.

And yet, what great matter is it, if you, who are but dust and nothing, subject yourself to man for God's sake, when I, the Almighty and the Most High, who created all things of nothing, humbly subjected Myself to man for your sake? I became of all men the most humble and the most abject (Luke 2:7; John 13:14), that you might overcome your pride with My humility. O dust, learn to be obedient! Learn to humble yourself, you of earth and clay, and to bow yourself under the feet of all men. Learn to break your own wishes, and to yield yourself to all subjection. Be fiercely against yourself and suffer no swelling of pride to dwell within you.[30]

Paul had a private revelation of the gospel. Paul was a great apostle who was called and instructed by God. But he wanted to be sure that his revelation was true and that he had not been working in vain. So Paul went up to Jerusalem with Barnabas and Titus and presented his gospel to the apostles there for discernment. This act was an accountability to the truth.

Accountability to others is necessary in my journey with Christ. An accountability partnership is an intentional relationship maintained by frequent and consistent meetings in which both persons share their hearts, minds and lives for the purpose of support, prayer, correction, and growth.

Relationships of accountability have great value. As demonstrated by Paul, they can prevent deception and help me know truth – the truth about myself and truth about the Lord. They help me resist temptations to which I am prone and from falling into sin in my life. My accountability relationships encourage and support me. If I face a significant challenge or struggle, I have persons that I trust and who care about me who support and pray for me. God offers this benefit in my spiritual journey and I am deemed foolish not to participate in it.

Meditation: Spend time reviewing your personal relationships. Accountability partnerships are regular, intentional, and defined. What is their connection with humility? What benefits have you received from these relationships? What actions do you need to take to increase benefit from relationships of accountability?

---

[30] *The Imitation of Christ*, pp.121-122.

III. Week Five, Day 6 (Date:) **SUBMISSION**

> A man of many companions may come to ruin, but there is a friend who sticks closer than a brother. **Pro 18:24**

There is a friend who sticks closer than a brother.

An accountability partnership is different than companionship or even friendship. An accountability partnership is intentional and defined. But, like most means of healthy growth in the kingdom of God, there is a cost.

The first cost is vulnerability and openness. In a healthy relationship, my heart is exposed for helpful input and insight. In one of my accountability relationships, I created and shared a matrix of my past and present sinful attitudes and actions. That chart was not a small one and contained multiple progressions. Vulnerability is why trust and discretion are necessary elements in the relationship – mindful, of course, that trust in a relationship is gradually developed. As my friend, Marcus, once shared on a Boyz Club leadership retreat, **"You can't drive a 20 ton truck of accountability over a 5 ton bridge of relationship."**

Another cost is time. Accountability meetings should occur regularly – weekly, every two weeks, or monthly. There is a discipline and intentionality to maintenance of the relationship. Failure to meet together results in loss of benefits quickly.

Finally, submission is a key. One purpose of an accountability relationship is to receive correction. Correction is sometimes hard to swallow. The deeper I go into the relationship, the more personality differences become evident. Diversity is a key value of the kingdom of God, but sometimes correction is hard to receive from a person who acts and thinks differently than me. But a person with different gifts and personality than me can see things about me and my situations that I cannot see.

> **Meditation:** Spend time seeking God about the relationships and connections in your life. Surrender those relationships to Him. Ask Him if He wants you to pursue or develop accountability relationships. Write down what He tells you. Then act on whatever He puts into your heart to do.

╬ ╬ ╬ ╬ ╬ ╬ ╬

> Speaking of accountability relationships, be careful to meet with your mentor or devotional partner regularly.

III. Week Five, Day 7 (Date:)　　　　　　**SUBMISSION**

Today is a day of review and of reckoning.

> **Meditation:** Review your journal over the past week. Note carefully your attitudes and feelings as you read about submission. Explore the sources or motivations behind those feelings.
>
> Then note any nudges that you sensed as you spent time with the Lord. Be careful to act on those nudges. Growth occurs in my personal life when I put into practice the applications that God reveals to me.

☩ ☩ ☩ ☩ ☩ ☩ ☩

NOTES:_____

_____

_____

_____

_____

_____

_____

_____

_____

_____

SECTION III – TRUST: WEEK SIX

III.Week Six, Day 1 (Date:)   **LOVE ONE ANOTHER**

> And one of the scribes came up and heard them disputing with one another, and seeing that he answered them well, asked him, "Which commandment is the most important of all?"
> Jesus answered, "The most important is, 'Hear, O Israel: The Lord our God, the Lord is one. And you shall love the Lord your God with all your heart and with all your soul and with all your mind and with all your strength.'
> The second is this: 'You shall love your neighbor as yourself.' There is no other commandment greater than these."
> And the scribe said to him, "You are right, Teacher. You have truly said that he is one, and there is no other besides him. And to love him with all the heart and with all the understanding and with all the strength, and to love one's neighbor as oneself, is much more than all whole burnt offerings and sacrifices."
> And when Jesus saw that he answered wisely, he said to him, "You are not far from the kingdom of God." And after that no one dared to ask him any more questions. **Mark 12:28-34**

You are not far from the kingdom of God.

We were sitting at the breakfast table in Alabama at the house of my Grandmother and Grandaddy (Papa and Meme). We had just finished a wonderful Meme breakfast. We were sitting there - Papa, Meme, Jimmy and my family.

I looked across the table and saw my grandfather - almost bald up top with tufts of gray hair on the sides and back of his head surrounding the bald middle. He was elderly, but wiry and in great shape. He had a distinct nose and clear eyes.

I saw my grandmother - kindness radiating from her eyes. Her silvery white hair was pinned in a bun at the top of her head. She had lost some teeth over the years and had a snaggletoothed smile. Yet that smile was one of the most pleasant ones I have ever seen, and she shared it often.

As I looked at my grandparents and thought of their years and of their lives, I imagined that vast wisdom must be stored in their hearts and minds. I turned to Papa and said, "Papa, if you could tell us anything, what would that be?"

I had opened the door and I waited expectantly. This question was actually a brave one. Papa could talk awhile. He usually let Meme carry social conversation. But if Papa got focused on a topic of interest to him, he could talk for hours. But I asked the question. I braced myself for what could be a long lecture or a list of life instructions.

Papa paused for a minute. He took a breath and looked me squarely in the eyes. He said three words – "Love one another."

Papa paused again. Silence filled the room. Every eye at that table was focused on him. We waited to see what else he would say. But he had no elaboration. Slowly and deliberately, he repeated, "Love...one...another."[31]

Jesus added a bonus. The scribe asked Jesus about the most important commandment. Jesus immediately pointed the scribe to the Shema. That is the greatest commandment. But Jesus didn't stop there.

Jesus added a second commandment from a different part of the Torah: *"You shall love your neighbor as yourself"* (Lev 19:18). Jesus' response in Mark 12:29-31 forms what Scot McKnight calls The Jesus Creed. Dr. McKnight suggests that Christians repeat The Jesus Creed daily just as a devout Jew would recite the Shema daily.[32]

So why did Jesus add a second commandment to the Shema? Because the two commandments to love God and to love your neighbor are inseparable.

God loves every being. He loves the thin and the fat; the hirsute and the hairless; the brown, black, yellow, and red. God loves the kind and the unkind; the just and the unjust. God loves people that love Him; and He loves people that deny Him or even hate Him. God loves His friends, and He loves His enemies. Love is an attribute of God that exists without regard to the decisions, thoughts, or actions of others. The love or hate of another creature does not determine the love that God has in return.

The love that comes from God loves other persons who are made in His image. Loving others organically flows from loving God. That is why John reminds us: *If anyone says, "I love God," and hates his brother, he is a liar; for he who does not love his brother whom he has seen cannot love God whom he has not seen. And this commandment we have from him: whoever loves God must also love his brother* (1 John 4:20-21).

The love of God in us is unconditional. We love without regard to the decisions, thoughts, or actions of another – even if those decisions, thoughts, or actions are contrary to our own or even detrimental and destructive to us. If we have the type of love that comes from God, then we love like God does.

Meditation: Meditate on the idea that we each are made in the image of God. A person who loves animals, for example, reflects the love of God for all of His creatures – even a sparrow finds a home at His altars (Psa 84:3).

Then consider 2 or 3 acquaintances and how each one reflects the image of God in unique ways. Does seeing the image of God help you to love those persons more?

---

[31] Excerpt from *Dod Knows* (by the author).

[32] *The Jesus Creed*, p. 12.

III. Week Six, Day 2 (Date:)   LOVE ONE ANOTHER

> As the Father has loved me, so have I loved you. Abide in my love.
> If you keep my commandments, you will abide in my love, just as I have kept my Father's commandments and abide in his love.
> These things I have spoken to you, that my joy may be in you, and that your joy may be full. This is my commandment, that you love one another as I have loved you.
> Greater love has no one than this, that someone lay down his life for his friends. **John 15:9-13**

This is My commandment, love one another as I have loved you.

My friend, Gretel, is a social worker. We were walking back from court one day and Gretel said, "Can you believe it, David? The Department of Social Services made its own social worker go through sensitivity training."

"What happened?" I asked.

"Some foreign woman came into the Department building. She needed to use the bathroom but she didn't know what the facilities were for. When the social worker walked into the bathroom, the woman was crouched down and peeing on the floor. The social worker tried to stop her, but that foreign woman couldn't speak any English. So the social worker yelled at her. So her supervisor made the social worker go through sensitivity training. Unbelievable!"

"Gretel," I said "the foreign lady was probably doing what they did in her native country."

"Yeah, but the social worker isn't the one peeing on the floor. That's disgusting!"

I paused for a moment. **"Gretel, don't you see? That is how we all appear to Jesus. What we think, what we say, the things that we do...it's disgusting to Jesus. To Him, we are peeing on the floor whenever He walks into the room.**

"But He doesn't yell at us or scold us. Instead He compassionately loves us and cares for us. He understands that we are in need of restoration."[33]

Jesus put the love of God on display. No person was too dirty, too ugly, too repulsive, too wretched, too disgusting, too evil, or too wealthy for Jesus to love. In fact, the less lovable the person, the more evident was the love of Jesus.

Every person has an intrinsic worth and value to God. In fact, the correct word is "precious." Every person is precious to God, because every person is

---

[33] David Thurman, *The Call: Book Three – Fruitful (Transforming Your Community)*, p. 14 (2017).

the object of the love of God.

"Dignity" can carry a negative connotation of superior social status or even arrogance. But every person has dignity. Dignity arises from the worth and value of each person to God. Love respects the dignity of each person, even if that person does disgusting, degrading, or repulsive things.

So Jesus chose to hang out with prostitutes, drunkards, and swindlers. The righteous people of Jesus' day, who felt that sinful behavior meant that the sinner had lost his dignity, condemned Jesus for His social interactions. But Jesus did not condone the behavior of sinful persons. He simply recognized their worth and administered His special form of grace.

Love is not irritable.

> **Meditation:** Choose a story about Jesus that you feel demonstrates His love. It can be a story about healing, redemption, restoration, or rejection. Read the story carefully. As you read the story, try to feel within yourself the love that Jesus felt as the story occurs. Imagine living your life with that kind of love within you. How would it change the way that you live? Write about it in your journal.

☩ ☩ ☩ ☩ ☩ ☩ ☩

NOTES:_____

_____

_____

_____

_____

_____

_____

_____

III. Week Six, Day 3 (Date:)　　　　　　　　　　　LOVE ONE ANOTHER

> We who are strong have an obligation to bear with the failings of the weak, and not to please ourselves. Let each of us please his neighbor for his good, to build him up.
> For Christ did not please himself, but as it is written, "The reproaches of those who reproached you fell on me." **Rom 15:1-3**

People need love the most when they deserve it the least.

Meme specialized in ministry to wounded souls. Catherine was one of those hurt souls. Catherine's husband rejected her and left her. He then divorced her. Catherine began a downward spiral emotionally and financially and, in the process, became alienated from her family. She had almost no friends and she was destitute when she met Meme. Meme was a stranger, but Meme opened her home to Catherine who needed a refuge.

It wasn't that Catherine was an unfriendly or antisocial person. In fact, she was too friendly. She tried to help in any way that she could, almost throwing herself at you. Catherine had such a need for belonging - such a craving for acceptance - that she tried way too hard to be helpful. She smothered other people with herself. It was almost repulsive. Then, when Catherine sensed a rejection of her good intentions from other people, it only injured her esteem more. Catherine was a wounded soul. But Meme specialized in wounded souls.

Meme took Catherine under her wing. She knew that Catherine needed to be busy and to do things that she could feel good about. Meme put Catherine to work cooking, cleaning, sewing and baking. Meme worked with her and praised her successes. During the next few months, Meme encouraged Catherine, listened to her, and counseled her. Meme prayed for her, and Meme prayed with her, sharing the love of God tangibly and intangibly.

Catherine's personal esteem slowly grew. Her self-destructive habits began to diminish. She received balm for her wounds and hope for her future. Catherine recovered to the extent that she was able to move out and live on her own. Yet she knew that if she needed support or a listening ear at any time, she had a friend in Meme that was faithful, caring and available.[34]

Meme prominently displayed a framed statement in her room that inspired her. It also described her calling. The statement read:

PEOPLE NEED LOVE THE MOST WHEN THEY DESERVE IT THE LEAST[35]

---

[34] See Appendix B for *Meme's Keys to Restore Wounded Souls*.

[35] David Thurman, *The Call: Book One – Functional (Keys to Effective Discipleship)*, pp. 70-71 (2007).

Bear with the failings of the weak. Bear one another's burdens. If I am strong – if I am blessed with God's love secure in my heart, my call is to love in such a way that I build up my neighbor. God's love is used to bless my neighbor who is weak, hurting, or even repulsive to me.

But the failings of the weak have a negative and sometimes destructive impact on me. It is unfair to me to have to put up with them. The burdens of others are their burdens, not my burdens. It is unjust for me to bear them!

The question is not one of fairness but of love. *Love bears all things.* When I practice the love of Jesus, I walk in His way – the way of the Cross. I put the love of Jesus on display.

Bearing another's burden is not just beneficial to my neighbor, it is beneficial to ME as I practice it and learn how to walk in it. God is helping me to grow through the weakness of my neighbor.

> **Meditation:** Consider a time when you needed grace from another person. It may be a failing, a burden, or a problem that you had, and another person assisted you, bore your burden, or was present in your crisis. Consider the manner in which that person supported you. What did it mean to you? Journal about it.

It is good to refer back to the instructional sections at the beginning of this devotional often. The Devotional Elements, for example, take practice in order to use them effectively. I make a short outline of important practices that I am trying to learn and I review the outline regularly. That way, I am reminded of them and can incorporate them into my devotional track.

III. Week Six, Day 4 (Date:)　　　　　　　LOVE ONE ANOTHER

> And behold, a lawyer stood up to put him to the test, saying, "Teacher, what shall I do to inherit eternal life?" He said to him, "What is written in the Law? How do you read it?"
> And he answered, "You shall love the Lord your God with all your heart and with all your soul and with all your strength and with all your mind, and your neighbor as yourself."
> And he said to him, "You have answered correctly; do this, and you will live."
> But he, desiring to justify himself, said to Jesus, "And who is my neighbor?"
> Jesus replied, "A man was going down from Jerusalem to Jericho, and he fell among robbers, who stripped him and beat him and departed, leaving him half dead. Now by chance a priest was going down that road, and when he saw him he passed by on the other side. So likewise a Levite, when he came to the place and saw him, passed by on the other side.
> But a Samaritan, as he journeyed, came to where he was, and when he saw him, he had compassion. He went to him and bound up his wounds, pouring on oil and wine. Then he set him on his own animal and brought him to an inn and took care of him. And the next day he took out two denarii and gave them to the innkeeper, saying, 'Take care of him, and whatever more you spend, I will repay you when I come back.'
> Which of these three, do you think, proved to be a neighbor to the man who fell among the robbers?"
> He said, "The one who showed him mercy." And Jesus said to him, "You go, and do likewise." **Luke 10:25-37**

You go and do likewise.

I see clearly that one element is needed here – something that I have difficulty with - TIME!

It takes TIME to become oriented to You and to Your ways, thoughts, and truths!

Help me to surrender time to You, to dedicate time with You each day to simply seek You and whatever You are wanting to show me!

<u>**O help me in this matter of TIME!!**</u>

O God, I want my life to be increasingly Oriented to You! I want to have You as the central axis of my life, for You to be what everything in my life rotates around. O how horrible things become when I am the axis and everything rotates around me, when it is "all about me."

Come and give me the humility needed for these changes to take place. Pride and Self ambition work against this. I want YOU! –Pastor Daniel Martin, 6/2/14

This account in Luke is another passage that references the Shema. The reference is in response to a question: *"What shall I do to inherit eternal life?"*

Scot McKnight says that Jesus reveals the first principle of spiritual formation in His response. A spiritually formed person loves God and loves others - thus the importance of repeating "The Jesus Creed" daily.[36]

And what part of this creed did Jesus emphasize here? Jesus told a story to illustrate loving your neighbor. The parable of the Good Samaritan is a story of compassion – compassion that bridged ethnic barriers.

The Good Samaritan demonstrated love in many ways – through compassion, healing, service, and money. But the first sacrifice was time. The Good Samaritan had to stop his journey and to put aside his own plans to minister to the wounded stranger. The Good Samaritan did what more religious persons did not do.

Love is demonstrated when I use my time for the interests or needs of another instead of my own interests and desires. This present generation spends a lot of time on the internet, social media, and video games. My older generation spent time on television, music, and sports. All of these "time consumers" can be used for the kingdom of God. But often they are used for pleasing myself and filling my desire for excitement.

One sacrifice of time is prayer for others. For a number of years, I have maintained a prayer list on my computer. I have friends, family, ministry coworkers, specific needs, and other items on my list. I keep the list on my computer so I can update it regularly – adding items or noting prayers that are answered. One goal is to pray through the list every day although I must confess that I miss some days.

Another goal is written at the top of my prayer list as a reminder: "Pray with love." And a secret of the kingdom of God is that the more time I spend praying for a person, the more my love for that person grows. If you spend significant time on the internet, social media, or video games, and you do not regularly pray through a list of other people, then you may want to consider how much you love and how you use your time.

> **Meditation:** Surrender your time to the Lord. Tell Him that you want Him to control your time and that you give it to Him. Then spend time seeking Him about how you can spend your time loving others. Consider the amount of time that you spend praying for others. Write down what God shows you about how much time you spend on yourself and on what you pleases you, and how much time you spend loving others.

---

[36] *The Jesus Creed,* Prologue and p. 12.

III. Week Six, Day 5 (Date:)   **LOVE ONE ANOTHER**

> By this we know love, that he laid down his life for us, and we ought to lay down our lives for the brothers. But if anyone has the world's goods and sees his brother in need, yet closes his heart against him, how does God's love abide in him? Little children, let us not love in word or talk but in deed and in truth. **1 Jn 3:16-18**

We ought to lay down our lives for the brothers.

My friend, Goose, is trying to live a sacrificial life based on the teachings of Christ. His work is to minister the Gospel to the needs of the community around him. Goose serves a very poor section of Charlotte. I had lunch one day with him to hear how the ministry was going. Goose said:

"I haven't been able to take a paycheck for 22 days. I am behind in my tax payments. But how am I supposed to keep the money for myself when the people that I know, and that I am called to love, are hungry and without food?

"My family and I have lost our health insurance coverage. My friends tell me that I am foolish. But earthly security is not a kingdom value. Almost none of the people that I tell about Jesus have insurance coverage. How can I spend money on my health insurance when they have such great needs? I have to rely on the Lord to protect me and my family. That is my witness.

"Right now we have two poor neighborhood children staying with us. We have taken young people into our home before who were physically and sexually abused. My friends tell me that I am stupid because I am exposing my young children to dysfunction and danger. But I want my children to participate in the gospel – to see it and to experience it. Just the other day, I overheard my little girl and her poor friend from the apartments talking about how they would like to make bracelets and sell them so they could use the money to give food to the poor and tell other people about Jesus.

"I can't live my life according to the values of the world. To me, the gospel is not something that you just say. The gospel is something that you are – something that you live. What good is the gospel if it does not change you? So many people come to the Lord, but it doesn't change how they live or who they are. Jesus calls us to change - to be different than the culture of the world."[37]

John writes about the type of love that lays down its life. Then he immediately writes about giving – the type of giving spirit that sees the need of a brother as just as important as your own need.

---

[37] *The Call: Book Three – Fruitful (Transforming Your Community)*, pp.76-77.

My friend, Goose, has been called to minister to the poor, to the needy, and to the destitute. Some people might disagree with his approach as irresponsible or even foolish. But I don't judge the way that the Lord has worked in Goose's heart just as I don't judge others that don't feel called to live this way. What I know is that Goose lives out the instructions from John in a remarkable way, and that Goose has helped many poor, destitute, and broken people through the years. He has offered a lifeline of love to them.

> **Meditation:** Identify an occasion that someone gave something to you that was significant to you, and that showed generosity or compassion. Think about the gift and the ways that it affected you. Write about the gift and its impact in your journal.

✝ ✝ ✝ ✝ ✝ ✝ ✝

NOTES:_____

_____

_____

_____

_____

_____

_____

_____

_____

_____

_____

III. Week Six, Day 6 (Date:)   **LOVE ONE ANOTHER**

> My brothers, show no partiality as you hold the faith in our Lord Jesus Christ, the Lord of glory. For if a man wearing a gold ring and fine clothing comes into your assembly, and a poor man in shabby clothing also comes in, and if you pay attention to the one who wears the fine clothing and say, "You sit here in a good place," while you say to the poor man, "You stand over there," or, "Sit down at my feet," have you not then made distinctions among yourselves and become judges with evil thoughts?
> Listen, my beloved brothers, has not God chosen those who are poor in the world to be rich in faith and heirs of the kingdom, which he has promised to those who love him? But you have dishonored the poor man. Are not the rich the ones who oppress you, and the ones who drag you into court? Are they not the ones who blaspheme the honorable name by which you were called? If you really fulfill the royal law according to the Scripture, "You shall love your neighbor as yourself," you are doing well. But if you show partiality, you are committing sin and are convicted by the law as transgressors. **James 2:1-9**

Outdo one another in showing honor.

Marriage counselors have told me that there are many issues, conflicts, or problems in a marriage that can be overcome. If a husband and wife come in for counseling and issues about finances, personality, in-laws, or children exist, then the counselor feels there is a good possibility that these issues can be discussed, addressed, and resolved.

But the counselors say that there is one significant problem that is a "red flag." If a couple come in for joint counseling and one spouse starts rolling eyes when the other one is talking, or the husband and wife start demeaning and belittling each other, the counseling may not be successful. If a husband and wife have lost respect for each other, then the marriage is probably over.

Respect is a key to a good relationship. If respect exists in a relationship, then many other differences, dysfunctions, or conflicts can be overcome.

Honor is another manner of showing love. Paul instructs the Romans: *Outdo one another in showing honor* (Rom 12:10b).

There are many motivations for showing honor. Honor can be bestowed so that it is returned – a kind of mutual self glorification for which Jesus condemned the Pharisees. Honor can be a means of manipulation to get what I want. If I show honor, then a person is more likely to come my way – to see things my way.

James encourages us to show honor without partiality. If your honor arises from a heart of love for every person, then the honor becomes encouragement. Respect provides a foundation for the restoration of many a weak or wounded soul. And respect provides the foundation to heal many relationships.

> **Meditation:** Consider how well you show honor to others. Is this something you do well or is it something you need to work on?
>
> Next, consider your motivations for the honor that you show. When you show honor, are you loving the person at the time that you do it or are you loving yourself? Write your thoughts in your journal.

☩ ☩ ☩ ☩ ☩ ☩ ☩

NOTES:_____

_____

_____

_____

_____

_____

_____

_____

_____

_____

_____

III. Week Six, Day 7 (Date:)   **LOVE ONE ANOTHER**

> Behold my servant, whom I uphold, my chosen, in whom my soul delights; I have put my Spirit upon him; he will bring forth justice to the nations.
> He will not cry aloud or lift up his voice, or make it heard in the street; a bruised reed he will not break, and a faintly burning wick he will not quench; he will faithfully bring forth justice.
> He will not grow faint or be discouraged till he has established justice in the earth; and the coastlands wait for his law. **Isa 42:1-4**

Today is a day of gentleness. Look back over your journal for the past week.

Today is a day to focus on the gentleness of God, and to rest in it. The verse below is one of my favorite verses:

…a bruised reed he will not break, and a smoldering wick he will not quench, until he brings justice to victory (Matt 12:20).

> **Meditation:** Imagine the gentleness – almost a delicate touch – that this verse describes. The verse in Matthew is quoted from Isaiah above.
>
> Meditate on the connection between the gentleness described in Isaiah and justice. How does the gentleness of the Chosen Servant bring about justice? Why is proclamation not the tool used *"He will not cry aloud,"* but gentle mercy instead?

> Incorporate love into your devotional life. Spend time receiving love from God and then reciprocate by loving Him. *Faith works through love. Let everything you do be done in love. Above all these, put on love. Above all, keep loving one another.* Dedicate periods of time to love. Make a focus on love a habit so that loving becomes a part of you. Then you will walk in love just as Jesus walked in love.

SECTION III – TRUST: WEEK SEVEN

III.Week Seven, Day 1 (Date:)   **JUDGMENT**

> Brothers, if anyone is caught in any transgression, you who are spiritual should restore him in a spirit of gentleness. Keep watch on yourself, lest you too be tempted.
> Bear one another's burdens, and so fulfill the law of Christ. For if anyone thinks he is something, when he is nothing, he deceives himself. But let each one test his own work, and then his reason to boast will be in himself alone and not in his neighbor. For each will have to bear his own load. Let the one who is taught the word share all good things with the one who teaches. Do not be deceived: God is not mocked, for whatever one sows, that will he also reap. **Gal 6:1-7**

You who are spiritual…

I have a special gift. I can't truthfully claim a gift of gentleness, but this gift is almost as good. And I call it a special gift because it comes so naturally to me and it seems that I have always possessed it. My keen insight, discernment, and wisdom combine to contribute to my gift. I call it my "gift of judgment."

My gift of judgment allows me to look into the lives of others and to discern how they are wrong. The gift goes deeper than just actions although I pretty handily judge their actions. My gift of judgment discerns thoughts, motivations, and evil intent. Because it is a gift, my gift of judgment is not reserved just for people that I know well. I can readily exercise the gift on people that I don't know well, or even people that I don't know at all, but who look untrustworthy or suspicious.

It sometimes strikes me as peculiar how I often bestow this gift on people that I don't like or who have different opinions than I have. That seems to stir the gift up within me. I haven't yet found this gift in lists of the fruit of the spirit or of spiritual gifts, but I am still hopeful that others around me will confirm the gift of judgment within me.

The "gift of judgment" has many causes and takes many forms. Paul seems to be familiar with it. In this beautiful passage in Galatians about a spirit of gentleness and bearing one another's burdens, Paul gives as much caution as encouragement. It is as if Paul says approach faults of others "gently, carefully, delicately, circumspectly, and lovingly."

Another theme in this passage is that each person needs to look to his own garden. I have so many weeds in my garden that I really don't need to be criticizing my neighbor's garden. It is beneficial to remember that my own garden will be judged in the same way that I judge the gardens of others. Meme told us: **"I used to search for the perfect church. Then one day I realized that even if I found the perfect church that the day I joined it, the church would become** imperfect. So I stopped searching for the perfect church."

> **Meditation:** Judgment is expressed not only through words but through attitude. Reread the scripture above. Meditate on the tension between the gift of judgment and loving others. How does judgment impact...bearing the failings of the weak? ...bearing the burdens of others? ...honoring the saints? ...restoration of the fallen? ...giving to others? Write your thoughts in your journal.

☩ ☩ ☩ ☩ ☩ ☩ ☩

NOTES:_____

_____

_____

_____

_____

_____

_____

_____

_____

_____

_____

III. Week Seven, Day 2 (Date:)   **JUDGMENT**

> Judge not, that you be not judged. For with the judgment you pronounce you will be judged, and with the measure you use it will be measured to you. Why do you see the speck that is in your brother's eye, but do not notice the log that is in your own eye? Or how can you say to your brother, 'Let me take the speck out of your eye,' when there is the log in your own eye? You hypocrite, first take the log out of your own eye, and then you will see clearly to take the speck out of your brother's eye. **Matt 7:1-5**

For with the judgment you pronounce, you will be judged.

O God, help me to see more and more seriously, this matter of being at one with You AND with all those You have bought with Your blood, all those who are Your children through receiving Your salvation—whether I agree with them or not, whether they do me wrong, do wrong, etc. or not.

<u>Help me to see how wrong I am at times and how much I, as well, need Your grace and mercy from them and from You!</u> **Help me to humble myself, to lay aside all my pride and walk in deep humility with my brethren!! O God, I need Your grace, strength, truth and guidance, power, and wisdom here!! Be with me, Lord!!**   -Pastor Daniel Martin, 6/17/12

This teaching is a reality check from Jesus. In this kingdom lesson about judgment, Jesus teaches a couple of basic principles.

The first principle is that I am deceived. Subject to deception because of my pride and fleshly desires, I don't comprehend my own sinfulness. I know this principle to be true for me because, in His mercy, God has revealed my faults and foibles to me over many years. How blind I am to my own failings!

And He continues to reveal those failings as I spend time with Him. I am so thankful He does not do it all at once. That would be overwhelming to me. He patiently works at a pace that I can sustain – first revealing one faulty area to change and then, when I am ready, another.

The second principle is that my most confident judgments occur because I suffer from the same fault that I am judging. I see the fault because I am personally familiar with it. My judgment of my brother only underscores my own guilt. *Therefore you have no excuse, O man, every one of you who judges. For in passing judgment on another you condemn yourself, because you, the judge, practice the very same things* (Rom 2:1). So my judgment of another serves to heap further condemnation on myself.

Meditation: Consider the principle that judging another is actually judging your own self. What does this principle mean to you? Why is this principle true?

III. Week Seven, Day 3 (Date:)   **JUDGMENT**

> Early in the morning he came again to the temple. All the people came to him, and he sat down and taught them. The scribes and the Pharisees brought a woman who had been caught in adultery, and placing her in the midst they said to him, "Teacher, this woman has been caught in the act of adultery. Now in the Law Moses commanded us to stone such women. So what do you say?" This they said to test him, that they might have some charge to bring against him. Jesus bent down and wrote with his finger on the ground. And as they continued to ask him, he stood up and said to them, "Let him who is without sin among you be the first to throw a stone at her." And once more he bent down and wrote on the ground.
> But when they heard it, they went away one by one, beginning with the older ones, and Jesus was left alone with the woman standing before him. Jesus stood up and said to her, "Woman, where are they? Has no one condemned you?" She said, "No one, Lord."
> And Jesus said, "Neither do I condemn you; go, and from now on sin no more." **John 8:2-11**

"Woman, where are they? Has no one condemned you?"

O the glory of Your Love, Desire, Acceptance, and Delight in me.

O, this child feeds (and needs to feed more) on Your great attitudes and "take" on my life! Your thoughts toward me are so life-giving, so full of grace, mercy, care, compassion, and love—seeing beyond my faults to my needs, overlooking faults and rushing in to meet needs—all so You can draw me closer to Yourself, so that You can begin dealing with the faults, lovingly and tenderly letting Your love over time wash them out of my life!

O the power of Your love as manifested by Your PATIENCE!! Your patience with me is so overwhelming, so consistent over long stretches of time. You continue to be patient with me, while at the same time overlooking the foul smell of my attitudes, actions, words—and especially Motives! O thank You for Your great mercy, forgiveness, and PATIENCE toward me!

I now see where the one place You may tend to "lose patience with me" is where I lose patience with others—especially Carolyn [his wife]—after You have been so patient with me! Help me here, Lord!! Come and help me to be as patient, as forgiving toward all, as You have been and are toward me!   –Pastor Daniel Martin, 12/9/11

This story starts with a "gotcha" moment by the scribes and Pharisees. They picked the temple as the scene of the test. And they felt so confident of the trap that they continued to press for an answer after they had presented the woman and her plight to Jesus.

The Pharisees were focused on the woman's standing under the law. The law judged her and it ministered judgment and condemnation. That is what the law does.

The Pharisees were correct on this point. The law did judge and condemn her. One almost feels apprehensive for Jesus and for His response. But Jesus simply pointed out that *every* person stands judged and condemned by the law. To possess *authority* to pass righteous judgment, a person needed perfection under the law. Slowly the implication of Jesus' response dawned on them. One by one, they skulked away.

So what did the only Person in the story who possessed perfection, and thus had the authority to pass judgment, do? Jesus ministered patience and grace to the woman.

Only the grace of God preserves me from judgment. God is so patient with me. When I exercise my gift of judgment, I minister condemnation. But I desire patience and grace from God for myself. So the question is – am I going to minister judgment and condemnation to my neighbor, or am I going to minister patience and grace? This question is an important one. My choice determines the judgment or grace that I receive in turn.

Meditation: *"Love is patient."* Give thanks to the Lord for His patience toward you. Meditate on the numerous ways that He has been patient with you. Write in your journal how you have benefited from the Lord's patience. Then write in your journal how you want the Lord to show patience to you in the future.

Next, write in your journal how you plan to show patience and grace to other persons in the future.

Grace, grace, and more grace. God offers grace to His children. Receive His grace as you discern your own heart and face your faults, failings, and depravity. God wants to cover you in great grace! One who has experienced great grace will likewise be one who shows great grace, patience, and mercy. Amazing grace!

III. Week Seven, Day 4 (Date:)　　　　　　　　**JUDGMENT**

> John said to him, "Teacher, we saw someone casting out demons in your name, and we tried to stop him, because he was not following us."
> But Jesus said, "Do not stop him, for no one who does a mighty work in my name will be able soon afterward to speak evil of me. For the one who is not against us is for us." **Mark 9:38-40**

We tried to stop him.

This judgment is the judgment of exclusivity. My church, my ministry, or my posse has got something unique as to truth…or as to doctrine…or in ministry values…or in method. So other believers not privileged to belong to my circle are somehow inferior, less called, less anointed, and less effective. In this story, the disciples tried to stop the work of an outsider. Jesus immediately rebuked them.

The judgment of exclusivity makes me feel special. Judging others elevates me and my group. It soothes my insecurities and it feeds my pride. My judgment assures me that I am something special.

Judgment of others often is nothing more than a means to cater to my flesh – flesh which I should be crucifying. Sadly, my fleshly life harms, or even tears down, another believer and the ministry to which that believer is called.

> **Meditation:** Think of an occasion that you felt unfairly judged by another believer. How did that make you feel? What impact did that judgment have on you? Write about it in your journal.

Why does the captain of a ship keep a captain's log? Because the information is useful, because the log informs his decisions, and because the log keeps him accountable to the purpose of the journey. Remember to journal every day as a part of your devotional journey. Your journal is your captain's log. A journal imprints what you experience and records the things that you learn. You will see patterns that emerge and you will see growth that is occurring through the movements in your heart as you journey to your destiny in the Lord.

III. Week Seven, Day 5 (Date:)   **JUDGMENT**

> Someone in the crowd said to him, "Teacher, tell my brother to divide the inheritance with me."
> But he said to him, "Man, who made me a judge or arbitrator over you?" And he said to them, "Take care, and be on your guard against all covetousness, for one's life does not consist in the abundance of his possessions." **Luke 12:13-15**

"Man, who made Me a judge or arbitrator over you?"

When a person carefully studies judgment in the Bible, it can be a little confusing. There are multiple commands that basically say *"Judge not lest you be judged"* (Matt. 7:1). But on other occasions, we are instructed to *"judge with right judgment"* (Jn. 7:24). So when do we have a right to judge?

The answer goes back to authority. I have the right to judge when I have been given the authority to judge. In this case, Jesus, Who was God in the flesh and Who had power to discern, refused to speak a judgment on the offended man's claim. In response to the request to intervene, Jesus declined. He declined on the basis of authority. Jesus was not the proper authority to resolve the dispute.

When I judge another person but have no authority to do so, I have seized authority that I do not possess. I have engaged in presumption before the Lord. When I judge another person without right, I not only commit an offense against that person, I also commit an offense against the Lord and His authority. Ouch!

I have authority over my own life and my own sins, and I can judge my own life. But I do not have authority over my brother. In a relationship of accountability though, my friend can give me authority to judge. If my friend grants me authority or asks for my judgment, then I can deliver it.

A church also has authority to judge its members. That is why the church has ultimate authority to judge sin of its members (Matt 18:17). In fact, Paul directs believers to submit their disputes with other believers to the church, not to the courts (1 Cor 6:1-7).

Meditation: Meditate on two things. First, meditate on God as the righteous Judge. Consider the judgments of God and the power and majesty of His judgments.

Second, meditate on the relationship between authority and judgment. Focus on the idea that judgment without authority is a fearful infringement on God's authority. Write your thoughts in your journal.

☦   ☦   ☦   ☦   ☦   ☦   ☦

III. Week Seven, Day 6 (Date:)   **JUDGMENT**

> And the angels who did not stay within their own position of authority, but left their proper dwelling, he has kept in eternal chains under gloomy darkness until the judgment of the great day— just as Sodom and Gomorrah and the surrounding cities, which likewise indulged in sexual immorality and pursued unnatural desire, serve as an example by undergoing a punishment of eternal fire.
> Yet in like manner these people also, relying on their dreams, defile the flesh, reject authority, and blaspheme the glorious ones. But when the archangel Michael, contending with the devil, was disputing about the body of Moses, he did not presume to pronounce a blasphemous judgment, but said, "The Lord rebuke you."
> But these people blaspheme all that they do not understand, and they are destroyed by all that they, like unreasoning animals, understand instinctively. **Jude 1:6-10**

He did not presume to pronounce a blasphemous judgment.

Meme was a person of great mercy. But she also knew the power of words and the freedom of truth. If Meme heard an unduly negative thought being expressed, or a dire foreboding about the future, she had a simple response: "Now, I'm just not going to believe that."

Meme was also a great encourager. If she heard someone express something negative about another person – a judgment or a condemnation, she had the same response: "Now, I'm just not going to believe that." It was a gracious, but effective rejection of gossip and judgment.

If anyone deserves a blast of judgment, it is the devil, right? After all, he is full of rebellion, evil intention, and perverse acts. But Michael, the archangel, refused to speak judgment against him. Even when the devil was trying to claim something that did not belong to him, Michael refrained from words of judgment!

The respect that Michael had for the authority of God was so great – so deep, that he refrained from infringing on it. In fact, if Michael had engaged in judgment, he would have aligned himself with the rebellion of the devil. That is why the word "presume" is used. If Michael had pronounced judgment on the devil, he would have presumed to infringe on the authority of God.

That is also why the judgment would have been blasphemous. It is blasphemous to infringe on the authority of God. In fact, the veiled purpose of the dispute by the devil may have been to tempt the archangel, Michael, to rebel and to blaspheme by judging him.

Further, the devil is the "accuser of the brethren" who accuses them day and night before God (Rev 12:10). An improper judgment against a fellow believer joins in that accusation and aligns with the devil and his accusations. Our call is to encourage, to exhort, to uplift, and to honor our fellow believer – the one that we love - and not to tear him or her down.

> **Meditation:** Ask the Lord to put a guard over your lips. Spend time in the Presence of the Lord. Write a prayer to the Lord about words and judgment. In your own words, ask Him to put a guard over your lips as to judgments and gossip.

☩ ☩ ☩ ☩ ☩ ☩ ☩

NOTES:_____

_____

_____

_____

_____

_____

_____

_____

_____

_____

_____

_____

III. Week Seven, Day 7 (Date:)　　　　　　　**JUDGMENT**

> There is therefore now no condemnation for those who are in Christ Jesus. **Rom 8:1**

Today is a day of review. Look back over your journal for the past week.

Meditation: Meditate on the verse above.

First, apply this verse to yourself. Feel the joy, relief, release, and freedom that come from no condemnation in Christ Jesus. Use this verse as a basis for worship of the great mercy and glory of our God.

Next, apply this verse to others around you. Think of other believers that rub you the wrong way, offend you, or that you just don't feel good about. Feel the joy, relief, release, and freedom that come to them from no condemnation in Christ Jesus. Use this verse as a basis for worship of the great mercy and glory of our God as it is shown to other believers.

✝　✝　✝　✝　✝　✝　✝

NOTES:_____

_____

_____

_____

_____

_____

_____

_____

SECTION III – TRUST: WEEK EIGHT

III.Week Eight, Day 1 (Date:) **CONSOLATION AND DESOLATION**

> For a day in your courts is better than a thousand elsewhere. I would rather be a doorkeeper in the house of my God than dwell in the tents of wickedness. For the LORD God is a sun and shield; the LORD bestows favor and honor. No good thing does he withhold from those who walk uprightly.
> O LORD of hosts, blessed is the one who trusts in you! **Psa 84:10-12**

No good thing does He withhold from those who walk uprightly.

Once upon a time there was an old farmer who had worked his crops for many years. One day his horse ran away. Upon hearing the news, his neighbors came to visit. "Such bad luck," they said sympathetically.

"Maybe," the farmer replied.

The next morning the horse returned, bringing with it three other wild horses. "How wonderful," the neighbors exclaimed.

"Maybe," replied the old man.

The following day, his son tried to ride one of the untamed horses, was thrown, and broke his leg. The neighbors again came to offer their sympathy on his misfortune.

"Maybe," answered the farmer.

The day after, military officials came to the village to draft young men into the army. Seeing that the son's leg was broken, they passed him by. The neighbors congratulated the farmer on how well things had turned out.

"Maybe," said the farmer.[38]

This ancient Chinese story illustrates that I do not really know whether an event or circumstance that happens in my life will turn out for my good or turn out for my bad. But I instantly judge events by my immediate expectations and by my felt wishes and desires.

St. Ignatius proposed a standard to determine the impact of events and circumstances on my life. Is my soul turning to God or is it turning away from God (and toward itself)? Is that circumstance drawing me closer to God or is it drawing me further away from God? In making that decision, will it increase my faith, hope, and love, or will it decrease my faith, hope, and love? Am I moving toward the courts of the Lord, or am I moving away from the courts of the Lord toward the kingdom of self?

---

[38] From **www.awakin.org** (author unknown).

St. Ignatius called the movements toward God "consolation," and the movements away from God "desolation." He taught that I need to attune my heart and mind to discern when I move toward God and when I move away from God.

> **Meditation:** Consider your internal movements over the past few days. Have you been moving closer to the Lord? Or have you been moving further away? Has it been a little of both – like a pendulum? Write your thoughts in your journal.
>
> Now read again the verses from Psalm above. Would you rather spend one day in the courts of the Lord than a thousand elsewhere? Is movement away from the Lord a desolation to you?

☩ ☩ ☩ ☩ ☩ ☩ ☩

NOTES:_____

_____

_____

_____

_____

_____

_____

_____

_____

_____

III. Week Eight, Day 2 (Date:) **CONSOLATION AND DESOLATION**

> And the people of Israel did what was evil in the sight of the LORD. They forgot the LORD their God and served the Baals and the Asheroth. Therefore the anger of the LORD was kindled against Israel, and he sold them into the hand of Cushan-rishathaim king of Mesopotamia. And the people of Israel served Cushan-rishathaim eight years.
> But when the people of Israel cried out to the LORD, the LORD raised up a deliverer for the people of Israel, who saved them, Othniel the son of Kenaz, Caleb's younger brother. The Spirit of the LORD was upon him, and he judged Israel. He went out to war, and the LORD gave Cushan-rishathaim king of Mesopotamia into his hand. And his hand prevailed over Cushan-rishathaim. **Jdg 3:7-10**

The people of Israel cried out to the Lord.

The Book of Judges reads like a broken record.

1. The people of Israel wander away from God and begin serving other gods.

2. God allows another nation to capture, enslave, or otherwise torment Israel.

3. The people of Israel turn back to God and cry out to Him.

4. God raises up a judge whom God empowers to liberate them from their latest oppression.

5. The people of Israel serve God for a time, but then drift away from God.

6. Repeat.

This pattern occurs time after time in the Book of Judges. The question is: Was the oppression of Israel which God allowed, and even orchestrated at times, a good thing or a bad thing? It certainly seemed bad at the time.

St. Ignatius said: **"I call it consolation when an interior movement is aroused in the soul, by which it is inflamed with love of its Creator and Lord, and as a consequence, can love no creature on the face of the earth for its own sake, but only in the Creator of them all...Finally, I call consolation every increase of faith, hope, and love, and all interior joy that invites and attracts to what is heavenly and to the salvation of one's soul by filling it with peace and quiet in its Creator and Lord."**[39]

Despite the perceived evils of oppression, slavery, hunger, labor, and subjugation, the torments of Israel's enemies were a consolation to Israel if those torments caused the hearts of Israel to turn back to the Lord.

---

[39] *The Spiritual Exercises of St. Ignatius* §316, p.142.

Something that I perceive as bad can actually be a consolation. Illness, suffering, loss, a challenge in life, or a personal crisis can prompt me to turn to God, to call on Him, or to draw closer to Him. My sister says that there are experiences in life for which I would not give a plug nickel on the front end, but wouldn't take a million dollars for after I have survived them.

Something that feels bad can actually be a consolation. I can be unhappy, sad, or afraid, but still find assurance of God's presence in the midst of distress. My soul has turned toward Him.

☩ ☩ ☩ ☩ ☩ ☩ ☩

> **Meditation:** Identify an occasion or an event in your life that you felt was awful at the time, but it prompted you to draw closer to God. Seek the Lord about whether that event was actually a mercy or a kindness from God in drawing you closer to Him.

NOTES:_____

III. Week Eight, Day 3 (Date:)   CONSOLATION AND DESOLATION

> All King Solomon's drinking vessels were of gold, and all the vessels of the House of the Forest of Lebanon were of pure gold. None were of silver; silver was not considered as anything in the days of Solomon. And the king made silver as common in Jerusalem as stone, and he made cedar as plentiful as the sycamore of the Shephelah.
> **1 Kings 10:21, 27**

The king made silver as common as stone.

In 1978, a trio of researchers at Northwestern University and the University of Massachusetts attempted to answer this [question about lottery winners and happiness] by asking two very disparate groups about the happiness in their lives: recent winners of the Illinois State Lottery — whose prizes ranged from $50,000 to $1 million — and recent victims of catastrophic accidents, who were now paraplegic or quadriplegic. In interviews with the experimenters, the two groups were asked, among other things, to rate the amount of pleasure they got from everyday activities: small but enjoyable things like chatting with a friend, watching TV, eating breakfast, laughing at a joke, or receiving a compliment. When the researchers analyzed their results, they found that the recent accident victims reported gaining more happiness from these everyday pleasures than the lottery winners.[40]

Winning the lottery is a dream for many. Very few people would refuse that cash. But a study shows that the daily happiness quotient of persons severely injured in accidents is actually higher than the lottery winners.

And what was the impact of the vast wealth of Israel in King Solomon's day? We know the rest of the story. The hearts of the king and of the people turned away from the Lord.

St. Ignatius said: "I call desolation...as darkness of soul, turmoil of spirit, inclination to what is low and earthly, restlessness rising from many disturbances and temptations which lead to want of faith, want of hope, and want of love. The soul is wholly slothful, tepid, sad, and separated, as it were, from its Creator and Lord."[41]

An event or circumstance that seems good may actually be a desolation. Success at work, coming into wealth, acclaim from our friends, or a comfortable lifestyle may lead us away from God or turn our attention and love toward ourselves. Something that feels good can be a desolation. I can

---

[40] Melissa Dahl, *A Classic Psychology Study on Why Winning the Lottery Won't Make You Happier* www.cut.com (2016).

[41] *The Spiritual Exercises of St. Ignatius,* §317 p.142.

feel happy and have a great time, yet be in inner turmoil in the quiet moments of my life.

Consolation leads to God. Desolation ultimately leads to death.

> **Meditation:** Identify an occasion or an event in your life that you felt was wonderful, great, or fantastic at the time, but it actually led you further away from God (such as increased wealth, a relationship, or an event of great fun). Seek the Lord about whether that event was actually a blessing or a temptation.

✟ ✟ ✟ ✟ ✟ ✟ ✟

NOTES:_____

_____

_____

_____

_____

_____

_____

_____

_____

_____

_____

III. Week Eight, Day 4 (Date:) **CONSOLATION AND DESOLATION**

> Behold, I am doing a new thing; now it springs forth, do you not perceive it? I will make a way in the wilderness and rivers in the desert. Isa 43:19

I will make a way in the wilderness and rivers in the desert.

Oswald Chambers is the credited author of the Christian devotional, *My Upmost For His Highest*. *My Upmost For His Highest* is a Christian classic, and is considered by some to be the greatest devotional ever written.

Oswald Chambers was a minister in England. He delivered many sermons and lessons. His wife was a stenographer and took shorthand notes of many of them.

When World War I broke out, Oswald Chambers served in Egypt as a chaplain to Allied troops there. While in Egypt, he suffered an attack of appendicitis. Complications developed from the appendicitis. After a period of painful illness, Oswald Chambers passed away in a foreign land at the age of 43.

After his death, Mrs. Chambers transcribed his sermons and lectures. She compiled them into a book and published it under the title *My Upmost For His Highest*. So Oswald Chambers never saw "his" book in print. In fact, when he died, Oswald Chambers did not know that it ever existed.[42]

I have often wondered what Oswald Chambers thought and felt as he fell ill and perished in a foreign land. Did he feel that his life was wasted and tragically would not fulfill the ministry to which the Lord called him? Or more likely he lived in such surrender to his plight that he understood that his illness was in fact a consolation. He trusted that the Lord can bring great success in the midst of perceived failure.

The Lord measures success and failure differently than we do. Events that seem to us like abject failure may be wondrous success in the Lord's eyes.

Further, many times success arises out of failure. The lessons that failure teaches; the character that failure builds; and the attitudes born out of failure - all may contribute to fulfilling good things that the Lord intends.

Meditation: Today we surrender our failures to the Lord. As past events or circumstances that you perceive as personal failures come to mind, surrender them to the Lord. Tell the Lord that you trust Him for each of those times. Ask for help to continue to trust Him as new events or circumstances arise.

---

[42] Source: Oswald Chambers, *My Upmost For His Highest*, Introduction by James Reimann (Discovery House 1992).

III. Week Eight, Day 5 (Date:)   **CONSOLATION AND DESOLATION**

> About this we have much to say, and it is hard to explain, since you have become dull of hearing. For though by this time you ought to be teachers, you need someone to teach you again the basic principles of the oracles of God. You need milk, not solid food, for everyone who lives on milk is unskilled in the word of righteousness, since he is a child. But solid food is for the mature, for those who have their powers of discernment trained by constant practice to distinguish good from evil. **Heb 5:11-14**

Constant practice.

Because of his pastoral position and his activities with the underground "confessing church" in Nazi Germany, Dietrich Bonhoeffer, the great German theologian, was in danger from the Nazi regime in 1939. Friends made arrangements for him to flee to New York where he was safe and protected. Bonhoeffer had not been in New York for twenty-four hours when he was already deeply out of sorts. He was sure that he must go back.

Bonhoeffer spent 26 days in New York in the summer of 1939 with a tempest in his soul. In July, he wrote: "I have come to the conclusion that I have made a mistake in coming to America. I must live through this difficult period of our national history with the Christian people of Germany. I shall have no right to participate in the reconstruction of Christian life in Germany after the war if I do not share the trials of this time with my people." So Bonhoeffer chose to return to Germany and to his eventual death by hanging at the hands of the Nazi regime.[43]

I attend to my daily physical needs. I get up in the morning. I comb my hair and wash my face. I dress and I eat breakfast. Physically, I prepare for a healthy day.

Likewise, I need to prepare for a healthy day spiritually as well.

In order to understand the movements of my soul, I attend to my daily spiritual needs. If I can attune myself to initial movement toward God, I can invite this movement and encourage it. If I can attune myself to recognize subtle movement away from God, I can reject the movement early on and reverse course.

Discernment grows from attentiveness to these movements within me. I need a daily devotional life attuned to God to train my heart, mind, and senses to discern movements of my heart and soul.

---

[43] Eric Metaxas, *Bonhoeffer* pp. 321, 329 (Thomas Nelson 2010).

The writer of Hebrews says that powers of discernment are trained by constant practice. A person who is mature spiritually has engaged in this practice. That person knows that a lapse in practice causes dullness of hearing, so that person strives to practice and not to stop.

Constant practice helps me better understand and react to the events and circumstances around me. It also assists my decision making through discernment of whether a decision actually draws me closer to God or pulls me further away from Him.

Dietrich Bonhoeffer had every right to flee to America in the face of mounting persecution. By any fleshly standard, the decision to survive and to self preserve was a sound one. But his mature spiritual discernment quickly told him that self preservation was a desolation, and that returning to the clutches of a mad and savage "wolf" was in fact a consolation.

> **Meditation:** Consider the level of discernment that caused Dietrich Bonhoeffer to return to Nazi Germany and to the dangers it held for him. He had the faith and trust to put his own life at risk based on his discernment.
>
> Explore the discernment that you use about the movements of your heart. How are you engaging in practice of your powers of discernment to distinguish good from evil? What steps do you need to take to engage in the constant practice that the writer of Hebrews encourages?

Sensitivity to the movements of your heart is very important. Many times our hearts drift astray and we don't realize it until some type of damage is done to ourselves or to others. You are trying to develop a form of spiritual radar. This radar senses trouble coming from without or from within. One term that I use is "God conscious" – an internal awareness that sees situations from a godly perspective and reacts to them with godly instinct. Some of the most sanctified persons I have known have carefully and lovingly developed God consciousness within them over many years through time with God.

III. Week Eight, Day 6 (Date:)   **CONSOLATION AND DESOLATION**

> But stay awake at all times, praying that you may have strength to escape all these things that are going to take place, and to stand before the Son of Man. **Luke 21:36**

Stay awake at all times, praying that you might have strength.

O Lead me in blessing Your name, in giving thanks to You, acknowledging, and BOWING MY KNEES in total surrender and yieldedness to You in everything by blessing You in the middle of the muddle!

When things are going great, and when things are going awful!

Help me to BOW as Job did with the words, "You give and take away; Blessed be Your name." With the words of Dave Roever "God, I still believe in You!" With the hymns and prayers lifted to You by Paul and Silas in the Philippians' jail!

With the prayers of Daniel in Daniel 9 as he cried out to You for mercy in the middle of bondage and defeat. With the prayers of Daniel as he faithfully opened his window and prayed publicly in boldness to You even when it meant the lion's den. With the prayers of Shadrach and company as they knew that it probably meant being thrown into the fire to burn.

With the cries of Habakkuk in 3:17-18 in the middle of the land of desolation!

O help me to BOW before You in All things—good and bad!
    –Pastor Daniel Martin, 6/12/15

In times of desolation – times when you do not sense or feel the mercy, grace, and Presence of God, St. Ignatius advises patience and constancy. These seasons have a purpose in God's good plan, but they require surrender and trust in God. Practice patience as you wait on God and endure the season. Use the circumstance as an impetus to increase piety and devotion.

St. Ignatius advises a person not to make major life changes during these times. The situation can seem murky and judgment can be obscured. Patience and constancy are the words for the seasons of desolation.[44]

> **Meditation:** Write down in your journal what you deeply desire from God. What are the desires that you seek from Him? Tell Him those desires and then submit them to Him.

---

[44] *The Spiritual Exercises of St. Ignatius*, §318-321 pp.142-143. For further material on spiritual discernment and decision making, see Appendix A - <u>Discernment: A Process for Making Godly Decisions</u>.

III. Week Eight, Day 7 (Date:)   **CONSOLATION AND DESOLATION**

Review your journal entries over the past week.

> **Meditation:** Today is a day of listening. Put aside all distractions. Try to quiet your mind.
>
> First, listen and discern the thoughts and intents of your own heart. Where is your heart in relationship to God? What have been the movements of your heart over the last week? Identify where you are.
>
> Next, spend time listening to the Holy Spirit. Invite Him to come and to dwell around you, with you, and in you. See what He speaks to you – such as a movement, an image, or a word He gives you. Ask Him to minister to your soul.

☩   ☩   ☩   ☩   ☩   ☩   ☩

NOTES:_____

_____

_____

_____

_____

_____

_____

_____

_____

SECTION III – TRUST: WEEK NINE

III.Week Nine, Day 1 (Date:)   **OFFENSE**

> Strive for peace with everyone, and for the holiness without which no one will see the Lord. See to it that no one fails to obtain the grace of God; that no "root of bitterness" springs up and causes trouble, and by it many become defiled; that no one is sexually immoral or unholy like Esau, who sold his birthright for a single meal. **Heb 12:14-16**

See to it...that no root of bitterness springs up and causes trouble.

As I knelt in prayer, seeking You, waiting on You, listening for You, I believe I heard You! It was not like most times on my knees (it was not even ten minutes, only nine)—it was You speaking as I was listening.

The response You were wanting from me, was submission to the truths You were sharing with me, with me acknowledging my wrong, with me admitting to the things You were sharing with me that weren't pleasant.

I learned the following things:

Where there is bitterness, there is:

- acknowledgement that others are wrong
- acknowledgment that I have been mistreated
- acknowledgement that I have been far more wronged that I am wrong
- ignoring of You / ignoring of the cross ("It's all about me!")
- PRIDE flowing full and free—wave after wave of it, with growing intensity
- NO humility / Filth
- Lack of Godliness / Godlessness
- Ugliness / Changing from glory to less glory
- Becoming more like the accuser of the brethren than like You
- Siding with the enemy/Siding with the darkness
- Failure to see others better than myself
- Success in seeing myself exalted
- Seeking the kingdom of darkness more than the kingdom of God/light
- I leave myself vulnerable to every kind of attack of the enemy

- The very bitterness itself is his attack, an attack that I not only am sort of accepting, an attack that I am eagerly embracing!
- I am willing to be separated from You on some important levels, all for the sake of clinging to MY righteousness in the matter!
- I am becoming more and more blind—and accepting my blindness as a badge or something to be treasured

The pile keeps growing and I am only partially scratching the surface of the list!
   -Pastor Daniel Martin, 8/6/15

Every person suffers an offense. It may be a public embarrassment, an unkind word, a dysfunction imposed, or a cruel injustice. The question is not whether I will suffer an offense. The question is what will I do with it and how will I respond to it.

An offense causes resentment. That is the fleshly outcome. But if the offense is not properly dealt with and allowed to fester, then the resentment turns to bitterness. Over time, bitterness causes rejection of the offender (or even rebellion if it is a person in authority). The rejection leads to broken relationship.

That is why scripture warns against a root of bitterness. It causes trouble, but it also defiles. Bitterness defiles the person who holds onto it. It tears at the emotions and brings searing negativity into the equation. Bitterness grabs hold of a person and binds like shackles. The person seeks comfort for the hurt and turns to destructive and sinful behaviors to soothe the hurt feelings, which is rebellion against God.

Even more, bitterness against another person hinders relationship with God. That is why scripture says that we cannot love God if we do not love our brother (1 Jn 4:20). Bitterness against another person is like a lid that blocks our prayers to God and that halts the flow of His Spirit.

And even worse, bitterness defiles many. When bitterness is shared through gossip or backbiting, other people take up the offense and they share the bitterness. Bitterness can extend to many generations within a family or within a people. One offense can ruin many lives.

An offense that remains, and does not go away, must be addressed.

> **Meditation:** *Love is not resentful."* Think about the progression of resentment to bitterness to rejection (or rebellion) to broken relationship. Have you seen this progression occur? Has it ever happened in your life?
>
> Then consider the impact of bitterness. Look at the list in Pastor Martin's devotion. Have you experienced any of these fruits of bitterness in your life?

III. Week Nine, Day 2 (Date:)   **OFFENSE**

> If your brother sins against you, go and tell him his fault, between you and him alone. If he listens to you, you have gained your brother. **Matt 18:15**

He should come and apologize to me!

I had a friend at church who passed me in the corridor one Sunday. My friend stopped to chat. He began to tell me about a wrong that another church member ("Joe") had done to him. Not wanting to be a party to backbiting, I asked my friend "Have you gone to Joe, told him about this problem, and talked about it with him?"

My friend paused for a minute. The most horrified look came over his face. Then he said "Are you crazy? Joe is the one that did wrong to me! Why should I have to go to him about it? He should come and apologize to me!"

The way of the Cross is a path of humility. Offense causes hurt and pain to me. Yet Jesus instructs that the person who has been hurt approach the offending person and seek to resolve the matter. This instruction seemed unfair to my friend.

But this instruction is based on the character of God. I have offended God by my sin and rebellion. But God didn't withdraw Himself in bitterness and let me suffer in my condition. God approached me in the form of His Son and suffered the pains of earth in order to address my sin. Now, the Holy Spirit comes and convicts my heart of the sin and offense that I commit. It is an action arising out of love, not offense. It is not just an obligation, but an honor, when God calls me to reflect His character to the world by either having enough love and grace to forgive an offense and to forget it, or to go and to seek out reconciliation with the offending person as Jesus did with me.

If there is an offense, I either must let the offense go or approach the offending person about it. The fact that I have to humble myself to make the approach may prompt me to let the offense go. But if signs of the offense – resentment and bitterness - remain even after I have "let it go," then I need go and address it. That reflects the character of God and what He did for me.

> **Meditation:** Read the devotion from Pastor Martin below. Decide if and how the devotion is applicable to your life. Then make Pastor Martin's prayer your own prayer. You can add to the prayer, personalize it, or change it as you are moved.

O Father, the roots of pride run far too deep inside me!

Come and show me how to deal fiercely with them.

Show me how to walk in humility before You, before my wife, before all those in my

world! Come and take over in me, and cause me to become more and more what You want me to become!

I need You, O I need You!

All the above gives me a deeper understanding of the truth You showed me several years ago about Prov. 3:7 - *"Don't be impressed with your own wisdom; Instead, fear the Lord, and turn away from evil."* (NLT)

You showed me that when I think that I am right, that I have been mistreated, that I know what is best, that I am in the right, that I have the wisdom about the situations around me in my world, and that others, even at times You or Your Word don't quite measure up to the way that I understand them to be — that I need to back off, and acknowledge that I am not to be impressed with MY own wisdom!

That my understanding and wisdom are never the standard of true understanding or wisdom...

That Your wisdom and understanding are always the standard...

That instead of stewing over how MY wisdom/understanding are not being recognized, followed, honored, exalted...

That I should instead be focusing on fearing You and then turning away from the evil things that You expose in me!

Doing the above always leads to life, humility, loss of pride, better relationships with You and those around me!

Pride always blocks the flow of life and humility that so enhance all my relationships!

O for the gift of humility, for the gift of being able to acknowledge and then successfully deal with all malice, anger, hatred, self-righteousness, pride, bitterness, etc.
  - Pastor Daniel Martin, 8/6/15

☩ ☩ ☩ ☩ ☩ ☩ ☩

NOTES:_____

_____

_____

_____

_____

_____

_____

III. Week Nine, Day 3 (Date:)   **OFFENSE**

> All this is from God, who through Christ reconciled us to himself and gave us the ministry of reconciliation; that is, in Christ God was reconciling the world to himself, not counting their trespasses against them, and entrusting to us the message of reconciliation.
> Therefore, we are ambassadors for Christ, God making his appeal through us. We implore you on behalf of Christ, be reconciled to God. For our sake he made him to be sin who knew no sin, so that in him we might become the righteousness of God. **2 Cor 5:18-21**

What is the purpose of my approach?

One thing I have done when offended is to write a letter to the person. Writing it helps me clarify my thoughts and emotions. In the letter, I express my feelings and share my viewpoint. I have shown the letter to my wife before. On one occasion, after she read it, she asked me "Is the purpose of this letter to reconcile with [the person]?"

"Yes!" I said.

"Then rewrite it" she responded. "It is too harsh."

Chastened, I went back to rewrite the letter. But my wife was right. I had written the letter to address the offense, but I had also written the letter to assert my correctness in the situation. I was trying to soothe my hurt feelings.

Before we approach a person who has offended us, there are some questions that we need to answer. These questions are important for the engagement process and we will explore them over the next few days. The first question is: *What is the purpose of my approach?*

Reconciliation is a ministry of Jesus. In Christ, God was reconciling the world to Himself. Now, the message of reconciliation has been entrusted to me. I carry it to the world. But how can I carry the message of reconciliation if I have separated from other people that have offended me?

The purpose of my approach to a person who has offended me is reconciliation. My attitude and the manner in which I approach the person are very important. If I lash out, strike back, condemn, or show bitterness, the approach will probably fail.

Meditation: Consider the impact of offense and hurt on our attitude and feelings toward another person. How do those feelings impact the way that we act toward that person? How can we still have the love of God toward that person – a love that desires to be reconciled?

III. Week Nine, Day 4 (Date:)   **OFFENSE**

> Search me, O God, and know my heart! Try me and know my thoughts! And see if there be any grievous way in me, and lead me in the way everlasting! **Psa 139:23-24**

How have I been wrong in the matter?

You spoke a 4-word phrase to me that always depicts the foundation of bitterness, resentment, and unforgiveness: <u>MORE WRONG THAN WRONGED!</u>

No matter how wronged I may have been, there is even more wrong in me!

When all I see is how wronged I have been I am totally ignorant of all "planks" in my own eye, while magnifying the "splinter" in the other's eye! O God, come and help me to become quicker and quicker to forgive.

Focus makes all the difference! Always I can focus on how wrong I am rather than how wronged I have been—If I choose to do so; If I decide that Life is better than Death!
–Pastor Daniel Martin, 8/6/15

The second question regarding the offense is: *How have I been wrong in the matter?* The basis for this question is my painful awareness of my own heart – my propensity to sin; my pride; my self-righteousness, and my ever present selfishness.

We don't realize how much affirmation of our beliefs, opinions, and our righteousness feeds our ego, pride, and self. And if someone disagrees with us, our need for affirmation - a craven desire - makes us oppose that person and argue with him even more vehemently because WE NEED TO BE RIGHT! We want more to be right than to be holy.

If an offense involves an interaction or an argument, rarely is one person fully to blame and the other person faultless. In order to see the offense as God sees it, I need to realize my fault in the matter as well as my dysfunctions in the area of personal affirmation. My own self righteousness and shame often drive me to shift blame to another person when, in fact, I bear the blame.

If I am in fault in the matter in any way, then I need to confess that fault and to seek forgiveness. My confession is necessary for my own soul, even if I believe that other party acted in a terrible and inexcusable manner.

Further, if I have a position of authority in the situation, I especially need to confess, repent, and to seek forgiveness. As the person with authority, I am responsible for the relationship and I need to rectify my error with humility. Therefore in a marriage, a husband must swallow his pride and seek reconciliation with his wife. He makes the approach – humbly, gently, and lovingly.

Meditation: Ask God to search your heart and to show you any need for personal affirmation based on being right. Take time and ask Him to go from room to room in your heart. Ask Him if there is any lingering bitterness or offense based on situations in which you needed to be right. What does He show you? Write it down.

✟ ✟ ✟ ✟ ✟ ✟ ✟

NOTES:_____

III. Week Nine, Day 5 (Date:)   **OFFENSE**

> And Joseph said to his brothers, "I am Joseph! Is my father still alive?" But his brothers could not answer him, for they were dismayed at his presence.
> So Joseph said to his brothers, "Come near to me, please." And they came near. And he said, "I am your brother, Joseph, whom you sold into Egypt.
> And now do not be distressed or angry with yourselves because you sold me here, for God sent me before you to preserve life.
> For the famine has been in the land these two years, and there are yet five years in which there will be neither plowing nor harvest. And God sent me before you to preserve for you a remnant on earth, and to keep alive for you many survivors. So it was not you who sent me here, but God. He has made me a father to Pharaoh, and lord of all his house and ruler over all the land of Egypt. **Gen 45:3-8**

How is God working in this situation?

"The truly patient man minds not by whom he is exercised, whether by his superior, by one of his equals, or by an inferior; whether by a good and holy man, or by one that is perverse and unworthy. But indifferently from every creature, how much or how often anything adverse befall him, he takes all thankfully as from the hand of God, and esteems it a great gain. For with God, it is impossible that anything, however small, if only it be suffered for God's sake, should pass without its reward."[45]

When I suffer an offense, I am often focused on myself, my hurt feelings, and my wounded pride. The third question about an offense is a question that I should ask in all situations in my life: *How is God working in this situation?* It is an attempt to see the offense from God's perspective.

God can allow an offense to occur for many reasons:

- Maybe He wants to do a work in your heart.
- Maybe He wants to "rub off some rough edges."
- Maybe He wants to do a work in the heart of the other party.
- Maybe He wants you to be a witness to the other party by the manner that you approach him and handle the offense.
- Maybe He wants you to be a witness of God's love to nonbelievers who see or hear about the offense.
- Maybe He just wants to save a nation.

---

[45] *The Imitation of Christ*, pp. 131-132.

In Joseph's situation, God wanted to save a nation. When Joseph's brothers betrayed him, Joseph could have wallowed in the mire of hatred, revenge, or self pity. But he was able to see the hand of God working through their offense. *"So it was not you who sent me here, but God."*

The manner in which followers of Christ respond to offenses, disputes, and wrongs against them is an area that should distinguish them in the eyes of the world. That is because followers of Christ understand grace and have received grace, so they give grace.[46]

> **Meditation:** Consider Joseph and the way that he handled his offense. He was in a position of power. When his conniving brothers appeared in Egypt, he could have beheaded them on the spot. But Joseph did not allow bitterness against God or against his brothers to destroy a nation. He aligned himself with God's purpose in the offense.

╬ ╬ ╬ ╬ ╬ ╬ ╬

NOTES:____

[46] For more detail on how to respond to offenses and other challenges in life, see Appendix C – Engaging With Christ In Your Everyday Life, by Steve Parker.

III. Week Nine, Day 6 (Date:)　　　　　　　　　　　　　　　　**OFFENSE**

> I say this to your shame. Can it be that there is no one among you wise enough to settle a dispute between the brothers, but brother goes to law against brother, and that before unbelievers?
> To have lawsuits at all with one another is already a defeat for you. Why not rather suffer wrong? Why not rather be defrauded?
> But you yourselves wrong and defraud—even your own brothers!
> Or do you not know that the unrighteous will not inherit the kingdom of God? Do not be deceived: neither the sexually immoral, nor idolaters, nor adulterers, nor men who practice homosexuality, nor thieves, nor the greedy, nor drunkards, nor revilers, nor swindlers will inherit the kingdom of God. **1 Cor 6:5-10**

What rights are You calling me to surrender to You?

[I]t is the very public nature of crucifixion that is of the greatest significance. Meant to be the supreme deterrent against challenging Roman authority, it is the public (shaming) nature of the death that is essential. Other deaths may have been more painful, but the slow death of crucifixion emphasized its main lesson: do not challenge Rome. Crucifixion was an efficient means to satisfy the lust for revenge and cruelty, but of even greater importance, "by the public display of a naked victim at a prominent place – at a crossroads, in the theater, on *high ground*, at the place of his crime – crucifixion also represented his highest humiliation..."[47]

This final question about an offense may be the most difficult question of all: *What rights are You (the Lord) calling me to surrender to You?*

Rights are an important part of my personal dignity. I have rights as a citizen of my country, and if I believe Thomas Jefferson, I have inalienable rights given by my Creator such as life, liberty, and the pursuit of happiness. When my rights are violated by a person, by a group, or by a system, it is an offense – an unjust offense.

But this question involves the way of the Cross. Jesus had rights as well. The will of His Father called Him to give up those rights and to suffer the pains of injustice. Jesus stood silently before His accusers as they concocted lies to condemn Him. He could have opposed them and corrected them. But He did not.

Jesus stood silently before the tribunal that judged Him. He could have argued and asserted His rights against the injustice being done against Him. But He did not.

---

[47] Philip D. Jamieson, *The Face of Forgiveness*, pp.107-108 (IVP 2016) (quoting Martin Hengel).

Then Jesus bore the highest humiliation as he hung publicly exposed on the Cross. The way of the Cross requires surrender to God and trust in Him. The Cross means surrender of my rights to His will. I trust in Him that He is working His good will in the same way that He worked His good will on the Cross.

Paul suggests that it is better to suffer wrong and to be mistreated rather than assert my rights in a way that causes any reproach to the kingdom of God.

Make no mistake - the way of the Cross is not about fairness. The way of the Cross is about surrender for the sake of the kingdom of God.

> **Meditation:** *"Love does not insist on its own way."* Consider the rights that you hold precious. Write them in your journal.
>
> Next, consider the level of trust that have in God. Spend time in worship of God. Surrender those rights to Him. Ask Him if there are any rights He is asking you to surrender through love and trust in Him.

Questions to ask about an offense:

1. What is the purpose of my approach?
2. How have I been wrong in the matter?
3. How is God working in this situation?
4. What rights are You (the Lord) calling me to surrender to You?

> If you experience ups and downs in your devotional life, rest in the assurance that is normal. Sometimes you are lifted and you feel encouraged, and other times something hurts and you feel discouraged. That is normal. Your feelings are important, but your feelings do not define your journey. Allow God to direct and to define your experience. Your goal is to walk with God and to live under His Kingship. Be consistent in seeking Him and don't be shaken by lesser things.

III. Week Nine, Day 7 (Date:)   **OFFENSE**

Review your journal over the last week. What struck your heart during this week?

> **Meditation:** How do these lessons on offense apply to you in your personal life? Spend time with God searching your heart. Write down anything that you need to address or other application that God has shown you during this week.
>
> Then seek God about actions that you need to take.

☩   ☩   ☩   ☩   ☩   ☩   ☩

NOTES:_____

_____

_____

_____

_____

_____

_____

_____

_____

_____

SECTION III – TRUST: WEEK TEN

III. Week Ten, Day 1 (Date:) **POWER OF CONFESSION**

> In the course of time Cain brought to the LORD an offering of the fruit of the ground, and Abel also brought of the firstborn of his flock and of their fat portions. And the LORD had regard for Abel and his offering, but for Cain and his offering he had no regard. So Cain was very angry, and his face fell.
> The LORD said to Cain, "Why are you angry, and why has your face fallen? If you do well, will you not be accepted? And if you do not do well, sin is crouching at the door. Its desire is for you, but you must rule over it."
> Cain spoke to Abel his brother. And when they were in the field, Cain rose up against his brother Abel and killed him.
> Then the LORD said to Cain, "Where is Abel your brother?" He said, "I do not know; am I my brother's keeper?"
> And the LORD said, "What have you done? The voice of your brother's blood is crying to me from the ground." **Gen 4:3-10**

His face fell.

I have spent years in ministry to groups of refugees from all over the world. I could not understand the actions of some of the refugee young men that I coached in soccer. If the team was winning, behavior on the field was good. My players acted with sportsmanship and decorum.

But if the team started to lose, some of my players despaired. I tried to encourage them to keep trying – that their effort and behavior was more important than the score of the game. If it became apparent, however, that the loss was going to occur, the players fell to pieces. They argued and picked fights. I tried to restrain them, but I had multiple games in which players were ejected for bad behavior. For some reason, fighting or getting kicked off the field seemed a better alternative than losing with sportsmanship and determination.

What I learned from coaching soccer teams with young men from other cultures is that the highest value of some cultures is respect. Receiving respect is the highest praise and experiencing disrespect is the worst insult. My players would rather fight, argue, or just plain quit, than suffer the ignominy of defeat.

To understand the power of confession, we must first understand the power of shame. When Cain's offering was not regarded, his face fell. He felt ashamed. In response, the Lord encouraged Cain to resist the sin that may result from shame and to overcome it.

But Cain allowed shame to determine his actions. In his wounded pride, he irrationally struck at the perceived cause of his shame – his brother. God was the One that did not regard Cain's offering. Yet Cain shifted blame to Abel. Then he killed him. When confronted with the murder, Cain denied his relationship with his own brother: *"Am I my brother's keeper?"*

In his book *The Soul of Shame*, Dr. Curt Thompson says shame does two major things:

1. Shame corrupts our relationships. These damaged relationships are with God and with each other; and

2. Shame disintegrates any and all gifts of vision and creativity. Shame is a primary hindrance to prevent us from using the gifts we have been given.

Shame's impact is to disintegrate any system it targets – our personal life, our story, family, marriage, friendship, church, school, community, business, or even a political system.[48]

I need to realize how much my own shame connects with my feelings of offense and hurt. Another person has disrespected me – maybe publicly. That disrespect makes me feel awful about myself. It ignites feelings of insufficiency or inadequacy that I already have. So I feel animosity toward that person. In fact, I may in truth want to kill him – just like Cain killed Abel. The offender deserves to be punished. Right?

> **Meditation:** Every family experiences shame. Consider shame that has occurred in your own family. It can be shame that you felt or that another family member felt.
>
> Then consider the impact of that shame. How did that shame affect behavior? How did it affect relationships? What destructive impact of shame occurred?

☩ ☩ ☩ ☩ ☩ ☩ ☩

> Worship is a good way to enter into the Presence of God. A shame response avoids the Presence of God. The Presence of God defeats shame because it restores relationship with Him and His Presence assures us that He loves and accepts His children. Incorporate regular times of worship into your devotional life.

---

[48] Curt Thompson, MD, *The Soul of Shame*, pp. 13, 146-147 (IVP 2015).

III. Week Ten, Day 2 (Date:)   POWER OF CONFESSION

> So when the woman saw that the tree was good for food, and that it was a delight to the eyes, and that the tree was to be desired to make one wise, she took of its fruit and ate, and she also gave some to her husband who was with her, and he ate.
> Then the eyes of both were opened, and they knew that they were naked. And they sewed fig leaves together and made themselves loincloths.
> And they heard the sound of the LORD God walking in the garden in the cool of the day, and the man and his wife hid themselves from the presence of the LORD God among the trees of the garden.
> But the LORD God called to the man and said to him, "Where are you?"
> And he said, "I heard the sound of you in the garden, and I was afraid, because I was naked, and I hid myself."
> He said, "Who told you that you were naked? Have you eaten of the tree of which I commanded you not to eat?"
> The man said, "The woman whom you gave to be with me, she gave me fruit of the tree, and I ate." **Gen 3:6-12**

The man and the wife hid themselves.

Public life means public exposure which can trigger feelings of shame. In politics, fear of exposure often leads to a "cover up" in the form of denial, perjury, stonewalling, or tampering with evidence. Many times, the cover up creates a much greater problem than the initial wrongdoing. In my lifetime, major political scandals have erupted not from the initial error, but from the cover up - Watergate, Iran contra, Bill Clinton and Monica Lewinsky. Presidents have been impeached and reputations have been ruined not so much due to the original trespass, but because the leader tried to hide it.

Shame may be described as a felt emotion such as inadequacy, insecurity, humiliation, or loss of dignity. Dr. Curt Thompson says shame is an emotion that would declare some version of:

- "I am not enough"
- "There is something wrong with me"
- "I am bad"
- "I don't matter"

Shame is a perception of who we are, not just what we have done.[49] Adam

---
[49] *The Soul of Shame*, p.24.

and Eve committed a sinful act, but the realization of their naked condition – how they perceived themselves – caused them to cover up.

My reaction to shame is to hide. That is what Adam and Eve did. They covered themselves and then hid from God's presence. I hide because I am ashamed, but I also have in my memory and my self-consciousness a sense that I am shameful. Shame is ingrained from early years. Because I have the feeling of shame, my mind believes it.

Finally, note the reaction of a shamed person when confronted. *"The woman whom You gave to be with me, she gave me fruit of the tree, and I ate."* Adam shifts blame to Eve and even attempts to include God in the circle of blame as well. Shame prompts the blame game. Shamed people shame other people.[50]

> **Meditation:** Explore your feelings about the shame declarations above from Dr. Thompson: "I am not enough;" "There is something wrong with me;" "I am bad;" or "I don't matter." Do you relate to any of those declarations? Have you ever felt them?
>
> What have you experienced as far as hiding or a cover up due to shame? What did you do to address the issue? Write about it in your journal.

NOTES:_____

_____

_____

_____

_____

_____

_____

_____

---

[50] *The Soul of Shame*, p. 29.

III. Week Ten, Day 3 (Date:)　　　POWER OF CONFESSION

> Therefore, since we are surrounded by so great a cloud of witnesses, let us also lay aside every weight, and sin which clings so closely, and let us run with endurance the race that is set before us, looking to Jesus, the founder and perfecter of our faith, who for the joy that was set before him endured the cross, despising the shame, and is seated at the right hand of the throne of God. **Heb. 12:1-2**

Shame exposed.

When I was a young child, I loved to play soldier. One day, I marched around the house with a curtain rod that was my spear. I entered an empty room that had a running box fan on the floor. I charged the fan and stabbed it with my spear. Curtain rods in box fans make an awful racket. Terrified, I left my spear in the fan and fled from the room. My parents ran toward the room as I ran out of it.

My father asked me if I knew anything about the curtain rod he found in the fan. Scared and ashamed, I denied any knowledge. He asked me if I knew how the curtain rod got into the fan. No knowledge. To my parents' credit, they did not discipline the young child despite the compelling circumstantial evidence.

That evening, my father and I went on a walk. My father told me the story of Peter and his fearful denial of Jesus. Peter fled in tears – ashamed and hurt by his own lies and betrayal. Next he told me of Jesus' restoration of relationship with Peter through love.

Then my father asked me if I had put the curtain rod into the fan. With conviction, I confessed my guilt and he forgave me. There was no further discipline.

It was an unforgettable lesson to a young child about truth, denial, shame, confession, and forgiveness. I also will never forget the relief that I felt as I unburdened myself and as the relationship between me and my father was restored.

Shame is self perpetuating. My feelings about myself lead to fear of exposure which in turn causes me to hide. Shame works through fear. Tragically, the more I hide my shame, the greater it grows. Shame leads to more shame. It is a vicious cycle. Some of the rooms of my heart that I have carefully walled off and protected are rooms filled with shame.

Exposure to the light facilitates healing from shame. In fact, exposure targets shame. That is why vulnerability helps me heal from shame. Vulnerability is the willingness to be seen. The practice of vulnerability with others helps me face my fears of rejection and find acceptance as a person.[51]

---

[51] *The Soul of Shame*, pp.110-111.

Please note that vulnerability is a two-edged sword. If my vulnerability is practiced among people that use it as an opportunity for judgment and condemnation, it can cause more hurt and rejection. That cuts deep and can increase my shame.

But if my vulnerability is practiced with persons that I trust and who love me, healing can be a life giving outcome. That is one reason relationships of accountability can be so wonderful. Healthy relationships with accountability help to heal shame.

Vulnerability is another area in which I practice surrender and trust. Through vulnerability, I surrender my pride, my reputation, and my self-righteousness. I entrust myself to the love of the Lord and to the love of my friends as I expose my heart of shame.

When Jesus was crucified, He was fully exposed. He was condemned, rejected, hated, and naked to the world. But unlike Adam, He did not hide. He *"despised the shame."*

Note also that Jesus despised the shame *"for the joy set before Him."* This joy arises from the joy of restored relationship with His Father and with His brothers and sisters – you and me. We can share in that joy when we walk in the way of the Cross with Him.

> **Meditation:** Do you identify with the vicious cycle of shame? Journal about an area in which you have struggled with shame.
>
> Consider contexts in which you participate that require vulnerability. How have those contexts been healthy for you? Journal about how those contexts have contributed toward healing and spiritual health for you.

Take your time in each devotion to explore it fully. You will get out of the devotional time what you put into it. Be slow and deliberate. If you need to spend more than one day on a devotion, that is fine. The ongoing work of God is the important thing, not a time table or that you met a deadline for completing devotions.

III. Week Ten, Day 4 (Date:) POWER OF CONFESSION

> Is anyone among you sick? Let him call for the elders of the church, and let them pray over him, anointing him with oil in the name of the Lord. And the prayer of faith will save the one who is sick, and the Lord will raise him up. And if he has committed sins, he will be forgiven.
> Therefore, confess your sins to one another and pray for one another, that you may be healed. The prayer of a righteous person has great power as it is working. **James 5:14-16**

Confess your sins to one another.

Keep me from secret sin, from sins that I know nothing about, from sins that I try to hide—even from myself.

Help me to be a quick confessor of sin, confessing them to You, confessing them to whomever I have wronged, and confessing them to others around me to hold me accountable to them in overcoming them. O I need Your help, Your anointing in this, O Savior and Friend!

Thank You for Your powerful patience with me, but help me to have a reverent fear of You that moves me to be quicker and more diligent in being instant in confession!!

O, I need Your help in this, O blessed Forgiver and Cleanser of all sin!
-Pastor Daniel Martin, 10/14/15

Confession is powerful. Confession exposes sin and it also exposes shame. Confession is a powerful tool to bring shame to the light. Confession overcomes shame and defeats its destructive effect on our lives.

In this passage from James, note the correlation between confession and healing. Confession facilitates healing of wounds of the heart and of wounds of the soul. Confession also alleviates stress, emotional turmoil, and guilt complexes that can cause or contribute to physical and mental illness. Yet confession is not a strong value in many Christian cultures. I want to protect my pride, dignity, and reputation carefully. It is so strange that I prefer to be sick rather than to confess.

The power of confession underscores the need for a direct and honest apology when there is an offense. Many times I want to make a proud or half-hearted confession when addressing an issue – an apology like "I'm sorry that you feel I said something wrong about you" or "I regret the fact that you didn't like what I did." These are not true confessions and actually play the blame game by implying there is something wrong with the other person instead of you.

A good confession specifically states my sin without excuse - whether it was my words, my actions, or my attitude. A good confession then asks for forgiveness from the other person.

And, in a healthy engagement, a good response to a confession grants forgiveness unequivocally. Absolution should be expressed with specificity, and grace should be accorded to restore the relationship.

> **Meditation:** Consider the impact of confession on shame. Seek the Lord about ways that you can incorporate confession into your life. Who are the believers to whom you can entrust your struggles, issues, and innermost thoughts? Write in your journal any prompting that the Lord gives you.

☦ ☦ ☦ ☦ ☦ ☦ ☦

NOTES:

III. Week Ten, Day 5 (Date:)   **POWER OF CONFESSION**

> A Psalm of David. O LORD, who shall sojourn in your tent? Who shall dwell on your holy hill?
> He who walks blamelessly and does what is right and speaks truth in his heart; who does not slander with his tongue and does no evil to his neighbor, nor takes up a reproach against his friend;
> in whose eyes a vile person is despised, but who honors those who fear the LORD; who swears to his own hurt and does not change;
> who does not put out his money at interest and does not take a bribe against the innocent. He who does these things shall never be moved. **Psalm 15**

He who does not slander with his tongue and does no evil to his neighbor.

I had a friend, a coworker in ministry, who did something that offended me. I went home and searched my heart. I wrote a letter to him about it. After more soul searching and "spousal accountability" that caused me to soften the letter, I sent it.

A couple of days later, my friend called me and said he received my letter. He asked if he could come see me immediately. I was in my backyard doing work, but agreed he could come.

When my friend arrived, he came straight to me in the backyard. He acknowledged his action and confessed it. He apologized profusely and asked for my forgiveness.

I granted the forgiveness verbally and we talked a little bit more. As my friend was leaving, I said "Wait a minute! I need to tell you one more thing. I want you to know that I have not discussed this matter with anyone else. The matter is now over and I will not discuss it with anyone else."

My friend said "Thank you!" I don't know how my friend felt but my respect for my friend increased from that day on.

Many people think the antithesis to confession is silence or even isolation. But the antithesis to confession is gossip. Gossip proclaims judgment and condemnation of another publicly instead of confession of my wrong. Gossip tries to pin sin on another person instead of facilitating its release through confession and forgiveness.

Gossip intends to increase the shame of another person while it feeds the pride of the slanderer through the pretense of superiority. But in fact gossip is a "shame shield" that connects to the inner shame of the person who gossips. The pride of the slanderer is a commonly used shield to hide and placate felt shame.

That is why the instruction in Matthew 18 about addressing an offense says

"Go and tell him his fault, <u>between you and him alone</u>" (Matt 18:15b). When I gossip about an offense, I have doubled the transgression.

Consider the impact of gossip. Gossip actually brings third parties into the offense, and tries to make them partake of the offense and to feel it. How hard will it be to reconcile with my friend after my friend hears that I have been talking with others about him? I have broken trust and destroyed the relationship, sometimes irreparably.

> **Meditation:** In scripture, there are lists of evils such as fornication, murder, and theft. Gossip is included as a serious sin in many of these lists. See Matt 15:19. Meditate on the reasons why gossip is treated so harshly in scripture. In your journal, write down reasons why gossip is so offensive.

☦ ☦ ☦ ☦ ☦ ☦ ☦

NOTES:_____

III. Week Ten, Day 6 (Date:)   **POWER OF CONFESSION**

> And he arose and came to his father. But while he was still a long way off, his father saw him and felt compassion, and ran and embraced him and kissed him. And the son said to him, 'Father, I have sinned against heaven and before you. I am no longer worthy to be called your son.'
> But the father said to his servants, 'Bring quickly the best robe, and put it on him, and put a ring on his hand, and shoes on his feet. And bring the fattened calf and kill it, and let us eat and celebrate. For this my son was dead, and is alive again; he was lost, and is found.' And they began to celebrate.
> Now his older son was in the field, and as he came and drew near to the house, he heard music and dancing. And he called one of the servants and asked what these things meant. And he said to him, 'Your brother has come, and your father has killed the fattened calf, because he has received him back safe and sound.'
> But he was angry and refused to go in. His father came out and entreated him, but he answered his father, 'Look, these many years I have served you, and I never disobeyed your command, yet you never gave me a young goat, that I might celebrate with my friends. But when this son of yours came, who has devoured your property with prostitutes, you killed the fattened calf for him!'
> And he said to him, 'Son, you are always with me, and all that is mine is yours. It was fitting to celebrate and be glad, for this your brother was dead, and is alive; he was lost, and is found.'
> **Luke 15:20-32**

Father, I have sinned against heaven and before you.

By our own attitudes we may determine our reception by Him. Though the kindness of God is an infinite, overflowing fountain of cordiality, God will not force His attention upon us. If we would be welcomed as the Prodigal was, we must come as the Prodigal came; and when we so come, even though the Pharisees and the legalists sulk without, there will be a feast of welcome within, and music and dancing as the Father takes his child again to His heart.[52]

This story is the second part of the parable of the prodigal son. The prodigal son came to his senses, returned home, and confessed his sin to his father. The father received him with open arms, rejoiced in his return, and celebrated

---

[52] A. W. Tozer, *The Knowledge of the Holy* p. 84 (Harper One 1961).

the restoration of relationship. The parable could have ended there and been a beautiful illustration of the love of God toward even the most wayward sinner.

But the parable of the prodigal son continues with the story of the elder brother. He believes what the younger brother did – he *"devoured the father's property with prostitutes"* - was shameful. Rather than being celebrated, the younger brother should be shamed, judged, and condemned.

Dr. Curt Thompson says that to be fully known and to be fully loved leads to absolute joy.[53] We can't be loved fully without being fully known. Shame makes me think that if I am known that I won't be loved.

But the love of the Father assures me that I can be fully known – fully vulnerable – and still be fully loved. Confession, like the confession of the prodigal son, leads to being fully known. Then love can be shared, and can bring joy.

The elder son sees himself as righteous and is not fully known as a result. He does not even truly see himself. His self-righteous heart renders him unable to participate in the joy of restoration of relationship.

But the father and the prodigal son are experiencing utter joy. Reconciliation of broken relationship is a Source of Joy.

> **Meditation:** Think of a time that a relationship you had was threatened or even broken, but then restored. What words or actions led to restoration? Journal about the joy that you experienced as a result of the restoration.
>
> Next, journal about the heart of God. How is the heart of God expressed in reconciliation and in this story? *"Love bears all things."*

> Consider whether you and your mentor or devotional partner should incorporate confession into your relationship. In healthy confession, correction and forgiveness are both administered in love. Confession is one of the keys to healing and to release of the work of the Holy Spirit and His power into your life.

---

[53] *The Soul of Shame*, p. 126.

III. Week Ten, Day 7 (Date:)   **POWER OF CONFESSION**

> Those who look to him are radiant, and their faces shall never be ashamed. **Psa 34:5**

Review your journals over the past week.

Meditation: Imagine that you are looking at the face of the Father. See His countenance as He gazes upon you. Look at the fullness of love that is in His eyes. Allow His love to make you radiant.

Next, imagine that you are looking at Jesus on the cross. He is condemned, rejected, hated, and naked to the world. But He is despising the shame that He bears – for it is in fact your shame that He bears so that you do not need to bear it. Allow His love to make you radiant.

✠   ✠   ✠   ✠   ✠   ✠   ✠

NOTES:_____

_____

_____

_____

_____

_____

_____

_____

SECTION III – TRUST: WEEK ELEVEN

III. Week Eleven, Day 1 (Date:)   **POWER OF FORGIVENESS**

> Seek the LORD while he may be found; call upon him while he is near; let the wicked forsake his way, and the unrighteous man his thoughts; let him return to the LORD, that he may have compassion on him, and to our God, for he will abundantly pardon.
> For my thoughts are not your thoughts, neither are your ways my ways, declares the LORD. For as the heavens are higher than the earth, so are my ways higher than your ways and my thoughts than your thoughts. **Isa 55:6-9**

So are My ways higher than your ways.

Difficult time getting over something said that hurt/wounded. I know what I have to do, but having a very hard time doing it. I guess it comes down to how much do I want to have a good hour with You, how much I value the relationship I have with You. This becomes a no-brainer when I put it in these terms—these are the terms they must be put in!

OK, Father, I choose to forgive. Empower me to do it, help me to know how to really do it, to let go of the hurt/wound, bless the offender, get over it. HELP ME TO SEEK TO HONOR YOU IN EVERY AREA WHERE I THINK I HAVE BEEN WRONGED—BY FORGIVING, TRULY FORGIVING!!

I must find my life, acceptance, love, and delight in You—not in anyone else, because ultimately, only You are the perfect One, only You can be what You say You will be at all times. All others will fail and in their failures will hurt and wound those around them.

I now choose to let go of the record of the wrong, to let the person go and tell myself that they owe me nothing, that I will to the best of my ability with God's help love them, bless them, be kind to them, not rejoice in negatives, not feel like a martyr, not have a pity party, do what love does for them, etc. Help me, Lord.

O the glory and life that flow where forgiveness flows, where I am so aware of how much I have been forgiven, that I easily and readily forgive.

I have lived with this unforgiveness for most of this day (Sunday), and it has dragged me down. I need to be free. I am free as I now forgive. I thank You that I can rise and be what You call for me to be in this.   –Pastor Daniel Martin, 3/17/14

God tells us that His ways are higher than our ways and His thoughts are higher than our thoughts. That is true in every facet. But the context of this passage from Isaiah is noteworthy. Immediately before this statement are the words *"He will abundantly pardon."*

Perhaps nothing distinguishes God more than His willingness to forgive the vilest creep. Forgiveness is necessary to restore relationship. So what does a perfect God Who desires relationship do? He forgives. What glory is here!

When we forgive, we honor God by following His example and His word. And when we fail to forgive, we dishonor Him because we reject His nature.

> **Meditation:** Consider how forgiveness is a part of the nature of God. Forgiveness flows from the very heart of God.
>
> Then spend time on the honor and exaltation in God's forgiveness. What do you want to say to God about His willingness to forgive? Write it in your journal.

☦ ☦ ☦ ☦ ☦ ☦ ☦

NOTES:_____

III. Week Eleven, Day 2 (Date:)   POWER OF FORGIVENESS

> Then Peter came up and said to him, "Lord, how often will my brother sin against me, and I forgive him? As many as seven times?"
> Jesus said to him, "I do not say to you seven times, but seventy-seven times.
> "Therefore the kingdom of heaven may be compared to a king who wished to settle accounts with his servants. When he began to settle, one was brought to him who owed him ten thousand talents. And since he could not pay, his master ordered him to be sold, with his wife and children and all that he had, and payment to be made. So the servant fell on his knees, imploring him, 'Have patience with me, and I will pay you everything.'
> And out of pity for him, the master of that servant released him and forgave him the debt. But when that same servant went out, he found one of his fellow servants who owed him a hundred denarii, and seizing him, he began to choke him, saying, 'Pay what you owe.' So his fellow servant fell down and pleaded with him, 'Have patience with me, and I will pay you.'
> He refused and went and put him in prison until he should pay the debt. When his fellow servants saw what had taken place, they were greatly distressed, and they went and reported to their master all that had taken place.
> Then his master summoned him and said to him, 'You wicked servant! I forgave you all that debt because you pleaded with me. And should not you have had mercy on your fellow servant, as I had mercy on you?' And in anger his master delivered him to the jailers, until he should pay all his debt.
> So also my heavenly Father will do to every one of you, if you do not forgive your brother from your heart." **Matt 18:21-35**

So also my heavenly Father will do to every one of you if…

Help me to be a "quick forgiver." Help me to decide at the beginning of the day not to take on the heavy loads that always come from unforgiveness. What horrible loads those are.

You call them TORMENTS—and that is exactly what they are! There is so much torment that comes from unforgiveness. The tormentor is the devil and his demons. They are empowered to bring that torment (and they always do) when I fail to forgive as I have been forgiven! (This is the truth of Matthew 18.)

O show me Your ways!!

Help me to walk in Your paths of righteousness in this area of my life!!
−Pastor Daniel Martin, 9/11/12

Jesus' parable in Matthew 18 is about forgiveness. But it also is about imprisonment and bondage and about torments.

When I hold onto an offense and don't forgive another person, I believe I have something on them. In my anger, I hold it "over their head" as a means to retaliate. I feel empowered. Because I have not released the sin, I believe I have kept them in bondage.

But Jesus' parable illustrates that my unforgiveness puts ME in prison! Not only have I allowed bitterness and contempt to enter my own soul, but I have damaged my relationship with my King. I put myself in torment. As those devices of the enemy continue to fester, they place me in great danger of unforgiveness from my heavenly Father.

> **Meditation:** Reflect on the impact of unforgiveness. Search your heart for any areas of bitterness, offense, or unforgiveness. Ask the Holy Spirit to help you. For each area that He reveals to you, ask Him for help in letting it go or in addressing it. Ask Him to help you walk in forgiveness in all areas of your life.

If your mind wanders during your devotional time, don't beat yourself up over it. Allow yourself simply to come back to the devotion and to enter back into it. Use discernment. Sometimes the Lord quickens something to our heart that you need to explore in detail. Other times, thought patterns take over and lead you to empty musings. In the latter situation, just return to the devotion when you realize it occurred.

III. Week Eleven, Day 3 (Date:) **POWER OF FORGIVENESS**

> Now when they heard these things they were enraged, and they ground their teeth at him. But he, full of the Holy Spirit, gazed into heaven and saw the glory of God, and Jesus standing at the right hand of God. And he said, "Behold, I see the heavens opened, and the Son of Man standing at the right hand of God."
> But they cried out with a loud voice and stopped their ears and rushed together at him. Then they cast him out of the city and stoned him. And the witnesses laid down their garments at the feet of a young man named Saul.
> And as they were stoning Stephen, he called out, "Lord Jesus, receive my spirit."
> And falling to his knees he cried out with a loud voice, "Lord, do not hold this sin against them." And when he had said this, he fell asleep. And Saul approved of his execution. **Acts 7:54-8:1a**

Lord, do not hold this sin against them.

This story is about Stephen, the first martyr of the church. But this story is also about Saul, the persecutor of the church who would become Paul, the great apostle.

Forgiveness is a release from death – the legal consequence of sin. It is a release from guilt, bitterness, and shame. Forgiveness releases the power of creativity and beauty. Maybe most importantly, forgiveness releases me to be the person that God called me to be – to walk in my true identity. Forgiveness is powerful.

Stephen did not have to seek forgiveness for his murderers. Nothing required him to follow the example of our Lord on the cross and to release them. But he did.

I believe that the attitude of forgiveness by Stephen released the power of the cross into Saul's life. Stephen's release allowed a work of grace in Saul's heart. Forgiveness paved the path for Saul to fulfill his call in the Lord. He became Paul, the great apostle of the kingdom of God.

> **Meditation:** Think of the billions of souls impacted by the ministry of Paul. How many persons did he convert? How many churches did he plant? How many coworkers did he mentor?
>
> Now consider the power of the words of Stephen that Saul heard. Do you think that Saul called those words to mind in the years that followed and received grace from them? Ask the Lord to make forgiveness of others a reality in your life.

III. Week Eleven, Day 4 (Date:)   **POWER OF FORGIVENESS**

> Come now, let us reason together, says the LORD: though your sins are like scarlet, they shall be as white as snow; though they are red like crimson, they shall become like wool. **Isa 1:18**

Come now, let us reason together.

Bitterness/Unforgiveness are like bad veils of the Lord – almost as bad as a head turned the wrong way! In fact the problem with unforgiveness, the reason we must forgive as we have been forgiven, is that…

When we are not forgiving someone, what we see is HOW WRONGED we have been, and we totally lose sight of HOW FORGIVEN we are, causing us to see our hurt, instead of seeing the love, forgiveness, sacrifice, and kindness of the Savior!

What do I want to be more filled with---my wound, or how forgiven and saved I am?

O Father, let me arise, come on the scene, and overcome the trifles and lies that act as veils in my life! They must be dealt with, they must be shunned, set aside, and conquered for the transformation that I need to take place—change that comes by beholding!!

If change comes by beholding the Savior, I will not be changed if I allow things to block my view of Him!

I want to be changed, transformed into Your image, into Your likeness, O blessed Redeemer! Come and give me deeper hatred, repulsion, and distaste for every trifle/lie that tries to block my view of the Savior!!

O this child/sheep needs the help of the Savior!!   -Pastor Daniel Martin, 11/12/14

Engagement. Through his prophet, Isaiah, the Lord wants to engage His people. But it is an engagement that has a premise – the removal of the stain of sin. The basis for reconciliation and restoration of relationship is forgiveness.

Listening is vital to reconciliation and restoration of relationship. Hearing the heart of another and their motivation is important. *"Let us reason together!"*

I hear the words or I see the action of another, and I judge the motivation. So I become offended. But maybe I misinterpreted or misunderstood. Many reconciliations begin with the words "I didn't mean to say that" or "I wasn't trying to do that."

But there is an important element to the listening. That element is a heart that wants to forgive. As Pastor Martin states, unforgiveness blocks my view. Unforgiveness blocks my view of the Lord and unforgiveness blocks my view of the other person. When I listen with a heart desiring to forgive, reconciliation is a likely outcome. The heart of the Lord desires to forgive!

Meditation: Today is a day of listening. Set aside a block of time. Eliminate distractions. Quiet your mind. Reread the scripture above. Then spend time in silence listening to your heart and listening to the Lord. Write in your journal what you sense or hear.

☦   ☦   ☦   ☦   ☦   ☦   ☦

NOTES:_____

III. Week Eleven, Day 5 (Date:)   **POWER OF FORGIVENESS**

> Bless those who persecute you; bless and do not curse them.
> Rejoice with those who rejoice, weep with those who weep.
> Live in harmony with one another. Do not be haughty, but associate with the lowly. Never be wise in your own sight.
> Repay no one evil for evil, but give thought to do what is honorable in the sight of all. If possible, so far as it depends on you, live peaceably with all.
> Beloved, never avenge yourselves, but leave it to the wrath of God, for it is written, "Vengeance is mine, I will repay, says the Lord." To the contrary, "if your enemy is hungry, feed him; if he is thirsty, give him something to drink; for by so doing you will heap burning coals on his head."
> Do not be overcome by evil, but overcome evil with good.
> Rom 12:14-21

Do not be overcome by evil, but overcome evil with good.

Looking back now at the issue of forgiveness, I see now how I blame the one doing the wrong for my lack of forgiveness, when You say the wrong is on my side in not being grateful for how much I have been forgiven.

<u>I tend to think that I could be patient with them if they would attempt to change. But this makes my ability to forgive be based on what they do or do not do. That leaves me helpless and totally under their control.</u>

The way You have set it up, my ability to forgive and be at peace stems solely on how I react to how much I have been forgiven! When this is the basis of how much I can forgive, there is no lack of power to forgive! O help me to see this in the middle of the hurts I feel from the wrongs done to me!

Again, help me to reach out and respond on the basis of how much I have been forgiven, instead of based on how much I have wronged!

How simple, clear, true, and powerful Your Ways are, O God! They are full of so much life and glory!   –Pastor Daniel Martin, 9/11/12

A frequent question about forgiveness is whether I am called to forgive another person when that person has not repented. What if the other person won't even talk to me about the matter?

I should always have a heart that wants to forgive and that is forgiving with the goal of reconciliation. But my attitude of forgiveness is not an exoneration of another person's misdeed. I can choose not to retaliate, not to hold the offense, and not to allow bitterness to dwell within me. But for reconciliation and restoration of relationship to occur, there must be repentance.[54] Reconciliation requires both parties to engage and I can't force it.

I can forgive though, even if the other person refuses to address the matter. The time that another person does not acknowledge the offense against me may be the most important time to forgive. Saul did not apologize for the stoning of Stephen. But Stephen still pronounced forgiveness.

And if the other person does engage, that person may not see the matter my way. We may disagree. People have different perspectives, different personalities and gifts, and even different memories of the same event. If I have humbly made an attempt to reconcile, I may need to resign myself to the disagreement, let it go, and move on.[55] In fact, the manner in which I disagree may be just as important as being right about the issue itself.

> **Meditation:** I have had godly people tell me that they refused to forgive an offense because the offending party did not repent. The stated reason for retaining the offense was that God requires repentance in order to forgive sin. Meditate on the dynamics of repentance, forgiveness, bitterness, reconciliation, and restoration. How much forgiveness will you extend to persons who do not apologize or repent of their offense against you?

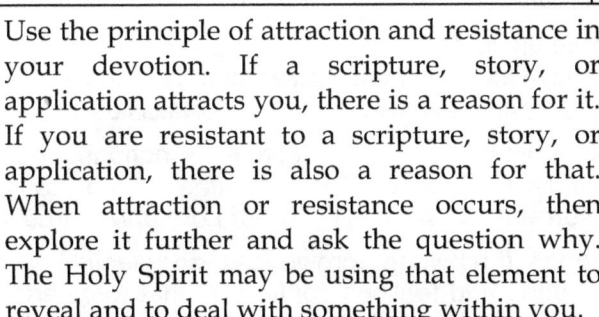

Use the principle of attraction and resistance in your devotion. If a scripture, story, or application attracts you, there is a reason for it. If you are resistant to a scripture, story, or application, there is also a reason for that. When attraction or resistance occurs, then explore it further and ask the question why. The Holy Spirit may be using that element to reveal and to deal with something within you.

---

[54] Brian Zahnd, *Unconditional? The Call of Jesus to Radical Forgiveness*, pp. 118-121 (Charisma House 2010).

[55] Note that Matthew 18 provides for further recourse in a church setting.

III. Week Eleven, Day 6 (Date:)   **POWER OF FORGIVENESS**

> Put on then, as God's chosen ones, holy and beloved, compassionate hearts, kindness, humility, meekness, and patience, bearing with one another and, if one has a complaint against another, forgiving each other; as the Lord has forgiven you, so you also must forgive.
> And above all these put on love, which binds everything together in perfect harmony. **Col 3:12-14**

As the Lord has forgiven you, so you also must forgive.

In her book, *The Hiding Place*, Corrie Ten Boom tells of her ministry of forgiveness after the Holocaust. Her family hid persecuted Jews from the Nazis, but were discovered and arrested. Her beloved father died. She and her sister were sent to a concentration camp where her sister died. Yet after the war, Ms. Ten Boom preached a message of forgiveness as she established a home to aid needy families.

Ms. Ten Boom spoke at a meeting in Munich. After the meeting, she was approached by a man she recognized as one of the most brutal Nazi guards at Ravensbruck where her sister had perished. The guard told her he had become a Christian. As he held out his hand to her, he thanked her for her message of forgiveness. She froze and kept her hand at her side.

"I tried to smile. I struggled to raise my hand. I could not. I felt nothing, not the slightest spark of warmth or charity. And so again I breathed a silent prayer. *Jesus I cannot forgive him. Give your forgiveness.*

"As I took his hand the most incredible thing happened. From my shoulder along my arm and through my hand, a current seemed to pass from me to him, while into my heart sprang a love for this stranger that almost overwhelmed me."[56]

Forgiveness is an act of the will. My flesh, my emotions, and all of my worldly instincts may resist forgiveness. But forgiveness, like many spiritual truths, occurs when I surrender my will to obey our Lord and to trust Him.

Note the disconnect between forgiveness and feeling. I may commit to forgive, but emotions and feelings contrary to that forgiveness can linger for years – particularly if I have suffered deep wounds or horrible abuse. Yet if I remain steadfast in the commitment to forgive, those hurts normally conform to my commitment over time. When I trust Him, God is working in my life at all times.

Or maybe God will give me the grace to feel immediately what Corrie Ten Boom felt – His deep love out of which His forgiveness flows.

---

[56] Corrie Ten Boom, Elizabeth and John Sherrill, *The Hiding Place* pp. 247-248 (Chosen 2006).

Meditation: Write a letter about a wound or abuse that you have suffered. The letter is addressed to the person that hurt you. It can be a hurt that is past or present. Describe your feelings of hurt in what you write. Tell the person what you want to tell them. Put in the letter your commitment to forgive that person.

☩ ☩ ☩ ☩ ☩ ☩ ☩

NOTES:_____

III. Week Eleven, Day 7 (Date:)   **POWER OF FORGIVENESS**

Today is a day of review.

> **Meditation:** Ask God to search the rooms of your heart. Eliminate distractions and open your heart to the Lord. Allow Him to go from room to room in your heart. Expose any hidden areas – particularly any areas that contain hurt, pain, or offense.
>
> For each place He shows you, ask Him what needs to be done to heal that room. Write in your journal what He shows you.

✟ ✟ ✟ ✟ ✟ ✟ ✟

NOTES:_____

_____

_____

_____

_____

_____

_____

_____

> It can be helpful to discuss hidden areas of your heart, particularly areas of offense, with your mentor. Our secrets can make us sick. Exposure can heal us.

SECTION III – TRUST: WEEK TWELVE

III.Week Twelve, Day 1 (Date:) **GOODNESS OF GOD**

> And when they came to the place that is called The Skull, there they crucified him, and the criminals, one on his right and one on his left. And Jesus said, "Father, forgive them, for they know not what they do."
> Luke 23:33-34a

He treats me in all respects as His favorite son.

I consider myself the most wretched of men, full of wounds and uncleanness. I have committed all sorts of crimes against my Sovereign. Prompted by heartfelt repentance, I confess all my wickedness to Him. I ask His forgiveness and give myself fully into His hands. He may do whatever He wants with me. But my Lord, Who is full of mercy and goodness, does not punish me. Instead he embraces me in love, seats me at His table, and serves me with His own hands. He hands me the key to His treasure trove. He converses with me and shows His delight in me incessantly in thousands of ways. He treats me in all respects as His favorite son. This is how I come into God's holy presence.[57]

Forgiveness is powerful. The power of forgiveness arises from the power of a love straight from the heart of a good God. Because of His love, this good God desires relationship with us. But He knew that the only path to relationship with fallen humans is a path paved by forgiveness. So forgiveness was proclaimed on the cross.

But for reconciliation and restoration to occur, engagement is necessary. God approaches me about my offense while offering His heart of forgiveness. I need to respond to His approach with repentance and confession.

Then, forgiveness must be received. Sometimes I struggle with receiving that forgiveness. I tend to beat myself up; or I dwell in guilt as if I can somehow earn forgiveness through my own action; or I live in fear of retribution because I don't understand the heart of God in the matter.

I regret to say that forgiveness for me must be received often…daily, even hourly. But that regret arises directly from my shame. So instead I rejoice to say that forgiveness is received by me…daily, even hourly!

---

[57] *The Practice of the Presence of God*, pp. 34-35.

Meditation: Today focus on how well you receive forgiveness. Sometimes there is a tendency to feel chagrin, shame, or insignificance because of what I have done. These feelings can have a positive effect if they lead to repentance and confession. But when forgiveness is granted, I need to trust that forgiveness.

How well do you receive forgiveness? Are you able to trust the power of God's forgiveness in your life? Can you allow yourself to be treated as His favorite son or daughter? Journal about your feelings.

╬ ╬ ╬ ╬ ╬ ╬ ╬

NOTES:_____

_____

_____

_____

_____

_____

_____

_____

_____

_____

_____

III. Week Twelve, Day 2 (Date:) **GOODNESS OF GOD**

> "Judge not, and you will not be judged; condemn not, and you will not be condemned; forgive, and you will be forgiven; give, and it will be given to you. Good measure, pressed down, shaken together, running over, will be put into your lap. For with the measure you use it will be measured back to you." **Luke 6:37-38**

Benefits of the kingdom of God.

"Thou are giving and forgiving, ever blessing, ever blest!"[58]

Not judged; not condemned; forgiven; and given – these blessings are all promised to me. They are not offered in short supply. They are offered in good measure and in abundance out of the goodness of God.

These blessings are the benefits of the kingdom of God. The law births revenge, retaliation, and condemnation. The kingdom of God births grace to the believer.

The last two sentences in this scripture are often applied to giving. But they apply to all of these four areas – judging, condemning, forgiving, and giving. The measure of the benefit is the measure with which I apply them.

Meditation: Meditate on the freedom and blessing that is being offered by God. Allow that meditation to lead you to joy. Spend time in worship and praise of the goodness of God to offer these benefits to you.

☩   ☩   ☩   ☩   ☩   ☩   ☩

> Try to remember the focus of your devotion as you go through your day. Keep a key phrase from the scripture or the application in mind so that you can apply it in your everyday routine or in other situations that arise. Change occurs when we apply the principles or virtues that God reveals.

---

[58] *Joyful, Joyful We Adore Thee*, Poem by Henry Van Dyke (1907).

III. Week Twelve, Day 3 (Date:)   **GOODNESS OF GOD**

> I believe that I shall look upon the goodness of the LORD in the land of the living!
> Wait for the LORD; be strong, and let your heart take courage; wait for the LORD! **Psa 27:13-14**

Do I really believe in the goodness of God?

The goodness of God is that which disposes Him to be kind, cordial, benevolent, and full of good will toward men. He is tenderhearted and of quick sympathy, and His unfailing attitude toward all moral beings is open, frank, and friendly. By His nature, He is inclined to bestow blessedness and He takes Holy pleasure in the happiness of His people.[59]

I previously wrote of my extended illness (I.Week Four, Day 3). My illness lasted 2 years and it was filled with intense physical pain, weakness, weight loss, and, at times, darkness. Many of my days were a matter of survival – physically and spiritually.

I was essentially bedridden for months. During my illness, I searched my heart and reviewed personal doubts, issues, and dysfunctions. One major issue for me was trust. For many reasons, I struggled to trust other people, and I struggled to trust God.

My conclusion in the area of trust in God came down to one key question: *Do I really believe in the goodness of God?* Yes, I had knowledge theologically that God is good. But in my soul, in my emotions, in my instincts, and in the core of my being, do I really believe in the goodness of God?

Almost paradoxically to me, as I slowly began to recover, I realized that I had a much deeper internal belief in the goodness of God. I had been stricken, but a belief in the goodness of God helped me to trust Him when I could not see it.

God is a good God!

> **Meditation:** *"Love is kind."* Spend time exploring your belief in the goodness of God. How do you view God – not just mentally, but emotionally, instinctively, and internally? Consider the connection between trust in God and the goodness of God. Journal about it.

╬   ╬   ╬   ╬   ╬   ╬   ╬

---

[59] *The Knowledge of the Holy*, p. 82.

NOTES:

III. Week Twelve, Day 4 (Date:)　　　　**GOODNESS OF GOD**

> Now when John heard in prison about the deeds of the Christ, he sent word by his disciples and said to him, "Are you the one who is to come, or shall we look for another?"
> And Jesus answered them, "Go and tell John what you hear and see: the blind receive their sight and the lame walk, lepers are cleansed and the deaf hear, and the dead are raised up, and the poor have good news preached to them.
> And blessed is the one who is not offended by me." **Matt 11:2-6**

Blessed is the one who is not offended by Me.

Trust is built in small increments. I don't go from meeting a person one minute to trusting that person completely the next minute. If I did that, I would make many bad business deals. Faithfulness in small things time after time and day after day builds trust.

Betrayal on the other hand can occur from one incident – even a small thing. Trust that has been built over decades can be destroyed in a flash by one act of unfaithfulness. Trust should be treated delicately and managed carefully.

A person can become offended at God. I have expectations – expectations for myself, expectations for others, and even expectations for God. John the Baptist had an anointed call from God that he fulfilled. But when John's time came, he was arrested and imprisoned by Herod. Isolated and languishing in prison, he sent word to Jesus, the Messiah, with a question. It is almost as if John is calling attention to his plight. He might have had an expectation of deliverance from the One called the Messiah. After all, they were cousins!

Many times my expectations are based on my flesh, on my selfish desires, or on my felt need to control circumstances and other people around me. Such expectations are false. But when my expectations are not met by God – even the false expectations, I feel let down. Trust has somehow been betrayed. I become offended at God.

Jesus did not deliver John. He affirmed John's call and ministry, but Jesus did not deliver John. He did send John a message – a message that essentially said "I am the Messiah, but don't be offended by Me if I don't meet your expectation and deliver you. Blessed is the one who is not offended by Me."

Meditation: Spend time considering what God owes you. Make a list in your journal of the things that you believe are due to you from God. Then think of times that you became upset, angry, or offended at God. Like John, those times are often times of questioning. What are the reasons those emotions occurred? Compare those reasons with the items on your list that are owed to you by God.

III. Week Twelve, Day 5 (Date:)   **GOODNESS OF GOD**

> So Jesus said to the Jews who had believed him, "If you abide in my word, you are truly my disciples, and you will know the truth, and the truth will set you free." They answered him, "We are offspring of Abraham and have never been enslaved to anyone. How is it that you say, 'You will become free'?"
> Jesus answered them, "Truly, truly, I say to you, everyone who practices sin is a slave to sin. The slave does not remain in the house forever; the son remains forever. So if the Son sets you free, you will be free indeed." **John 8:31-36**

The truth will set you free.

That our idea of God correspond as nearly as possible to the true being of God is of immense importance to us. Compared with our actual thoughts about Him, our creedal statements are of little consequence. Our real idea of God may lie buried under the rubbish of conventional religious notions and may require an intelligent and vigorous search before it is finally unearthed and exposed for what it really is. Only after an ordeal of painful self-probing are we likely to discover what we actually believe about God. A right conception of God is basic not only to systematic theology but to practical Christian living as well.[60]

Embracing truth is important because truth is the key to freedom – freedom from sin, freedom from fear, and freedom from the enemy.

The truth about myself is important – the truth about the thoughts and intents of my heart and about my actions. The truth about my true identity in the Lord is vital to my soul and to my destiny.

Truth about doctrine is important - truth about redemption, atonement, salvation, and grace. This truth arises from the word of God illuminated to my heart by the Holy Spirit Who guides me into all truth (John 16:13).

But the most important truth is truth about God Himself – Who He is, His attributes, and His love and acceptance of me. Wrong beliefs about God ("ungodly beliefs") are the cause of many issues, dysfunctions, and illnesses. God is a good God and I can trust Him. That truth leads to freedom.

Meditation: *":Love rejoices with the truth."* Write a letter to God in your journal. In the letter, tell God what you believe about Him. Focus especially on aspects of His goodness and your trust in Him. Be truthful with God about your feelings and about any incidents or events that come to mind that impact what you feel about God.

---

[60] *The Knowledge of the Holy*, p. 2.

III. Week Twelve, Day 6 (Date:)   **GOODNESS OF GOD**

> Lamech said to his wives: "Adah and Zillah, hear my voice; you wives of Lamech, listen to what I say: I have killed a man for wounding me, a young man for striking me. If Cain's revenge is sevenfold, then Lamech's is seventy-sevenfold." **Gen 4:23-24**

Seventy-seven times.

One evening, shortly before he died, Papa told me the story of Charlie Hale and Papa's brother, Ray. The story was as much about Papa's heart as it was about Charlie Hale.

Charlie Hale was not a savory character. He was a notorious criminal. Papa's brother, Ray, fell in with him and they started "doing business" together. When Papa was young, Ray and Charlie Hale had an argument. Charlie Hale shot and killed Ray. Papa said he hated Charlie Hale for years after the shooting. There were times when Papa considered killing Charlie Hale, and if he had a gun and the opportunity, he would have pulled the trigger.

Through the early years of their marriage, Meme began to talk with Papa about forgiveness. At first, Papa refused to forgive Charlie Hale. Meme kept encouraging him, and reminded him of the forgiveness that Jesus offers to all of us. Eventually, over forty years after the shooting, Papa forgave Charlie Hale and removed the hate from his heart. He experienced a deeper peace in his life when he did. [61]

I cannot tell you how much that act of forgiveness changed and re-directed the culture of my family. Descendants of Papa like myself, Pastor Martin, and many others were eternally impacted by that act of forgiveness.

We read about Lamech in the Bible as a descendant of Cain. This vignette about Lamech appears in the lineage of Cain. Lamech boasted that he would expand the revenge of Cain, which was pronounced by the Lord, from sevenfold to seventy sevenfold. By his own hand and decree, Lamech expanded the cycle of revenge.

Families have cycles of dysfunction that are passed down from generation to generation. Alcoholism, divorce, dependency, abuse, and poverty are only a few of the issues that run in families. The dysfunction is passed from parent to child as if some spirit is writing the script.

Cultures have cycles as well. Violence, abuse, racism, addiction, and greed pervade many cities, nations, and tribes. These patterns are written into the history of a people as if they were etched in stone – just like revenge attached itself to Cain and his descendants.

---

[61] Excerpt from *Dod Knows* (by the author).

What can break a negative cycle? When Peter asked Jesus how many times he should forgive his brother, Jesus didn't just pick His answer out of thin air. Jesus gave Peter a number that had specific meaning – seventy-seven times (Matt 18:21-22).

<u>A seventy-sevenfold cycle of revenge is broken by a seventy-sevenfold cycle of forgiveness.</u>

Forgiveness arises out of the goodness of God. Forgiveness is the key to breaking the cycles of dysfunction and illness in my family. Forgiveness is also the key to breaking the patterns of dysfunction in my culture. But forgiveness must begin within the church which means that forgiveness must ultimately begin with you and with me.

> **Meditation:** Identify generational patterns of dysfunction that have impacted you. Write about them in your journal. Then consider how forgiveness can impact those patterns. Seek the Lord about forgiveness in your life and what forgiveness needs to occur regarding those dysfunctions.

☦ ☦ ☦ ☦ ☦ ☦ ☦

NOTES:_____

_____

_____

_____

_____

_____

_____

_____

_____

_____

III. Week Twelve, Day 7 (Date:)   **GOODNESS OF GOD**

Review your journal over the past week.

> **Meditation:** Select a devotion over the past week that impacted you. Read the devotion again and spend more time with it. Seek the Lord about how you can apply the devotion to your life.

☩   ☩   ☩   ☩   ☩   ☩   ☩

NOTES:_____

_____

_____

_____

_____

_____

_____

_____

_____

_____

> Now that we are near the end of Section III, consider a quarterly retreat or an extended time to review your devotional journal with your mentor or spiritual director.

SECTION III – TRUST: WEEK THIRTEEN

(This week is a practicum in the practice of stillness before the Lord. One goal of stillness is to quiet every part of our being – mind, body, and emotion so that the Holy Spirit can commune with our spirit uninterruptedly.

This practice, which is called contemplation, may be a little unusual for some people. It is analogous to the old trust exercise in which one person releases control and falls backward trusting the other person to catch him. In stillness, I release control over myself and trust the Holy Spirit to come as I fall into His arms.

Please note that there is not a specific expectation from stillness. Stillness is offering myself to the Lord to dwell in silence in His Presence. He can act or not act. He can move or not move. I am simply trusting Him with myself.

For each day, please try to find a place of quiet that is devoid of stimulation of your senses – sound, sight, or smell. Eliminate all distractions that you can – be alone, cell phones off, no music, etc. Set aside a period of time for the meditation. If you have not done this type of meditation before, a recommendation for the actual time of stillness is 20 minutes. You may want to set an alarm or other device for 20 minutes so that you are not concerned about time as you meditate. You can increase time for stillness as you practice it more and become more familiar with it.)

NOTES:_____

_____

_____

_____

_____

_____

_____

_____

III. Week Thirteen, Day 1 (Date:)   PRACTICUM: STILLNESS

> But the LORD is in his holy temple; let all the earth keep silence before him. **Hab 2:20**

Let all the earth keep silence before Him.

We need to find God and He cannot be found in noise and restlessness. See how nature, the trees, the flowers, and the grass grow in perfect silence. See the stars, the moon, and the sun, how they move in silence. The apostle said, "We will give ourselves continually at prayer and to the ministry of the Word." For the more we receive in silent prayer, the more we can give in our active life. We silence to be able to touch souls. The essential thing is not what we say, but what God says to us.[62]

Today, the Lord is in His holy temple – your body. So keep silence before Him. We will practice "re-collection" which is a way to be still and try to focus all of our mind and emotion on Him.[63]

Meditation: 1. Begin with repentance and cleansing. Examine yourself over the past day. Repent of any sins, confess them to the Lord, and receive forgiveness.

2. Quiet your mind, senses, and emotions. Hold out your hands with your palms down. "Palms down" is a symbolic gesture to release all concerns, weights, or worries to the Lord. With your palms down, you are giving the Lord all of your burdens. You can silently mouth the items to be released if you wish.

Then turn your palms up. "Palms up" is receiving the Holy Spirit. You are opening yourself for the Holy Spirit to enter. You can silently mouth invitations to the Holy Spirit. If you feel a worry or concern with your palms up, you can turn them down to release it.

Repeat "palms up, palms down." Spend the remaining time in silence before the Lord. You can continue to use "palms up, palms down" during your time of silence, or you can stop as you dwell in silence and center your being in the Lord.

☦   ☦   ☦   ☦   ☦   ☦   ☦

---

[62] *Total Surrender*, p. 107.

[63] See Richard J. Foster, *Celebration of Discipline*, pp.30-31 (Harper One 1998) for a more detailed description of the meditation exercise elements.

III. Week Thirteen, Day 2 (Date:)   **PRACTICUM: STILLNESS**

> But, as it is written, "What no eye has seen, nor ear heard, nor the heart of man imagined, what God has prepared for those who love him"— these things God has revealed to us through the Spirit. For the Spirit searches everything, even the depths of God.
> For who knows a person's thoughts except the spirit of that person, which is in him? So also no one comprehends the thoughts of God except the Spirit of God. **1 Cor 2:9-11**

No one comprehends the thoughts of God except the Spirit of God.

Spinoza wrote of the intellectual love of God; and he had a measure of truth there; but the highest love of God is not intellectual, it is spiritual. God is spirit and only the spirit of man can know Him really. In the deep spirit of a man the fire must glow or his love is not the true love of God.[64]

Today, practice stillness of the mind. In your heart and in your mind you know He is God and you love Him, so you allow that knowing to rest within you.

Meditation: 1. Begin with a focus on the love of God. Spend time receiving His love.

2. Take time to examine the blessings of the last 24 hours. Give thanks for them.

3. Quiet your mind, senses, and emotions. As much as you can, empty your mind.

4. Spend time in silence before the Lord. Keep your mind quiet. If anything stirs in your mind, simply say "You are God." Then focus on Him.

☦   ☦   ☦   ☦   ☦   ☦   ☦

> Remember to give yourself grace during this exercise. If you struggle to keep still or to silence your thoughts, that is not unusual. Just keep working at it. If your mind wanders, don't beat yourself up. Just bring it back to your meditation. If you can bring yourself back to where you were, then do it. If you need to start over, that is fine. Just do that. Grace, grace, and more grace.

---

[64] *The Pursuit of God*, pp.25-26.

III. Week Thirteen, Day 3 (Date:)   **PRACTICUM: STILLNESS**

> Awake, O north wind, and come, O south wind! Blow upon my garden, let its spices flow. **Songs 4:16a**

Today we focus on breath.

Accordingly, such persons should not mind if the operations of their faculties are being lost to them; they should desire rather that this be done quickly so there may be no obstacle to the operation of the infused contemplation God is bestowing, so they may receive it with more peaceful plentitude and make room in the spirit for the enkindling and burning of the love that this dark and secret contemplation bears and communicates to the soul. For contemplation is nothing else than a secret and peaceful and loving inflow of God, which, if not hampered, fires the soul in the spirit of love.[65]

Breath and wind are symbolic of the Holy Spirit in scripture in many ways – linguistically, illustratively, aurally, etc. In the verse above, spices can be symbolic of our virtues, love, spiritual gifts, or inspiration that is stirred by the Presence and work of the Holy Spirit.

Meditation: 1. Begin with repentance and cleansing. Call to mind sins over the past day. Repent of those sins, confess them to the Lord, and receive forgiveness.

2. Quiet your mind, senses, and emotions.

3. As you enter stillness before the Lord, use your breath as a device to invite the Holy Spirit. Slowly breathe in. As you inhale, ask the Holy Spirit to enter your being. Then slowly exhale. As you exhale, you release everything within you that is not the Holy Spirit – thoughts, worries, concerns, pains, or your agenda for the day.

As you breathe, use your exhalation as a release – a way to empty yourself. As you inhale, invite and receive the Holy Spirit.

☩   ☩   ☩   ☩   ☩   ☩   ☩

> If you sense that the Lord is speaking to you or giving you something during times of stillness, then pursue it. Be open to it and pursue it. But often in times of stillness, there are "rabbit trails" which are distractions from your mind, body, or external factors that interfere with your meditation. Use discernment, but prioritize silence and stillness.

---

[65] St. John of the Cross, *The Dark Night*, I.11.6 (From *The Collected Works of St. John of the Cross*, Kavanaugh and Rodriguez (ICS Publications 1991)).

III. Week Thirteen, Day 4 (Date:)   **PRACTICUM: STILLNESS**

> [F]ear not, for I am with you; be not dismayed, for I am your God; I will strengthen you, I will help you, I will uphold you with my righteous right hand. **Isa 41:10**

Today is a day to yield pain, wounds of the heart, or discomfort to the Lord.

When I was ill, I had sleepless nights filled with pain and weakness. Before I went to bed, I would try to grab hold of a verse, a word, or even just an image, and then hold onto that verse, word, or image through the night. It might be the word "rest;" or a verse like "Be still, and know that I am God" or "the Lord is my Shepherd;" or an image of Jesus as the Good Shepherd. A word, a phrase, or an image could be a "lifeline" to get me through the night. In the intense moments, my mind didn't function very well, but I could hold onto a word, a phrase, or an image. I repeated it over and over, and doing that was often helpful. Interestingly, the same word, verse, or image seemed to last only one night, and did not have much beneficial effect the second night.

But there were times when I could not hang on any longer. I had a recurring image that helped me then. I saw myself at the edge of a cliff and I was hanging on by a rope or by a branch sticking out the bank. But I could not hold on any longer. My strength was gone. So I let go of it. But when I let go, I fell into the soft, loving hand of the Lord. I lay there nestled, safe, and comforted in the palm of His hand.

Today you are going to be still before the Lord with any pain, wounds of the heart, or personal discomforts.

> **Meditation:** 1. Begin with focus on acceptance by God. God asks you to come to Him – just as you are – even hurting, broken, or proud.
>
> 2. Quiet your mind, senses, and emotions.
>
> 3. Be still before the Lord but allow yourself to feel pain, wounds, or discomforts. Give them to the Lord. Ask the Holy Spirit to come and to bring salve to you. If it helps you to imagine yourself in the palm of His hand, then do so. Rest in Him.

III. Week Thirteen, Day 5 (Date:)   **PRACTICUM: STILLNESS**

> The hairs of his head were white, like white wool, like snow. His eyes were like a flame of fire, his feet were like burnished bronze, refined in a furnace, and his voice was like the roar of many waters.
> **Rev 1:14-15**

His voice was like the roar of many waters.

The traits of the solitary bird are five: first, it seeks the highest place; second, it withstands no company; third, it holds its beak in the air; fourth, it has no definite color; fifth, it sings sweetly. These traits must be possessed by the contemplative soul. It must rise above passing things, paying no more heed to them than if they did not exist. It must likewise be so fond of silence and solitude that it does not tolerate the company of another creature. It must hold its beak in the air of the Holy Spirit, responding to his inspirations, that by so doing it may become worthy of his company. It must have no definite color, desiring to do nothing definite other than the will of God. It must sing sweetly in the contemplation and love of its Bridegroom.[66]

Often in my times of stillness and silence, music runs through my head. The music can be good music, but most times for me, the music is another distraction in my mind.

Today sit in stillness and silence.

Meditation: Meditation: 1. Begin with repentance and cleansing. Call to mind sins over the past day. Repent of those sins, confess them to the Lord, and receive forgiveness.

2. Sing a Psalm. Recall a Psalm that is set to music, or find a favorite Psalm, and then sing it to the Lord.

3. Quiet your mind, senses, and emotions.

4. Ask the Lord to quiet your mind from all music except for heavenly music. Ask the Holy Spirit to come and be with you. If music enters your mind that is a distraction, try to quiet it. Or you can replace it with the sound of many waters – like the voice of the Lord is described in scripture. Sit in stillness and quiet and hear only the music that the Lord may put in your heart.

☦ ☦ ☦ ☦ ☦ ☦ ☦

---

[66] St. John of the Cross, *The Sayings of Light and Love*, 2.121 (From *The Collected Works of St. John of the Cross*, Kavanaugh and Rodriguez (ICS Publications 1991)).

III. Week Thirteen, Day 6 (Date:) **PRACTICUM: STILLNESS**

> For God alone, O my soul, wait in silence,
> for my hope is from him. **Psa 62:5**

A habitual, silent, and secret communion of the soul with God.

I have stopped practicing all forms of devotion and set prayers, except those which I am obliged to participate in. I make it my practice only to persevere in His holy presence. I do this simply by paying attention to, and directing my affection to, God. It is a habitual, silent, and secret communion of the soul with God. This often causes such joys and raptures inwardly, and sometimes also outwardly, that I am forced to prevent their appearance to others.[67]

Meditation: 1. Think of where you have encountered God in the last few days. Give thanks for these times.

2. Quiet your mind, senses, and emotions.

3. Set your affection toward God. Direct every part of your being toward loving Him. Then wait in silence for Him. Allow Him to move within you as He desires.

☫   ☫   ☫   ☫   ☫   ☫   ☫

NOTES:_____

_____

_____

_____

_____

_____

_____

---

[67] *The Practice of the Presence of God*, p. 34.

III. Week Thirteen, Day 7 (Date:)   **PRACTICUM: STILLNESS**

> For thus said the Lord GOD, the Holy One of Israel, "In returning and rest you shall be saved; in quietness and in trust shall be your strength." **Isa 30:15a**

Today is the seventh day, a day of rest.

Meditation: 1. Begin with repentance and cleansing. Call to mind sins over the past day. Repent of those sins, confess them to the Lord, and receive forgiveness.

2. Quiet your mind, senses, and emotions.

3. Be still before the Lord. Ask Him for a time of rest – not just physical rest, but rest for your soul. Enter into His rest as His Holy Spirit ministers to you.

╬   ╬   ╬   ╬   ╬   ╬   ╬

NOTES:_____

_____

_____

_____

_____

_____

_____

_____

_____

_____

SECTION IV – POWER AND GLORY

Week One: Power

Week Two: The Cup

Week Three: Weakness

Week Four: Triumph

Week Five: Refiner's Fire

Week Six: Leadership

Week Seven: Fear of Man

Week Eight: The Cave

Week Nine: Generational Thinking

Week Ten: Restoration

Week Eleven: Glory

Week Twelve: The Bride

Week Thirteen: Practicum – My People

A WORD BEFORE SECTION IV – POWER AND GLORY

You have reached the beginning of *Section IV – Power and Glory*. Congratulations on the completion of Section III! Please take some time to review what God is doing in your heart and in your life as you have journeyed through *Section III – Trust*. Especially look at changes He has made in your heart in the areas of surrender and trust.

As you journey through Section IV, you will note some changes in focus. One change is a focus on suffering and the way of the Cross. As I read scripture, suffering and the Cross are closely connected with power and glory. In fact, my impression is that when power and glory are mentioned in scripture, suffering and the Cross are not far away.

Suffering and the way of the Cross are not always negatives that lead to despair or to depression. The truth is that many events of suffering and the Cross find their source in the love and mercy of God.

Another change in focus will be from individual to corporate. I believe that, as a believer grows in maturity and in understanding of the kingdom of God, that believer becomes attentive to the corporate aspects of the kingdom of God – to the body of Christ. The believer adopts God's perspective and begins to see as God sees.

Emergence theory is the idea that smaller parts interact or connect in a way that forms a larger entity. When the smaller parts connect, traits or realities emerge that only occur from the unity of the parts.

Consider the human body. Atoms connect to form cells. Cells connect to form organs and other body parts. The organs and body parts form a body. When I see you though, I don't think about the individual cells or individual organs. I see a person – a whole. There are countless atoms in a human body (the estimated number has over 25 zeroes), trillions of cells, over 70 organs, but only 1 body. Paul describes this corporate entity. *For just as the body is one and has many members, and all the members of the body, though many, are one body, so it is with Christ* (1 Cor 12:12). [68]

Some people may view the body of Christ in scripture as figurative – just an allegory that helps the church unite and work together. But the question needs to be asked: When God sees His people, does He just see us individually, or does He also see a Body that is greater than the sum of its parts? And if He sees a Body, what is my role and place in that Body? The spiritual health and function of each member is important (1 Cor 12:22).

---

[68] For more exploration of emergence theory, go to https://bibleproject.com/podcast/emergence-sin/.

SECTION IV – POWER AND GLORY: WEEK ONE

IV.Week One, Day 1 (Date:)   **POWER**

> He said to me, 'It is Solomon your son who shall build my house and my courts, for I have chosen him to be my son, and I will be his father. I will establish his kingdom forever if he continues strong in keeping my commandments and my rules, as he is today.'
> Now therefore in the sight of all Israel, the assembly of the LORD, and in the hearing of our God, observe and seek out all the commandments of the LORD your God, that you may possess this good land and leave it for an inheritance to your children after you forever.
> "And you, Solomon my son, know the God of your father and serve him with a whole heart and with a willing mind, for the LORD searches all hearts and understands every plan and thought. If you seek him, he will be found by you, but if you forsake him, he will cast you off forever. Be careful now, for the LORD has chosen you to build a house for the sanctuary; be strong and do it." **1 Chr 28:6-10**

Serve Him with a whole heart.

Brené Brown has written books on wholeheartedness. She has defined some basic traits of people that are wholehearted. Wholehearted people have:

1. A sense of courage which is different than bravery. These people have the courage to be imperfect. Wholehearted people fully embrace vulnerability. They can tell their stories of who they are with their whole heart.

2. Compassion to be kind to themselves and to others. You can't be compassionate with someone else if you are not kind to yourself.

3. Connection as a result of authenticity. Wholehearted people let go of who they think they should be in order to be who they are. They are willing to take risks in their relationships and lives.[69]

David is a man after God's own heart – in worship and in truth. But his time on earth is coming to an end. David has called a great assembly in Israel in order to instruct the people and also to instruct his son, Solomon.

Final instructions are important. When the end is near, instructions tend to be somber and significant. David instructs Solomon to build a dwelling place for

---

[69] Brené Brown, *The Gifts of Imperfection* pp.12-21 (Hazelden 2010).

God. He gave Solomon the plans for the temple along with vast resources of gold, silver, bronze, iron, wood, and precious stones to build it.

David also gives Solomon instructions about the Lord - to serve the Lord with a whole heart and with a willing mind. Then, in the presence of the great assembly, he installs Solomon as king of Israel.

It is a coronation and a consecration – the temporal and the divine. The event is full of anticipation and full of promise.

> **Meditation:** Focus on the word "wholehearted." What did David mean when he instructed Solomon to serve the Lord with a whole heart? How did David do this? Spend time searching your heart. How can you serve the Lord wholeheartedly in your life? How does a whole heart relate to your call and destiny?

☩ ☩ ☩ ☩ ☩ ☩ ☩

NOTES:

IV. Week One, Day 2 (Date:)   POWER

> As soon as Solomon finished his prayer, fire came down from heaven and consumed the burnt offering and the sacrifices, and the glory of the LORD filled the temple. And the priests could not enter the house of the LORD, because the glory of the LORD filled the LORD's house. When all the people of Israel saw the fire come down and the glory of the LORD on the temple, they bowed down with their faces to the ground on the pavement and worshiped and gave thanks to the LORD, saying, "For he is good, for his steadfast love endures forever." 2 Chr 7:1-3

For He is good, for His steadfast love endures forever.

Solomon built the temple in accordance with the plans his father, David, had given him. At the dedication of the temple after its completion, Solomon gathered the people and delivered a long prayer. At the end of the prayer, the Presence of the Lord fell and it was palpable. The Lord visited His people wondrously. The glory of the Lord was so strong that the priests, even though they were consecrated, could not enter into the temple.

The people bowed, worshiped, and gave thanks. His steadfast love endures forever.

> **Meditation:** Think of an occasion when you sensed a visitation by the Lord – a time when you sensed His Presence or a time when you knew the glory of the Lord had come. Consider the setting and the circumstances when that occurred. Journal about it.
>
> Do you think there is a connection between a corporate gathering and the visitation of the Lord? Seek the Lord for His heart about where He desires to dwell in His glory and fullness. What is His desire?

╬   ╬   ╬   ╬   ╬   ╬   ╬

> Speaking of presence, seek the Presence of the Lord often in your devotional times. The Lord is present in you and around you. Your role is to invite and to welcome His Presence and then to abide in it as your awareness increases.

IV. Week One, Day 3 (Date:)   POWER

> Solomon brought Pharaoh's daughter up from the city of David to the house that he had built for her, for he said, "My wife shall not live in the house of David king of Israel, for the places to which the ark of the LORD has come are holy."
> Then Solomon offered up burnt offerings to the LORD on the altar of the LORD that he had built before the vestibule, as the duty of each day required, offering according to the commandment of Moses for the Sabbaths, the new moons, and the three annual feasts—the Feast of Unleavened Bread, the Feast of Weeks, and the Feast of Booths. **2 Chr 8:11-13**

My wife shall not live in the house of David king of Israel.

O Savior, come and break down every IDOL and remove all that I place above You or anywhere close to You in value. I want to value You and You alone with all my being, my choices, my time, and my words!

O come and change me more and more into what You are calling for in this!

Come and "cast out every foe"! Show me the "foes" that I allow access to my time, my emotions, my thoughts! I need them all gone, all cast down to their right place, evicted from my premises!

Come and walk with me today in this battle, O Sharer of Life! This sheep needs You coming and correcting, disciplining, and instructing him powerfully today!

Come and have Your own Way, Jesus!!   –Pastor Daniel Martin, 11/8/14

We know the story of Solomon. He loved foreign women and they ultimately led him astray to worship gods other than the One true God.

To me, the most telling verse in the story of Solomon is 2 Chr 8:11 above. Solomon loved the daughter of Pharaoh. He loved numerous foreign women, but Solomon seemed to favor her more than his other wives. He built a palace just for her (1 Kg 9:24).

But Solomon did not build her palace in Jerusalem. The fact that Solomon removed Pharaoh's daughter from Zion shows that he knew she was not honoring to the Lord. Something about the relationship was wrong. But Solomon continued to conduct the worship, liturgy, sacrifices, and feasts before the Lord.

Solomon did something that I tend to do. He compartmentalized his heart. On one hand, he honored religious practice at his place of worship, the Temple. But on the other hand, he continued to do things separate and apart from the place of worship that were unholy and were not pleasing to God.

The fact that Solomon moved Pharaoh's daughter away from Jerusalem was a clear demonstration of the division of his heart. His desire for her was an idol.

- An idol is not just something that you worship as god. An idol is not just something that you worship instead of the One true God.
- An idol is any longing, any thought, or any possession that keeps you from a total surrender to God.
- An idol is that affection that keeps you from a complete devotion to God.
- An idol is anything that keeps you from serving God with a whole heart.[70]

Solomon had idols in his heart long before he began active worship of Ashtoreth, Milcom, Chemosh, and Molech (1 Kings 11:5-7). The idols simply became more manifest as Solomon grew older.

> **Meditation:** Consider the idea of idols and of compartmentalization – a division of the heart. Seek the Lord about any idols and compartmentalization in your own life. Ask the Holy Spirit to show you ways in which your heart has been divided. For each thing, He shows you, seek Him about what you should do in order to serve Him with your whole heart. Ask Him for His help to serve Him with your whole heart. Write down what He shows you in your journal.

✠ ✠ ✠ ✠ ✠ ✠ ✠

NOTES:_____

_____

_____

_____

_____

_____

---

[70] See Appendix D for a more complete *List of Idols* in our lives.

IV. Week One, Day 4 (Date:)   POWER

> Now King Solomon loved many foreign women, along with the daughter of Pharaoh: Moabite, Ammonite, Edomite, Sidonian, and Hittite women, from the nations concerning which the LORD had said to the people of Israel, "You shall not enter into marriage with them, neither shall they with you, for surely they will turn away your heart after their gods." Solomon clung to these in love.
> He had 700 wives, who were princesses, and 300 concubines. And his wives turned away his heart. For when Solomon was old his wives turned away his heart after other gods, and his heart was not wholly true to the LORD his God, as was the heart of David his father.
> **1 Kings 11:1-4**

He had 700 wives, who were princesses.

Fallen powers exist in our world. They do not desire the Presence of God. They fear His Presence and resist it. "[The powers] are forces much larger than human energies, much more complex than human discernment, beyond merely the natural world." – Marva Dawn[71]

The old saying is that there are two ways to expand a kingdom – by conquest and by marriage. Although he amassed a large military, Solomon was a man of peace so he exercised the latter option. The marriages to foreign women catered to Solomon's lust of the flesh. But they also forged political alliances that enabled Solomon to increase his power, wealth, and influence to dizzying heights.

The 700 wives which Solomon had in his lifetime were princesses. His marriage to them expanded the territory and wealth of Israel exponentially. In Solomon's reign, the kingdom of Israel reached the zenith of its power and prestige. It was literally the golden age. Solomon became the most powerful man on earth.

And who can blame Solomon for his shrewd political moves? After all, this was a kingdom established by God and the Israelites were God's people. Surely, expansion of the kingdom of God's people must be a good thing – even if it is accomplished by marriage to foreign wives!

But fallen powers were hard at work.

---

[71] Marva Dawn, *Powers, Weakness, and the Tabernacling of God* p. 16 (Eerdmans 2001).

Meditation: Consider the influence that the cultures around Solomon had on his heart. How did they impact Solomon and the kingdom of Israel during his reign?

Now consider the impact of the culture of our world on the people of God today. Are there any parallels in the way that worldly culture today impacts the people of God? Write your thoughts in your journal.

☦ ☦ ☦ ☦ ☦ ☦ ☦

NOTES:_____

_____

_____

_____

_____

_____

_____

_____

_____

_____

_____

_____

IV. Week One, Day 5 (Date:)   **POWER**

> In those days also I saw the Jews who had married women of Ashdod, Ammon, and Moab. And half of their children spoke the language of Ashdod, and they could not speak the language of Judah, but only the language of each people.
> And I confronted them and cursed them and beat some of them and pulled out their hair. And I made them take an oath in the name of God, saying, "You shall not give your daughters to their sons, or take their daughters for your sons or for yourselves. Did not Solomon king of Israel sin on account of such women? Among the many nations there was no king like him, and he was beloved by his God, and God made him king over all Israel. Nevertheless, foreign women made even him to sin. Shall we then listen to you and do all this great evil and act treacherously against our God by marrying foreign women?"
> **Neh 13:23-27**

Did not Solomon king of Israel sin on account of such women?

Because of the unfaithfulness of Israel in following after other gods, the Lord allowed destruction and desolation to fall upon Israel, and delivered them into captivity and exile. But our God is a God of restoration and redemption! When the exile ended, the man God called to rebuild Jerusalem and to restore the worship of the Lord was Nehemiah.

After he oversaw the rebuilding of the wall of Jerusalem, Nehemiah gathered the people in a great assembly. When the people wept in response to the reading of the law, Nehemiah encouraged them not to mourn saying *"Do not be grieved, for the joy of the Lord is your strength"* (Neh 8:10). It was a season of rejoicing.

Then, Nehemiah forced Jewish men who married foreign women to take an oath against foreign marriage. This action seems harsh, but it was deemed necessary because the worship of foreign gods in Israel was a direct result of Solomon's marriage to foreign women. Nehemiah insured the worship of only the One true God in Jerusalem at the Second Temple.

> **Meditation:** Consider the parallel between fidelity in marriage and fidelity in the worship of God. Scripture is very clear about the heart of the Lord for marriage. In what ways does faithfulness in marriage reflect faithfulness to the Lord? Consider reasons why fallen powers desire to attack and undermine the Biblical institution of marriage. Write about it in your journal.

IV. Week One, Day 6 (Date:)   **POWER**

> Then Jesus said to the crowds and to his disciples,
> "The scribes and the Pharisees sit on Moses' seat, so do and observe whatever they tell you, but not the works they do. For they preach, but do not practice. They tie up heavy burdens, hard to bear, and lay them on people's shoulders, but they themselves are not willing to move them with their finger.
> They do all their deeds to be seen by others. For they make their phylacteries broad and their fringes long, and they love the place of honor at feasts and the best seats in the synagogues and greetings in the marketplaces and being called rabbi by others." Matt 23:1-7

They love the place of honor.

Powers and principalities are spiritual forces that influence (or ally with) fleshly and human forces to shape, influence, and try to control the world. They can work independently from humans, but more often they work inside of human constructions. Fallen powers impact our political, military, economic, sociological, media, technological, and religious institutions.[72]

So what became of worship at the Second Temple in the time of Jesus? There was a certain purity of the people. But in the mind of powerful sects such as the Pharisees, this purity had become exclusivity. And the Pharisees fully understood the concept of power. They exercised it artfully – carefully guarding it and the prestige that accompanied it.

The chief priests and the Pharisees were very powerful. They controlled the temple and the Jewish religion. They had territory that they were jealous to protect and they intended to guard it carefully – even to the point of extinguishing threats to it, like Jesus. After all, what was good for the Jewish religion must have been good for the worship of God and for His kingdom - right?

> **Meditation:** Consider the Pharisees of Jesus' day. What authority did they have based on the positions that they occupied? How did Jesus honor that authority?
>
> What idols did the Pharisees have in their hearts? List them in your journal. How can we avoid similar idols in our worship of God today?

☦   ☦   ☦   ☦   ☦   ☦   ☦

---

[72]See *Powers, Weakness, and the Tabernacling of God,* pp. 21, 32-34.

IV. Week One, Day 7 (Date:)   **POWER**

Today is a day of review. Review the devotions and your journal entries over the past week.

> **Meditation:** Select an area or a theme from the past week that struck you. Spend more time with that area or theme asking the Holy Spirit to quicken it to your heart. Then ask for discernment that the eyes of your heart may be opened to see truth in that area.

✟ ✟ ✟ ✟ ✟ ✟ ✟

NOTES:_____

_____

_____

_____

_____

_____

_____

_____

_____

_____

_____

SECTION IV – POWER AND GLORY: WEEK TWO

IV.Week Two, Day 1 (Date:)   **THE CUP**

> Then Simon Peter, having a sword, drew it and struck the high priest's servant and cut off his right ear. (The servant's name was Malchus.) So Jesus said to Peter, "Put your sword into its sheath; shall I not drink the cup that the Father has given me?" So the band of soldiers and their captain and the officers of the Jews arrested Jesus and bound him. **John 18:10-12**

Shall I not drink the cup that the Father has given Me?

Blessed be Thy Name, O Lord, forever (Ps 113:2) who hast willed that this temptation and tribulation should come upon me. I cannot escape it, but must needs flee to Thee, that Thou mayest help me, and turn it to my good.

Lord, I am now in tribulation, and my heart is ill at ease, for I am much troubled with the present suffering. And now, O beloved Father, what shall I say? I am caught amid straits; "Save me from this hour: but for this cause came I unto this hour" (John 12:27), that Thou mayest be glorified, when I shall have been greatly humbled, and by Thee delivered. "Be pleased, O Lord, to deliver me" (Ps 40:13), for, poor wretch that I am, what can I do, and where shall I go without Thee? Grant me patience, O Lord, even now in this moment.[73]

Jesus knew that His Father, Who loved Him perfectly, had given Him a cup that He must drink. It was a cup filled with pain, suffering, anguish, and ridicule.

This scripture summarizes the polarized understanding of the kingdom of God by Jesus and by His disciples. Peter and the disciples understood the establishment of the kingdom of God in terms of power, violence, strength, and conquest. So when threatened by a show of force, Peter bravely pulled out his sword and began to fight. He expected Jesus to join in and to prevail.

But Jesus understood the establishment of the kingdom of God in terms of the cup. He told Peter to put the sword back into its sheath, and he submitted Himself to arrest and to being bound. Jesus was willing to drink the cup in weakness in order to accomplish the will of His Father.

---

[73] *The Imitation of Christ*, p.151.

Meditation: Imagine that you are Peter. What are your expectations of Jesus when you pull out your sword and begin fighting? What emotions do you feel when Jesus tells you to put your sword back into its sheath and you see Jesus being arrested and bound? Maybe you even feel betrayal?

Shortly before this event, Jesus had shared the Last Supper with His disciples and they all had drunk from a cup. What did it mean to Jesus' disciples when He said that He must drink from the cup the Father had given Him? What does it mean to you?

☦ ☦ ☦ ☦ ☦ ☦ ☦

NOTES:_____

IV. Week Two, Day 2 (Date:)   **THE CUP**

> From that time Jesus began to show his disciples that he must go to Jerusalem and suffer many things from the elders and chief priests and scribes, and be killed, and on the third day be raised. And Peter took him aside and began to rebuke him, saying, "Far be it from you, Lord! This shall never happen to you."
> But he turned and said to Peter, "Get behind me, Satan! You are a hindrance to me. For you are not setting your mind on the things of God, but on the things of man."
> Then Jesus told his disciples, "If anyone would come after me, let him deny himself and take up his cross and follow me." Matt 16:21-24

Get thee behind Me, Satan!

Jesus' rebuke of Peter may seem harsh. It was certainly immediate. But Jesus recognized the temptation and reacted to it decisively.

We have already seen how the three temptations of Jesus appealed to Jesus' humanity - to the lust of the eyes, the lust of the flesh, and the pride of life. (See II.Week Two). We have further seen the craftiness of the temptations in connecting to the call of the Father on Jesus' life – as the Bread of life, as the King of glory, and as the King of kings. (See III.Week Three, Day 4).

But the temptations were even more devious than that. The temptations offered Jesus a shortcut – an easy road. In His life and ministry, Jesus put up with the misconceptions and bumbling of His disciples. He tolerated burdens and dysfunctions of every person He met. Jesus experienced ridicule and suspicion from the authorities. And He drank from the cup.

Satan was offering Jesus a way to fulfill His destiny without the cup – the right end, so to speak, but by the wrong means. All that Jesus had to do was to agree. All pain, sweat, and humiliation would be removed immediately. Satan tried to make Jesus think that He could realize His destiny with just a word of assent. And He wouldn't have to worry about those pesky Pharisees.

But Jesus came to accomplish the will of His beloved Father. He rebuked Satan's "easy street" offer immediately. And He rebuked Peter's view of conquest through worldly power, might, and prestige in the same way. That view came straight from the enemy.

> **Meditation:** Imagine again that you are Peter. You have just affirmed Jesus as the Christ and been commended for it. Now what do you feel as Jesus rebukes you? What do you think that Jesus means by what He says? What does Jesus' subsequent statement of discipleship mean to you today?

IV. Week Two, Day 3 (Date:)   THE CUP

> Many of the Jews therefore, who had come with Mary and had seen what he did, believed in him, but some of them went to the Pharisees and told them what Jesus had done. So the chief priests and the Pharisees gathered the council and said, "What are we to do? For this man performs many signs. If we let him go on like this, everyone will believe in him, and the Romans will come and take away both our place and our nation."
> But one of them, Caiaphas, who was high priest that year, said to them, "You know nothing at all. Nor do you understand that it is better for you that one man should die for the people, not that the whole nation should perish."
> He did not say this of his own accord, but being high priest that year he prophesied that Jesus would die for the nation, and not for the nation only, but also to gather into one the children of God who are scattered abroad. So from that day on they made plans to put him to death. **John 11:45-53**

The Romans will come and take away both our place and our nation.

The crucifixion of Jesus did not occur by accident. There were elements and persons who conspired to put Him to death and succeeded. There were "visible historic forces – namely, the *religious* leaders, Jewish and Roman *politics*, and the crowd (i..e., *social* forces) – which served as agents of more sinister invisible powers."[74]

Jesus had just raised Lazarus from the dead. By all accounts, it was an amazing miracle – something that had happened in scripture historically only by the spirit and power of Elijah. Many people rejoiced with Mary and Martha and believed in Jesus.

But the Pharisees were not rejoicing. They controlled the temple, the Jewish religion, and the nation. They had political territory that they were jealous to protect and they intended to guard it carefully. A man who could raise the dead and who could sway the people was dangerous. Any anointing He may possess from the Lord was a secondary consideration.

Jesus threatened their power and control. So the high priest, whose authority John recognized, prophesied that one man should die for the people. That man was Jesus. So they conspired to put Him to death using all of the human power and force they could muster.

---

[74] *Powers, Weakness, and the Tabernacling of God*, p.9 (quoting James S. Stewart).

Meditation: Consider the idea of fallen powers at work in the crucifixion of Jesus. Do you agree with the idea that fallen powers influence institutions of man, including religious, political, and social forces? If so, can you identify any similar powers that are at work in the world today? Journal your thoughts about it.

☦ ☦ ☦ ☦ ☦ ☦ ☦

NOTES:_____

IV. Week Two, Day 4 (Date:)   **THE CUP**

> And they were on the road, going up to Jerusalem, and Jesus was walking ahead of them. And they were amazed, and those who followed were afraid. And taking the twelve again, he began to tell them what was to happen to him, saying, "See, we are going up to Jerusalem, and the Son of Man will be delivered over to the chief priests and the scribes, and they will condemn him to death and deliver him over to the Gentiles. And they will mock him and spit on him, and flog him and kill him. And after three days he will rise."
> And James and John, the sons of Zebedee, came up to him and said to him, "Teacher, we want you to do for us whatever we ask of you." And he said to them, "What do you want me to do for you?"
> And they said to him, "Grant us to sit, one at your right hand and one at your left, in your glory."
> Jesus said to them, "You do not know what you are asking. Are you able to drink the cup that I drink, or to be baptized with the baptism with which I am baptized?"
> And they said to him, "We are able." And Jesus said to them, "The cup that I drink you will drink, and with the baptism with which I am baptized, you will be baptized, but to sit at my right hand or at my left is not mine to grant, but it is for those for whom it has been prepared." **Mark 10:32-40**

The cup that I drink you will drink.

James and John want power and prestige. They understand the kingdom of God and its authority in worldly terms – position, honor, and rule. So Jesus corrects them.

Initially, Jesus corrects their desire for authority. *"You do not know what you are asking."* James and John see the power and control that accompany authority and they want that. But Jesus asks them a pointed question about responsibility. If James and John want the authority, they must bear the responsibility! All authority properly exercised comes with responsibility. In this case, the responsibility involves a cup and baptism. Can James and John bear such great responsibility?

Then, when James and John respond affirmatively, Jesus confirms the cup and baptism they will experience. Jesus is making it clear to His disciples that He is walking the way of the Cross and that they must walk the way of the Cross as well.

Finally, after affirming the cross that James and John must bear, Jesus does not even grant their request for position and honor. That request remained unanswered as it is in the hands of His Father and subject to His authority.

> **Meditation:** Consider the correlation that Jesus made between authority and responsibility. How fearful is the authority that James and John sought?
>
> Next, what is the cup that Jesus said James and John must drink? Describe it in your journal.

☩ ☩ ☩ ☩ ☩ ☩ ☩

NOTES:_____

_____

_____

_____

_____

_____

_____

_____

_____

_____

> Be faithful in your journal entries. They serve as a reminder of what you learn and how God is working through your dedication of time.

IV. Week Two, Day 5 (Date:)   THE CUP

> For God, who said, "Let light shine out of darkness," has shone in our hearts to give the light of the knowledge of the glory of God in the face of Jesus Christ. But we have this treasure in jars of clay, to show that the surpassing power belongs to God and not to us.
> We are afflicted in every way, but not crushed; perplexed, but not driven to despair; persecuted, but not forsaken; struck down, but not destroyed; always carrying in the body the death of Jesus, so that the life of Jesus may also be manifested in our bodies. For we who live are always being given over to death for Jesus' sake, so that the life of Jesus also may be manifested in our mortal flesh.
> So death is at work in us, but life in you. **2 Cor 4:6-12**

Always carrying in the body the death of Jesus.

Marva Dawn draws an important distinction between what has been called since Luther's time "a theology of glory" as opposed to the biblical "theology of the cross." "In Gnostic Christianity, the enlightenment of the mind enables the avoidance of suffering. In classical Christianity, the gift of the Holy Spirit leads one through the same path of suffering that was followed by the Messiah."[75]

Luther's *Heidelberg Disputation* addresses the theology of glory and the theology of the cross. The theologian of glory "does not know God hidden in suffering. Therefore he prefers works to suffering, glory to the cross, strength to weakness, wisdom to folly, and, in general, good to evil."[76] **This approach is natural for humans with human desires using human minds. A theologian of the cross though sees the cross (pain, suffering, weakness, and reproach) as the source of God's involvement in the world and of the revelation of His work.**

The distinction between the theology of glory and the theology of the cross is stark. The implications of the theology I follow are significant. Of which cup do I intend to drink?

Under the theology of glory:

- I have dominion. I exercise a divine power over other people and over my circumstances.

---

[75] *Powers, Weakness, and the Tabernacling of God*, p.90 (quoting, in part, Luke Timothy Johnson).

[76] The Heidelberg Disputation, Proof to Thesis XXI (Source: **www.bookofconcord.org/heidelberg.php**).

- I am entitled to financial prosperity. If I feel deprived of some possession, I am entitled to get it now.
- I have irresistible favor with all men and with all animals and I can behave accordingly.
- If I am sick, ill, or in pain, I am entitled to immediate recovery.

I call the theology of glory my "personal rewards program" in which I receive all the benefits of the world without being "worldly minded." Otherwise, of course, I carry about in my body the death of Jesus Christ, as Paul so eloquently reminds me.

> **Meditation:** Spend time meditating on the theology of glory and the theology of the cross. How have you seen or heard the two theologies presented in churches or in other Christian teachings? Compare your beliefs to each theology. Ask the Holy Spirit to reveal truth to you about these two views.

☦ ☦ ☦ ☦ ☦ ☦ ☦

NOTES:_____

_____

_____

_____

_____

_____

_____

_____

_____

_____

IV. Week Two, Day 6 (Date:)   THE CUP

> About that time Herod the king laid violent hands on some who belonged to the church. He killed James the brother of John with the sword, and when he saw that it pleased the Jews, he proceeded to arrest Peter also. This was during the days of Unleavened Bread.
> **Acts 12:1-3**

He killed James the brother of John with the sword.

Jesus has now many lovers of His heavenly kingdom, but few bearers of His cross. Many He has who are desirous of consolation, but few of tribulation. Many He finds who share His table, but few His fasting. All desire to rejoice with Him, few are willing to endure anything for Him. Many follow Jesus to the breaking of bread; but few to the drinking of the cup of His passion (Luke 22:42). Many reverence His miracles; few follow the shame of His cross. Many love Jesus so long as no adversities befall them. Many praise and bless Him so long as they receive any consolation from Him. But if Jesus hide Himself, and leave them but a little while, they fall either into complaining, or into dejection of mind.

But they who love Jesus for the sake of Jesus, and not for some special comfort of their own, bless Him in all tribulation and anguish of heart, as well as in the highest comfort. Yea, although He should never give them comfort, they would ever praise Him notwithstanding, and wish to always give thanks. Oh, how powerful is the pure love of Jesus, which is mixed with no self-interest or self-love![77]

Scripture records very simply, matter of factly, and without much elaboration, the cup that James drank. In the subsequent story in Acts 12, God rescued Peter miraculously. But in His divine wisdom, God allowed James to be martyred.

According to the theology of the Cross, I may suffer, I may hurt, I may experience deprivation, and I deny my selfish desires. Why?

- I must drink the cup in order to draw closer to Christ and to be conformed to His image.
- I must drink the cup in order to build true character that God wants to instill in me.
- I must drink of the cup in order to follow the pure example of Christ and to become more like Him through fellowship with His suffering.
- I must drink of the cup to grow into a mature believer to His glory and praise.

---

[77] *The Imitation of Christ*, pp.83-84.

- I must drink of the cup to witness to the world and to heavenly powers that Christ alone is sufficient in all places and in all circumstances.

But my tendency is to present to God the sacrifice that I want to give rather than the sacrifice that He desires. Many times the sacrifice He desires lies within me – a yielding and surrender to His plan for my life and my character.

One more note: The killing of James pleased the Jews. So Herod arrested Peter. Fallen powers were still at work.

> **Meditation:** *"Love believes all things."* What do you think James experienced as he was apprehended by Herod and then executed? Do you think he recalled what Jesus told him about drinking from the cup, and that he believed it?
>
> The execution of James occurred during the "days of Unleavened Bread" – the Passover. Do you think James recalled Jesus' own suffering and execution during the Passover? Write your feelings in your journal. Scripture says that the cross is a stumbling block for many (1 Cor 1:23). Why is this true?

☩ ☩ ☩ ☩ ☩ ☩ ☩

NOTES:_____

_____

_____

_____

_____

> Slow movement of the heart can be very good. Healthy growth is often slow and meticulous. But it is solid. Be encouraged that God is moving in your life to mature you as you dedicate time to Him.

IV. Week Two, Day 7 (Date:) **THE CUP**

Today is a day of review. Look back over your journal for the last week.

> **Meditation:** Consider the cup of which the Lord drank. How has the Lord asked you to drink of the cup in your own life? Identify areas in which the cup is real to you today. Journal about these areas and then compose a prayer to the Lord about them.

☦ ☦ ☦ ☦ ☦ ☦ ☦

NOTES:_____

_____

_____

_____

_____

_____

_____

_____

_____

_____

_____

SECTION IV – POWER AND GLORY: WEEK THREE

IV.Week Three, Day 1 (Date:)   **WEAKNESS**

> For though we walk in the flesh, we are not waging war according to the flesh. For the weapons of our warfare are not of the flesh but have divine power to destroy strongholds. We destroy arguments and every lofty opinion raised against the knowledge of God, and take every thought captive to obey Christ, being ready to punish every disobedience, when your obedience is complete. **2 Cor 10:3-6**

For the weapons of our warfare…have divine power to destroy strongholds.

Change me and change me and change me from glory to glory into Your image! I want You more!! When the enemy attacks, I don't want it to be that he is only resisting, fighting against: Me, My flesh, My knowledge about the armor, My words, or <u>My Strength</u>.

I want it to be that he is actually facing and dealing with: You, Your Truth, Your Word, Your blood, Your Name, Your power, Your righteousness, Your Good News, Your Shalom, Your shield of faith, Your Love, Your hope, Your Presence, Your Grace and Mercy! Your Glory!!

O God, I thank You that You are so equipping, so inspiring, so empowering, so strengthening, so enabling, so encouraging, and so uplifting! Come and lift me up into all that You are and have for me!   –Pastor Daniel Martin, 5/31/14

Paul speaks of ongoing warfare – a warfare against strongholds, fallen powers, and institutions whose arguments and lofty opinions are raised against the knowledge of God. The Greek word translated "stronghold" only appears once in the New Testament – in this passage. That word is a military term for a fortress or even a prison.[78]

Paul makes it clear that worldly power – human strength – cannot overcome these strongholds. The power to overcome is divine. It is a power that comes only from God and its deployment begins with our obedience.

Fallen powers are overcome through the power and Presence of God alone.

> **Meditation:** Reread the scripture passage above, but as you do it, keep in mind the idea that fallen powers work through, and in conjunction with, worldly institutions. Determine what this passage means to you. Write about that meaning in your journal.

---

[78] Arndt and Gingrich, *A Greek-English Lexicon of the New Testament (by Walter Bauer)*, p. 601 (University of Chicago Press 1979).

IV. Week Three, Day 2 (Date:)   **WEAKNESS**

> On behalf of this man I will boast, but on my own behalf I will not boast, except of my weaknesses—though if I should wish to boast, I would not be a fool, for I would be speaking the truth; but I refrain from it, so that no one may think more of me than he sees in me or hears from me.
> So to keep me from becoming conceited because of the surpassing greatness of the revelations, a thorn was given me in the flesh, a messenger of Satan to harass me, to keep me from becoming conceited. Three times I pleaded with the Lord about this, that it should leave me.
> But he said to me, "My grace is sufficient for you, for my power is made perfect in weakness." Therefore I will boast all the more gladly of my weaknesses, so that the power of Christ may rest upon me. For the sake of Christ, then, I am content with weaknesses, insults, hardships, persecutions, and calamities. For when I am weak, then I am strong. **2 Cor 12:5-10**

My power is made perfect in weakness.

Therefore I take pleasure in infirmities - for Christ's sake: for when I am weak, then am I strong (2 Corinthians 12:10). A pastor who was accomplishing great things for God was asked the key to his success. Everyone thought he would respond with, "You need charisma," or "the ability to relate to people." They were astounded when, instead, he replied, "I have found <u>the most important characteristic for anyone who wants to accomplish great things in the kingdom of God is weakness</u>."

No accomplishment of eternal value in God's kingdom is a result of men's efforts. It is a result of God using individuals who cannot do things by themselves. Remember, if you can do it, then you don't need God. Become radically dependent upon Him. Your independence from God gives Satan a foothold into your life. Your weakness recognized and admitted is the Spirit's opportunity to use you as His vessel for ministry and service.

As you start your day, put God in charge. Ask Him to do what you cannot do through your own ability.[79]   –Pastor Daniel Martin, 2/13/13

This scripture passage has context. Immediately before it, Paul tells of a person who was caught up into the third heaven – into paradise – a great vision and revelation of the Lord. What an experience that must have been! Immediately after it, Paul defends his status as a true apostle.

---

[79] Quoted from a *Charisma* devotion, 2/11/12.

In this passage, Paul tells the Corinthian church of a lesson learned – a mystery that Paul learned about power: The power of the Lord is made perfect in my weakness. Weakness in my life invites the power of Christ to rest upon me. Insults, hardships, persecutions, and calamities invite the power of Christ to dwell within me. As a result, when I am weak, then I am strong in Him.

When my fleshly power ends, it invites the power of God to dwell within me. The power of God Almighty is encouraged by my weakness – a brokenness which makes room for God's strength. The strength and power of the Lord is manifested through the weakness and humility of the saints.

We enter the Presence of God in weakness so that there is no trace of flesh to boast in the Presence of God. *"Love does not boast."* That is why Paul says he will not boast except of his weaknesses. Surrender is yielding our ability, our power, our will, and our strength to God. Surrender is a means of humility and brokenness and it yields the power of God – the type of divine power which overcomes strongholds.

> **Meditation:** Consider this view of weakness in relationship to the power of God. Write in your journal your feelings as you read this devotion and as you consider the paradoxes of the kingdom of God – die to live, deny yourself to fulfill, the way of the Cross to glory, and my weakness and the power of God.

☩ ☩ ☩ ☩ ☩ ☩ ☩

NOTES:_____

_____

_____

_____

_____

_____

_____

_____

IV. Week Three, Day 3 (Date:)   **WEAKNESS**

> To me, though I am the very least of all the saints, this grace was given, to preach to the Gentiles the unsearchable riches of Christ, and to bring to light for everyone what is the plan of the mystery hidden for ages in God who created all things, so that through the church the manifold wisdom of God might now be made known to the rulers and authorities in the heavenly places.
> This was according to the eternal purpose that he has realized in Christ Jesus our Lord, in whom we have boldness and access with confidence through our faith in him. **Eph 3:8-12**

That through the church the manifold wisdom of God might now be made known.

Even as Christ accomplished atonement for us by suffering and death, so the Lord accomplishes witness to the world through our weakness. In fact, God has more need of our weakness than of our strength. Just as powers overstep their bounds and become gods, so our power becomes a rival to God.[80]

The church has a role in relationship to rulers and authorities in heavenly places, including fallen powers. The church makes known the manifold wisdom of God – a mystery hidden for ages.

The role of the church is to be a witness of Christ's Lordship – to fellow humans and to the powers and principalities, and to call them into submission to Christ's Lordship which has been established through the Cross. God's power in us is a witness to the world (including the people of the world) and to the rulers and authorities in heavenly places.

The church accomplishes this role through weakness, humility, and service as the church conforms to the Cross of Christ. The church is not called to be prestigious, domineering, or well-heeled. Only through submission and obedience to Christ and to His Cross, His Lordship is put on display to all.

> **Meditation:** Do you agree with this role of the church in relationship to fallen powers – to witness to them and to call them into submission to Christ's Lordship? If so, what means do you think that the church uses to accomplish this witness? How does your church act to accomplish this witness?

╬   ╬   ╬   ╬   ╬   ╬   ╬

---

[80] *Powers, Weakness, and the Tabernacling of God*, p.47.

NOTES:_____

_____

_____

_____

_____

_____

_____

_____

_____

_____

_____

_____

_____

_____

> Be sure to meet regularly with your mentor or devotional partner. Meeting will help your perspective on the devotions and can give you better insight on approach, focus, and direction.

IV. Week Three, Day 4 (Date:)					WEAKNESS

> For this is a gracious thing, when, mindful of God, one endures sorrows while suffering unjustly. For what credit is it if, when you sin and are beaten for it, you endure? But if when you do good and suffer for it you endure, this is a gracious thing in the sight of God.
> For to this you have been called, because Christ also suffered for you, leaving you an example, so that you might follow in his steps. He committed no sin, neither was deceit found in his mouth. When he was reviled, he did not revile in return; when he suffered, he did not threaten, but continued entrusting himself to him who judges justly.
> **1 Pet 2:19-23**

Christ also suffered for you, leaving you an example, so that you might follow in His steps.

Our call to stand against the powers and principalities must be seen as synonymous with our calling to be the people of God. These are not two calls but one. We are called as His people to participate in Christ's triumph over these powers by submitting to the way of the cross. *We are called to be a cruciform people – to live according to the cross-shaped way of Jesus.* **We are called to receive power in weakness, not power in our strength or in ourselves.** *We are the people known by their love.* **We are called proclaim, "Without You, Jesus, we can do nothing."**[81]

We do not view the suffering of Christ in historical isolation. His suffering was an example for His church so that we might follow in His steps. That is why Peter encourages his flock to do good and to suffer for it, for that finds favor in the sight of God.

The Church lives in weakness because this life of submission is Christ's model for His Body. I tend to shape the Cross to my life – to make it work for what I want. That tendency is selfish and fleshly. Instead, I am called to conform my life and my body to the shape of the Cross – even if it is painful to me. Where in scripture does it say that the Cross fulfills my fleshly desires?

If I am operating out of my strength (worldly power, influence, and reputation) rather than out of the weakness in which God dwells, there is something drastically amiss. So I bear the cross of Christ, and through it, I overcome.

> **Meditation:** Consider the suffering and humiliation of Christ as an example to you so that you can follow in His steps. To what extent are you willing to allow that suffering to occur to you? Spend time with God in surrender as you tell Him your thoughts and feelings about it. Then write a prayer in your journal to Him about the way of the Cross.

---

[81] Jamin Goggin and Kyie Strobel, *The Way of the Dragon or the Way of the Lamb* pp.78-79 (HarperCollins 2017).

IV. Week Three, Day 5 (Date:)   **WEAKNESS**

> "Behold, I am sending you out as sheep in the midst of wolves, so be wise as serpents and innocent as doves. Beware of men, for they will deliver you over to courts and flog you in their synagogues, and you will be dragged before governors and kings for my sake, to bear witness before them and the Gentiles. When they deliver you over, do not be anxious how you are to speak or what you are to say, for what you are to say will be given to you in that hour. For it is not you who speak, but the Spirit of your Father speaking through you.
> "Brother will deliver brother over to death, and the father his child, and children will rise against parents and have them put to death, and you will be hated by all for my name's sake. But the one who endures to the end will be saved." **Matt 10:16-22**

I am sending you out as sheep in the midst of wolves.

Jesus did not only leave His followers an example. He gave instructions. Jesus sent out His disciples two by two as part of their discipleship training. But in the instructions He made clear their status in relationship to the world and its powers. The disciples are sheep going out into wolves. The disciples are called to have the wisdom and insight of serpents, but to be as innocent (also interpreted as "gentle" or "harmless") as doves. The disciples are commissioned as Christ's ambassadors who bear His demeanor.

What are the implications of living and ministering in weakness? Here are three starters:

- To suffer injustice without resentment.
- To suffer hurt without destruction.
- To suffer humiliation without retaliation.

The believer lives in surrender and trust. He entrusts his weakness to God's power. He entrusts his rights to God's justice. And he entrusts his faith to God's goodness.

At times, when I hear from a friend who is going through turmoil or anguish while walking in the way of the Cross, what I tell my friend is this: "God entrusts extraordinary burdens to His best people."

Meditation: Review the three starters above. Apply them to your life to date. How have you lived them out? How would you like to live them? Journal about your responses.

☩   ☩   ☩   ☩   ☩   ☩   ☩

IV. Week Three, Day 6 (Date:)   **WEAKNESS**

> Then he brought them up into his house and set food before them. And he rejoiced along with his entire household that he had believed in God. But when it was day, the magistrates sent the police, saying, "Let those men go."
> And the jailer reported these words to Paul, saying, "The magistrates have sent to let you go. Therefore come out now and go in peace."
> But Paul said to them, "They have beaten us publicly, uncondemned, men who are Roman citizens, and have thrown us into prison; and do they now throw us out secretly? No! Let them come themselves and take us out."
> The police reported these words to the magistrates, and they were afraid when they heard that they were Roman citizens. So they came and apologized to them. And they took them out and asked them to leave the city. So they went out of the prison and visited Lydia. And when they had seen the brothers, they encouraged them and departed. **Acts 16:34-40**

Do they now throw us out secretly? No!

A question that I regularly hear is "How do I know when to stand up and when to back down? When do I assert my rights and when do I lay them down and yield?"

This scripture is the end of the story about the Philippian jailer. Paul and Silas are evangelizing Philippi. They exercise the power of God in casting a spirit of divination out of a fortune-teller. As a consequence of this righteous act, they are dragged before the authorities, attacked by the crowd, stripped of their clothes, beaten with rods, and cast into prison.

Miraculously, an earthquake occurs. Paul persuades the jailer not to commit suicide and then leads him and his household to Christ. So it is time for Paul to go. But Paul does not go meekly. He asserts his rights as a Roman citizen and demands a public accounting.

As I read this story, I go "Wait a second, Paul! You decide to assert your rights now? What happened when you were being accused, attacked, stripped, beaten, and imprisoned? Those actions were certainly unjust. Fallen powers were hard at work. Why didn't you assert your rights as a Roman citizen then?"

We all know the outcome of Paul's initial sacrifice of his rights. Through the yielding of Paul and Silas, God worked a mighty miracle. The jailer and his household were saved as a result.

The Holy Spirit must reveal to us when to assert rights and when to yield them. Paul was obviously led by the Holy Spirit as to timing. After the work of the Lord was finished, then Paul asserted his rights so that disrepute would not fall on the church.

In conjunction with the leading of the Holy Spirit, there is another question to ask (courtesy of my friend, Mitch): "Is it beneficial to the kingdom of God?" Which option will serve as the better witness and will bring the most glory to the Lord?

> **Meditation:** Explore your attitude over the last few days with regard to the kingdom of God. Have you lived your life as a witness to the Lord? Have you been concerned for the kingdom of God? Write your thoughts in your journal and then tell the Lord how you want to live your life.

☩ ☩ ☩ ☩ ☩ ☩ ☩

NOTES:_____

_____

_____

_____

_____

_____

_____

_____

_____

_____

IV. Week Three, Day 7 (Date:)   **WEAKNESS**

Today is a day of review. Review your journal over the last week.

> **Meditation:** Spend time with the Lord. List in your journal the ways in which you are willing to walk in weakness, submission, and yielding in your life. This exercise is not one of condemnation. You are stating your desires to Him even if some of them are not a reality yet. Take your time and list the ways that you want to walk the way of the Cross for His glory.
>
> Then present the list to the Lord as a sacrifice to Him. Ask the Holy Spirit for help in living them out.

☥ ☥ ☥ ☥ ☥ ☥ ☥

NOTES:_____

_____

_____

_____

_____

_____

_____

_____

_____

SECTION IV – POWER AND GLORY: WEEK FOUR

IV.Week Four, Day 1 (Date:)   **TRIUMPH**

> Now I rejoice in my sufferings for your sake, and in my flesh I am filling up what is lacking in Christ's afflictions for the sake of his body, that is, the church, of which I became a minister according to the stewardship from God that was given to me for you, to make the word of God fully known, the mystery hidden for ages and generations but now revealed to his saints.
> To them God chose to make known how great among the Gentiles are the riches of the glory of this mystery, which is Christ in you, the hope of glory. Him we proclaim, warning everyone and teaching everyone with all wisdom, that we may present everyone mature in Christ. For this I toil, struggling with all his energy that he powerfully works within me. **Col 1:24-29**

I am filling up what is lacking in Christ's afflictions for the sake of His body, that is, the church.

This passage gives insight to Paul's understanding of the suffering of the church. Paul says he is filling up what is lacking in Christ's afflictions for the sake of the body. Paul knows that warfare is ongoing and the afflictions of Christ's body have not ended.

Now make no mistake. The work of Christ and the atonement for our sins was completed on the cross, period. When Christ said *"It is finished"* (Jn 19:30) on the cross immediately before He died, He proclaimed the fulfillment of the redemption of God offered for humankind.

But there is a sense in which the afflictions of the church are the afflictions of Christ. The church is the Body of Christ and its sufferings are thus sufferings of Christ. When a believer suffers for the sake of Christ's body, a believer joins with the way of the Cross and conforms to the image and work of Christ.

It is instructive that Paul speaks of maturity in Christ. <u>Walking in the way of the Cross produces this maturity.</u>

Finally, note how Paul toils. He toils with energy from Christ which Christ powerfully works within him. Paul had learned to allow Christ to work within Him powerfully and not in his own strength.

Meditation: Read this scripture passage carefully. Identify one or two themes or phrases that strike you. Meditate on those themes or phrases. Ask God to make them a reality in your life.

IV. Week Four, Day 2 (Date:)   TRIUMPH

> Then I saw in the right hand of him who was seated on the throne a scroll written within and on the back, sealed with seven seals. And I saw a mighty angel proclaiming with a loud voice, "Who is worthy to open the scroll and break its seals?" And no one in heaven or on earth or under the earth was able to open the scroll or to look into it, and I began to weep loudly because no one was found worthy to open the scroll or to look into it.
> And one of the elders said to me, "Weep no more; behold, the Lion of the tribe of Judah, the Root of David, has conquered, so that he can open the scroll and its seven seals."
> And between the throne and the four living creatures and among the elders I saw a Lamb standing, as though it had been slain, with seven horns and with seven eyes, which are the seven spirits of God sent out into all the earth. And he went and took the scroll from the right hand of him who was seated on the throne.
> And when he had taken the scroll, the four living creatures and the twenty-four elders fell down before the Lamb, each holding a harp, and golden bowls full of incense, which are the prayers of the saints. And they sang a new song, saying, "Worthy are you to take the scroll and to open its seals, for you were slain, and by your blood you ransomed people for God from every tribe and language and people and nation, and you have made them a kingdom and priests to our God, and they shall reign on the earth." **Rev 5:1-10**

Worthy are You to take the scroll and to open its seals for

You were slain and by Your blood ransomed people for God.

"This is the root of grace: the dismantling of our power. Whenever even a little power rises up in us, the Spirit and authority of God will retreat to the corresponding degree. In my estimation this is the single most important insight with regard to the kingdom of God." – Eberhard Arnold[82]

When does a Lion become a Lamb? The Lion of the tribe of Judah - the root of David the king - has conquered. A lion is the king of the jungle – powerful, predatory, and dominant. In this case, the Lion is truly regal as He is the root of David.

But the actual power is manifested in the form of a Lamb – and a Lamb that had been slain at that. He, and only He, has the power to open the scroll and

---

[82] *Powers, Weakness, and the Tabernacling of God,* p.62 (quoted by Johann C. Arnold).

the seven seals. No other being in the presence of the Father has that power – only a Lamb who was slain.

Isn't that just like God? Isn't that the type of thing that God does – that comes directly from His heart? He chooses a sacrificial Lamb to display His awesome power!

The power of the Lamb is the greatest power in the universe. When I walk in weakness, in surrender, and in sacrifice, it is this power of the Lamb that arises within me. God ordained this power to open the seals of the scroll and to triumph over powers and principalities.

> **Meditation:** Reread this scripture again slowly. As you read it, imagine the scene that it describes. Feel what John felt when no one can open the scroll. Then hear the announcements. Sense the appearance, power, and worship of the Lamb. Journal what arises within you.

╬ ╬ ╬ ╬ ╬ ╬ ╬

NOTES:_____

_____

_____

_____

_____

_____

_____

_____

_____

_____

_____

_____

IV. Week Four, Day 3 (Date:)   **TRIUMPH**

> And you, who were dead in your trespasses and the uncircumcision of your flesh, God made alive together with him, having forgiven us all our trespasses, by canceling the record of debt that stood against us with its legal demands. This he set aside, nailing it to the cross.
> He disarmed the rulers and authorities and put them to open shame, by triumphing over them in him. **Col 2:13-15**

This He set aside, nailing it to the cross.

Yes, You conquered all death, all death causing things, all evil, all injustices, all wrongs, all wrongs people have caused each other, all wrongs we have committed against each other. You are so mighty, so strong, so powerful against all ungodliness!

In Your Majesty, Purity, Justice, Compassion, Hatred of evil, Love of truth, come and deliver me from all that is in opposition to You, that in any way honors Your enemy, that in any way blesses and pleases him.

I want only You to be Honored, Blessed, Pleased, Glorified, Magnified, Worshiped, Exalted, Delighted by everything I do, say, meditate, think, plan, emote, walk in!
  -Pastor Daniel Martin, 6/16/20

This passage proclaims the triumph of the cross. Through the cross, those who were dead were made alive. Through the cross, trespasses were forgiven and the debt, with its legal demands, was canceled. Through the cross, rulers and authorities were disarmed and put to open shame. The triumph of the cross brings great rejoicing in heaven and on the earth!

The cross is the means of triumph. The victory of the cross is etched in eternity. So the question is "If the triumph of the Cross was sufficient and complete, why is the church of Christ engaged in warfare and in fighting fallen powers today rather than simply enjoying the fruits of this triumph?"

> **Meditation:** The question above has broad implications for our lives, our expectations, and how we live. Spend some time with this question. Write down your thoughts and feelings.

☫   ☫   ☫   ☫   ☫   ☫   ☫

> Remember to rest in God as you do your devotions. There are times to cease striving and just fall into Him.

IV. Week Four, Day 4 (Date:)   TRIUMPH

> It has been testified somewhere, "What is man, that you are mindful of him, or the son of man, that you care for him? You made him for a little while lower than the angels; you have crowned him with glory and honor, putting everything in subjection under his feet."
> Now in putting everything in subjection to him, he left nothing outside his control. At present, we do not yet see everything in subjection to him. But we see him who for a little while was made lower than the angels, namely Jesus, crowned with glory and honor because of the suffering of death, so that by the grace of God he might taste death for everyone. For it was fitting that he, for whom and by whom all things exist, in bringing many sons to glory, should make the founder of their salvation perfect through suffering. **Heb 2:6-10**

At present, we do not yet see everything in subjection to Him.

O Yes, Let forever come in and take over in every detail of my life. I want to live for Eternity - not waste all my life on me...now...on empties. I want my life to count, to be full of Eternity Issues now! I want to know where I end, then once I know it, help me to embrace coming to the end of myself and all I am and have. Where I end is where You begin! What an awesome place that is!!

O please stay with me until Now has transformed into forever! Please help me to die to myself, so my future can come alive in You!!

O please take everything I treasure and do with it whatever You want done with it. Whatever has to die, let it die. Whatever needs to be set aside for now, please help me to set it aside for as long as needed, even into eternity if necessary!

O what a blessed Place! Where all I am holding onto is the Cross, where it is all that matters, where the deaths it causes are a form of Life, where You come forth with all Your Glory!!

O what awesome Love You had for me which won me over in 1975, and has continued to do so ever since! What an awesome God You are to me, O Sovereign Lord!
        -Pastor Daniel Martin, 3/23/20

A tension exists in the timing of the triumph. Jesus has triumphed and has been crowned with glory and honor. Everything has been put in subjection to Him.

So the victory of the Cross has been accomplished, yet we do not yet see everything in subjection to Him. Fallen powers are still at work in our world. Scripture is clear that Satan and his forces will not be fully restrained until the end.

Part of the answer to the tension lies in bringing many sons to glory. The fallen powers exist for a purpose. They are part of God's plan for His saints just as they were a part of His plan for Jesus. The battle against fallen powers – the fight, the wounds, the lessons learned – all work toward the sanctification, purification, strengthening, and growth to maturity of the saints.

Also, the way of the Cross accomplishes its perfect work. The saints become His instrument in the war. As they learn to walk in the way of the Cross, they ally with Him in the fray.

God perceives time differently than we do. His purposes existed before the foundation of the world. But in our finiteness, we pray *"Thy Kingdom come, Thy will be done, on earth as it is in heaven."* And we wait on His timeless punctuality with trust in His plan and in confidence in the outcome.

> **Meditation:** Spend time meditating on this phrase from today's scripture reading "should make the founder of their salvation perfect through suffering." Does this phrase refer to Jesus? If so, in what ways can a sinless person be made perfect (or complete)? And how does suffering accomplish this?

☩ ☩ ☩ ☩ ☩ ☩ ☩

NOTES:_____

_____

_____

_____

_____

_____

_____

_____

_____

IV. Week Four, Day 5 (Date:)   **TRIUMPH**

> But thanks be to God, who in Christ always leads us in triumphal procession, and through us spreads the fragrance of the knowledge of him everywhere. For we are the aroma of Christ to God among those who are being saved and among those who are perishing, to one a fragrance from death to death, to the other a fragrance from life to life. Who is sufficient for these things? **2 Cor 2:14-16**

We are the aroma of Christ to God.

The image that we get in this passage is not of the church triumphing, but of one who has been triumphed over. The image of triumph has a cultural correspondence for the Corinthians in Paul's day...What the apostle Paul is telling us here is that in Christ God has triumphed over us, and in him we are now paraded before a watching world. We are caught in the victory parade of Christ, celebrating his defeat of the world, the flesh, and the devil. The image is not of our power, but God's. We are viewed in a position of weakness. And yet, as the church embraces the role of Christ's captive, we make Christ's way known in the world.[83]

The church participates in the triumphal procession of Christ. It participates in the display – a part of the demonstration and parade. But its role is to witness to Christ and to His triumph and glory, not to its own triumph. The church is the conquered – vanquished and transformed by the Cross, not the Conqueror. But this conquest is a conquest of love.

In the triumphal procession, the church emits a fragrant aroma – an aroma akin to a sacrifice. This aroma is not pleasing to those perishing. Nor should the church expect it to be pleasing. To them, it is the aroma of death.

But to those being saved, it is the aroma of life. The sacrifice, humiliation, and weakness of the saints please those persons experiencing life in Him.

Most importantly, the aroma is pleasing to God. When the church walks in the way of the Cross, the aroma of Christ's triumph lifts upward to God.

Meditation: Imagine the triumphal procession envisioned by this scripture passage. What do you see?

Next, consider the aroma of the sacrifice of the saints. What type of aroma is pleasing to God? What aroma is produced by your life? What aroma is produced by your church? Journal about it.

☩   ☩   ☩   ☩   ☩   ☩   ☩

---

[83] *The Way of the Dragon or the Way of the Lamb,* p. 188 (citing Paul Barnett).

NOTES:

IV. Week Four, Day 6 (Date:)   **TRIUMPH**

> Beloved, do not be surprised at the fiery trial when it comes upon you to test you, as though something strange were happening to you.
> But rejoice insofar as you share Christ's sufferings, that you may also rejoice and be glad when his glory is revealed.
> If you are insulted for the name of Christ, you are blessed, because the Spirit of glory and of God rests upon you. **1 Pet 4:12-14**

That you may also rejoice and be glad when His glory is revealed.

A positive outlook without negativity was something that Papa and Meme worked on constantly. They faced significant challenges throughout their lives. In order to survive the rough patches, they trained their minds to focus on cheerful expectations rather than dark imaginations. It was one of the many ways that they practiced their faith. Positive thoughts, words of faith, and words of gratitude are a few of the weapons that Papa and Meme used in the battle of the mind.

Jimmy was a capable grumbler. We called it "fussing and complaining." Jimmy invariably expressed just how he felt. If he didn't like something, every person around him knew about it, and they usually knew about it in detail - detail which he repeated over and over again.

Meme encouraged Jimmy many times not to "fuss and complain." She encouraged Jimmy to have a "happy face," not a sad face. Jimmy tended to focus intensely on a matter. If that matter was a problem or a difficulty, Jimmy just couldn't let it go. The "storm clouds," as we called it, would roll in, and they usually hung around for awhile. If Jimmy grumbled about a problem, I said, "Jimmy, are you fussing and complaining?"

"No me futh tompain!" Jimmy responded.

"Good! We don't like that fussing and complaining."

"No me doey." Jimmy said, shaking his head sullenly.

"Where's that happy face, Jimmy?"

"Yeah have happy faith." Jimmy's face looked dour as if he had just swallowed gasoline.

"I don't see a happy face, Jimmy. Where is it?"

Jimmy turned and grinned at me - except the "grin" was not very convincing. Jimmy's teeth were clenched together with his lips parted in some sort of forced grimace. "Thee?" he said, almost yelling at me.

I knew when it was time to back off, and at least appreciate the effort. "Yes, I see, Jimmy. That is a good happy face, buddy."

Sometimes the fact that Jimmy had been accused of fussing and complaining was just one more thing to grumble about. Many times, though, Jimmy would take stock of his attitude. An hour or two after a particularly grumpy spell, Jimmy came to me and said, "Thorry, Davy. Thorry futh tompain."

"That's okay, Jimmy. We all have our moments."

"Me pway Jesus help me. Pway Jesus help me no futh tompain."

"That's good, Jimmy. Prayer is important. We all feel sad sometimes."

"No me feel thad. Feel happy! Feel Jesus in my heart!"[84]

"Feel Jesus in my heart" was Jimmy's version of joy – a joy that existed even if the circumstances were not to Jimmy's liking.

Like gratitude, joy is a choice that is made not because of circumstance, but in the middle of every circumstance – even ones that don't feel good. Peter encourages his flock to rejoice when they share Christ's sufferings so that they also can rejoice and be glad when His glory is revealed.

There is a revelation of the glory of Jesus Christ in the trial. Joy arises from a realization that the fiery trial has a purpose - that God is lovingly and artfully working in us, through us, and around us. But joy also arises when we receive illumination of the glory that will result from the fiery trial.

A source of joy is found in the <u>overcoming of the sense of the uselessness of suffering,</u> a feeling that is sometimes very strongly rooted in human suffering.[85]

> **Meditation:** *"Love hopes all things."* Take time to write about the sources of joy in your life. As you review your list, seek the Lord about joy in the middle of trials. What are the sources of joy during fiery trials?

☦ ☦ ☦ ☦ ☦ ☦ ☦

> Allow time for God to move in your heart and in your spirit. We are not just trying to learn His lessons, but we are trying to implant them into our core in such a way that they become a part of us. Lasting change requires deep work.

---

[84] Excerpt from *Dod Knows* (by the author).

[85] Pope John Paul II, *Salvifici Doloris (On the Christian Meaning of Human Suffering)*, §27 (1984).

IV. Week Four, Day 7 (Date:)   **TRIUMPH**

Today is a day of review. Look back over your journal for the past week.

> **Meditation:** Today is a day of artistic or physical expression. As you review the week, pick one devotion or a theme that struck you. Then express that devotion or theme to God in a physical or artistic way – a picture, a poem, a letter, a dance, or other interpretive expression. Ask the Holy Spirit to guide your expression to God and to make it a pleasing aroma.

☩ ☩ ☩ ☩ ☩ ☩ ☩

NOTES:_____

_____

_____

_____

_____

_____

_____

_____

_____

_____

_____

SECTION IV – POWER AND GLORY: WEEK FIVE

IV.Week Five, Day 1 (Date:)   **REFINER'S FIRE**

> In the whole land, declares the LORD, two thirds shall be cut off and perish, and one third shall be left alive.
> And I will put this third into the fire, and refine them as one refines silver, and test them as gold is tested. They will call upon my name, and I will answer them. I will say, 'They are my people'; and they will say, 'The LORD is my God.'" **Zech 13:8-9**

I will put this third into the fire.

I want all the dross, <u>all that is not You, not like You,</u> to be consumed, burned up by Your fire and cleansing. I want the Gold of what You have, to be in me, what You want in my life, what You designed me for, to come forth and shine out from me!

Come, Holy Spirit, I need You doing this in me. I don't want my flesh dominating, running, ruining my life.

I want what counts to become what I follow, pursue, feed on, and run after! Come and change me, and change me, and change me!   -Pastor Daniel Martin, 12/9/13

Scripture speaks of a remnant. In Zechariah, that remnant is one-third of the land. But there is a process that Lord has for the remnant. It is a process of refining.

Refining is hard on the metal being refined. The metal is subjected to extreme heat until it becomes liquid. Dross – impurities in the metal – is removed so that the metal can become cleaner, purer, and more valuable. Then the metal is poured into the desired form and cooled.

The Lord promises a refining process for His people. The refining occurs through discipline, through temptation, through offense, and through suffering. It is not a pleasant process. But the result is purity. The heat and melting of the refiner's fire results in a purity and holiness that is beautiful to behold and is pleasing to the Lord, and thus a source of great joy!

Note the result of refining in this scripture. The Lord's people say *"The Lord is my God."* The process of refining increases the faith of God's people.

> **Meditation:** Identify a time in your life that you felt the Lord was refining your life. What were the circumstances of the refining? How did it feel? How did you react to it?
>
> What was the Lord doing in your life? Write about it in your journal.

╬   ╬   ╬   ╬   ╬   ╬   ╬

IV. Week Five, Day 2 (Date:)   **REFINER'S FIRE**

> The crucible is for silver, and the furnace is for gold, and the LORD tests hearts. **Pro 17:3**

The Lord tests hearts.

So I am bold to name the threads out of which this inner veil [*over our hearts*] is woven. It is woven of the fine threads of the self-life, the hyphenated sins of the human spirit. They are not something we do, they are something we are, and therein lies both their subtlety and their power.

To be specific, the self-sins are these: self-righteousness, self-pity, self-confidence, self-sufficiency, self-admiration, self-love and a host of others like them. They dwell too deep within us are too much a part of our natures to come to our attention till the light of God is focused upon them...

Self is the opaque veil that hides the Face of God from us. It can be removed only in spiritual experience, never by mere instruction. We might as well try to instruct leprosy out of our system There must be a work of God in destruction before we are free. We must invite the cross to do its deadly work within us. We must bring our self-sins to the cross for judgment. We must prepare ourselves for an ordeal of suffering in some measure like that through which our Savior passed when He suffered under Pontius Pilate.

Let us remember: when we talk of the rending of the veil we are speaking in a figure, and the thought of it is poetical, almost pleasant; but in actuality there is nothing pleasant about it. In human experience that veil is made of living spiritual tissue; it is composed of the sentient, quivering stuff of which our whole beings consist, and to touch it is to touch us where we feel pain. To tear it away is to injure us, to hurt us and to make us bleed. To say otherwise it to make the cross no cross and death no death. It is never fun to die. To rip through the dear and tender stuff of which life is made can never be anything but deeply painful. Yet that is what the cross did to Jesus and it is what the cross would do to every man to set him free.[86]

There are parts of us that only the Lord can change. There are sinful issues that only the Lord can resolve. We cannot force them out. We can only seek God for help and ask Him, in His mercy, to remove them just as a surgeon cuts and divides in order to remove malignant masses. It is painful and messy. But to the extent we submit to the authority of the Surgeon, we benefit from healing and wholeness of our soul.

---

[86] *The Pursuit of God*, pp. 29-30.

Meditation: Focus on the idea that only God can remove certain parts of us that need to change. How do you feel about asking God to crucify your flesh and to do work within you that is effective but deadly?

During this devotional journey, have you identified any areas of your heart that need to change, but you seem helpless to do so? As you are led, submit those areas to the Lord for His surgery and ask Him to make the changes that He desires. Spend time with God seeking Him about His will and plan for your heart.

☩ ☩ ☩ ☩ ☩ ☩ ☩

NOTES:_____

IV. Week Five, Day 3 (Date:)   **REFINER'S FIRE**

> But whatever gain I had, I counted as loss for the sake of Christ. Indeed, I count everything as loss because of the surpassing worth of knowing Christ Jesus my Lord. For his sake I have suffered the loss of all things and count them as rubbish, in order that I may gain Christ and be found in him, not having a righteousness of my own that comes from the law, but that which comes through faith in Christ, the righteousness from God that depends on faith—that I may know him and the power of his resurrection, and may share his sufferings, becoming like him in his death, that by any means possible I may attain the resurrection from the dead. Not that I have already obtained this or am already perfect, but I press on to make it my own, because Christ Jesus has made me his own.
> Brothers, I do not consider that I have made it my own. But one thing I do: forgetting what lies behind and straining forward to what lies ahead, I press on toward the goal for the prize of the upward call of God in Christ Jesus.
> Let those of us who are mature think this way, and if in anything you think otherwise, God will reveal that also to you. **Php 3:7-15**

Let those of us who are mature think this way.

Down through the centuries and generations it has been seen that *in suffering there is concealed* a particular *power that draws a person interiorly close to Christ,* a special grace...[The individual] discovers a new dimension, as it were, of *his entire life and vocation*. This discovery is a particular confirmation of the spiritual greatness which in man surpasses the body in a way that is completely beyond compare. When this body is gravely ill, totally incapacitated, and the person is almost incapable of living and acting, all the more do interior *maturity and spiritual greatness* become evident, constituting a touching lesson to those who are healthy and normal.[87]

Suffering joins the believer to Christ in profound and spiritual ways. The suffering servant gains intimate knowledge of Christ through experience of the cross. He shares sufferings like Christ. It is one thing to have knowledge of the cross. It is another thing to experience it.

The believer draws closer to Christ by being conformed to the cross willingly. The suffering servant bears an image that is a likeness of Christ and begins to reflect Christ's passion and character. Through suffering, the believer attains interior maturity and spiritual greatness.

---

[87] *Salvifici Doloris (On the Christian Meaning of Human Suffering)* §26.

Meditation: Identify a person (or persons) that you respect or admire spiritually. Then ask the question of how suffering shaped or influenced that person's life and walk with the Lord. You can research a historical figure or inquire of that person if (s)he is a contemporary. Write what you find in your journal.

☦ ☦ ☦ ☦ ☦ ☦ ☦

NOTES:_____

_____

_____

_____

_____

_____

_____

_____

_____

_____

> Keep in mind that God has a call for you – a spiritual destiny for your life. God has a role for each believer – a special place in His body and in His kingdom. Take time to seek the Lord frequently about His will for your life.

IV. Week Five, Day 4 (Date:)   **REFINER'S FIRE**

> Therefore do not be ashamed of the testimony about our Lord, nor of me his prisoner, but share in suffering for the gospel by the power of God, who saved us and called us to a holy calling, not because of our works but because of his own purpose and grace, which he gave us in Christ Jesus before the ages began, and which now has been manifested through the appearing of our Savior Christ Jesus, who abolished death and brought life and immortality to light through the gospel, for which I was appointed a preacher and apostle and teacher, which is why I suffer as I do. But I am not ashamed, for I know whom I have believed, and I am convinced that he is able to guard until that Day what has been entrusted to me. **2 Tim 1:8-12**

Share in suffering for the gospel by the power of God.

My close friend and law partner, Judge Sam Wilson, called October 18, 2002 both the worst day of his life and the best day of his life. That day was the worst day of his life because, after deteriorating health and increased pain for months, Sam Wilson was diagnosed with incurable Stage 4 lung cancer. It was a death sentence.

Later, Sam told me that day was also the best day of his life because the Lord revealed something to him. Sam Wilson had an epiphany on that date. He realized not just that he knew the Lord, but that the Lord knew Him. And so despite the horrible news, Sam Wilson committed to share the gospel with every person that he could. Sam not only accepted his cross willingly and graciously, he embraced it. A little later that fall, Sam announced to me that he would not return to the practice of law, but commit the remainder of his life to the spread of the gospel.

And share the gospel he did. In cancer wards in the hospital, with long time friends, publicly and privately with anyone who would listen – Sam Wilson shared about Jesus. Sadly, on Christmas Eve, 2002, the doctors, having exhausted their medical skill, sent him home from the hospital in the care of hospice. They told Sam he had less than 2 weeks to live.

But two weeks later Sam Wilson was still alive, confined to a hospice bed in his home. Without medical treatment, Sam slowly recovered until a few months later, scans did not show any tumors left in his body. God had performed a miracle.

Sam continued to share the gospel. He confided in me that he felt guilty at times. "David," he said "some of the cancer patients with whom I have shared were in much better shape than I was when I visited them. But they are now gone and I am still here."

Sam Wilson lived four more years until he passed in January of 2007. He had struggles, but I never heard him complain or express bitterness about his cross. The power of his testimony impacted many hearts and lives. My gratitude for the extra time we had with Sam still overflows. That season was precious and unforgettable for me and for many

others.

The power of the testimony of a cross borne well is incredible. That is why the crucifixion of Christ strikes a universal chord. Jesus didn't just drink of the cup. He did so willingly, lovingly, and even joyfully.

The power of God meets us at the cross. The measure of His grace increases as the demands of the moment increase as well. That is why Paul was confident that God would fulfill the purpose and calling in his life even as Paul suffered as he did. Paul knew, as Sam Wilson came to know, that suffering was linked to the power of God and to the sharing of the gospel.

> **Meditation:** Today is a day of meditation on suffering, the power of God, and the gospel. Begin your time with repentance and then ask the Holy Spirit to show you connections between these areas. Follow the leading of the Holy Spirit but move toward a time of contemplation in silence as you progress. Write in your journal what the Holy Spirit shows you.

☫ ☫ ☫ ☫ ☫ ☫ ☫

NOTES:_____

_____

_____

_____

_____

_____

_____

_____

IV. Week Five, Day 5 (Date:)   **REFINER'S FIRE**

> Bless our God, O peoples; let the sound of his praise be heard, who has kept our soul among the living and has not let our feet slip.
> For you, O God, have tested us; you have tried us as silver is tried.
> You brought us into the net; you laid a crushing burden on our backs; you let men ride over our heads; we went through fire and through water; yet you have brought us out to a place of abundance.
> **Psa 66:8-12**

We went through fire and through water; yet You have brought us out to a place of abundance.

My friend, Steve, has a dance that he calls his "thank you, Jesus" dance. This dance is not reserved for occasions in which Steve hits a good lick or wins a big prize. In fact, it is quite the opposite. The "thank you, Jesus" dance is danced on occasions that Steve receives bad news, does not get what he wants, or experiences offense of some type.

The "thank you, Jesus" dance is Steve's response to a negative emotional reaction – often a reaction of his flesh. Steve is trying to give thanks in all circumstances, even if his emotional reaction is the opposite. It is a demonstration of Steve's faith that God is working in all circumstances in his life.

The Lord gave me four lifelines during my illness. I still pray these lifelines when I am under stress or when I am in a difficult situation. The fourth lifeline is: "Thank You for these circumstances, O Lord, because You are a good God and I believe You are working all things in my life for good."

A significant question for our lives is whether we choose to live in the reality of God in our lives or in the reality that is limited to what our senses and emotions tell us. The reality of God is a matter of faith in God and in His promises. One of the promises is that He works all things together for good if we love Him and if we are called according to His purpose (Rom 8:28). We may not see the good that God sees or intends. So we exercise our faith to align with God's promise.

The good that God intends is usually for us in our life. Sometimes the good that God intends is good for another person or for a group of people. Other times, the good may impact rulers and authorities in earthly or heavenly realms. But a key word is "all." Give thanks in ALL circumstances. He works ALL things for good. We need to trust Him ALWAYS.

Meditation: *"Love believes all things."* Spend time with God reviewing difficult circumstances that have occurred in your life. Review your ability to give thanks in those circumstances. This response is not "hokey" or disgenuine. Be honest with God about your feelings as to gratitude for those circumstances. Ask the Holy Spirit to give you the ability to react with faith and gratitude in all circumstances.

Lifelines:
- I believe in You, O Lord, Maker of the heavens and the earth.
- I trust You, O my God, at all times and in all places.
- I glorify you, O Lord, above all other beings.
- Thank You for these circumstances, O Lord, because You are a good God and I believe You are working all things in my life for good.

╫ ╫ ╫ ╫ ╫ ╫ ╫

NOTES:_____

_____

_____

_____

_____

_____

_____

_____

IV. Week Five, Day 6 (Date:) **REFINER'S FIRE**

> Shadrach, Meshach, and Abednego answered and said to the king, "O Nebuchadnezzar, we have no need to answer you in this matter. If this be so, our God whom we serve is able to deliver us from the burning fiery furnace, and he will deliver us out of your hand, O king. But if not, be it known to you, O king, that we will not serve your gods or worship the golden image that you have set up."
> And these three men, Shadrach, Meshach, and Abednego, fell bound into the burning fiery furnace. Then King Nebuchadnezzar was astonished and rose up in haste. He declared to his counselors, "Did we not cast three men bound into the fire?" They answered and said to the king, "True, O king."
> He answered and said, "But I see four men unbound, walking in the midst of the fire, and they are not hurt; and the appearance of the fourth is like a son of the gods."
> Then Nebuchadnezzar came near to the door of the burning fiery furnace; he declared, "Shadrach, Meshach, and Abednego, servants of the Most High God, come out, and come here!" Then Shadrach, Meshach, and Abednego came out from the fire.
> **Dan 3:16-18, 23-26**

And the appearance of the fourth is like a son of the gods.

The fiery trial which Shadrach, Meshach, and Abednego suffered was a clear witness to the greatest human power on earth, the proud Nebuchadnezzar. The witness occurred before, during, and after the fiery furnace.

But these three men of God did not suffer the fire alone. Some One else appeared to suffer the furnace with them.

I may drink of the cup and I may go through the fire. But I am never alone in them. Some One else drinks the cup with me and walks through the fire at my side. He has gone before me and He abides with me and in me. I am joined with Him and nothing can separate the bond of love between us.

Meditation: Set time aside and seek the Presence of the Lord. Ask Him to assure your heart of His Presence without regard to the circumstance – even in the middle of a burning fiery furnace. Rest in His Presence.

☦   ☦   ☦   ☦   ☦   ☦   ☦

IV. Week Five, Day 7 (Date:)	**REFINER'S FIRE**

Today is a day of review. Read back over your journal for the past week.

> **Meditation:** Select a theme over the past week that struck a chord with you. You can go back over the devotion with that theme or just focus on that theme. As you spend time with God on that theme, also spend time loving Him. The word is "lavish." Lavish your love upon the Lord.

☩ ☩ ☩ ☩ ☩ ☩ ☩

NOTES:_____

_____

_____

_____

_____

_____

_____

_____

_____

_____

_____

SECTION IV – POWER AND GLORY: WEEK SIX

IV.Week Six, Day 1 (Date:) **LEADERSHIP**

> And when the ten heard it, they began to be indignant at James and John. And Jesus called them to him and said to them, "You know that those who are considered rulers of the Gentiles lord it over them, and their great ones exercise authority over them. But it shall not be so among you. But whoever would be great among you must be your servant, and whoever would be first among you must be slave of all. For even the Son of Man came not to be served but to serve, and to give his life as a ransom for many." **Mark 10:41-45**

The Son of Man came not to be served but to serve, and to give His life as a ransom for many.

"The good shepherd gives his life for the sheep"— Protector. Lord, show me in my decisions and actions, thoughts and motives, where I am thinking about the costs in my life, instead of the good of the sheep, when I decide what decisions and actions to take in protecting the sheep.

Lord, deliver me from fear of man, fear for myself, instead of ONLY having a deep fear of You! O, Lord, fear of man is so deeply ingrained in me that only You can deliver. But You, by Your Spirit can do it. Holy Spirit, come and deliver me from all fear of man. Set me free. It is not by my might, not by my power, but by Your Spirit, Father, that this mountain can be removed. Come and deliver me from it—whatever the cost of deliverance might be. I want to be free. Whatever it takes to make me into the man, shepherd, pastor, that I need to be, do it!! -Pastor Daniel Martin, 1/2/12

This teaching of Jesus follows the request of James and John to sit in the positions of power and prestige at the right and left hand of Jesus. The other disciples were indignant. They probably desired the requested positions for themselves. So Jesus continues His teaching about authority, its purpose, and its exercise.

Rulers of the world use their power for domination. They exercise their power to manipulate others for their selfish ends – money, prestige, more power, and admiration. They are jealous of other persons with power because they themselves want that power.

But Jesus forbids that use of power among His followers. God shares His authority with people for a purpose. That purpose is to serve those persons who are subject to that authority. A person who is under Godly authority should feel served, not dominated. So the proper exercise of that authority is service of other people as Pastor Martin prayed.

Meditation: *"Love does not envy."* Consider the contrast between the desire for power in the world and the heart of the servant with authority as instructed by Jesus. Choose examples of exercise of authority in Christian circles that you have seen or experienced. How well were Jesus' teachings followed in those examples?

☩ ☩ ☩ ☩ ☩ ☩ ☩

NOTES:

IV. Week Six, Day 2 (Date:)   LEADERSHIP

> Yet among the mature we do impart wisdom, although it is not a wisdom of this age or of the rulers of this age, who are doomed to pass away. But we impart a secret and hidden wisdom of God, which God decreed before the ages for our glory.
> None of the rulers of this age understood this, for if they had, they would not have crucified the Lord of glory. **1 Cor 2:6-8**

None of the rulers of this age understood this.

The other side of the dialectic is given here: that earthly rulers (principalities) crucified the Lord of glory. This text also underscores the powers' functioning in religious, as well as political, spheres. This alerts us to the disturbing fact that *churches* today can similarly be principalities acting for evil instead of good.

Why are a large proportion of today's churches in North America not living out of weakness? If the church is most faithful to its true vocation as a created power through the weakness that gives way to God's tabernacling, then we must ask questions such as:

- **Why have we turned pastors into successful CEO's instead of shepherds for the weak?**
- **Why do we search for pastors who are sophisticated and charismatic - instead of models of suffering?**
- **Why do our churches adopt practices of business life and its achievement models?**
- **Why do we resort to gimmicks...instead of practicing an "unadulterated handling of the Word"?**[88]

Marva Dawn's assertion that fallen powers can influence and ally with religious institutions, including churches and ministries, is a sobering thought for leadership. The temptation to accumulate corporate wealth, prestige, and influence can be insidious if, like Solomon, leaders have the justification that what is good for their organization must be good for the kingdom of God. The exact opposite may be true.

I can see Jesus and the devil at the third temptation when the devil is showing Him all the kingdoms of the world. If it were I, the devil would be tempting me with all of the fleshly pleasures and delights that I could enjoy from ruling over all the kingdoms of the world.

---

[88] *Powers, Weakness, and the Tabernacling of God*, pp. 7, 50, and 57.

But I don't think that is what he is saying to Jesus. To Jesus, the devil may be saying "Think of all the good you could do with all of this - how much good you can do if you rule the world and control all worldly goods! How many people can you help with this money, power, and control? Surely you can do more good as ruler than if you die a humiliating death nailed to a tree!"

Marva Dawn's questions should be asked fearfully and with respect for the positions of authority to whom they are addressed. But they should be asked. Churches who are intent on the accumulation of funds, property, influence, or prominence need to engage in some serious soul searching.

> **Meditation:** Meditate on the idea that churches, like individuals, should operate out of weakness to encourage the power and Presence of the Lord. How does this idea inform qualifications for church leaders?

☩ ☩ ☩ ☩ ☩ ☩ ☩

NOTES:_____

IV. Week Six, Day 3 (Date:)   **LEADERSHIP**

> And I, when I came to you, brothers, did not come proclaiming to you the testimony of God with lofty speech or wisdom. For I decided to know nothing among you except Jesus Christ and him crucified. And I was with you in weakness and in fear and much trembling, and my speech and my message were not in plausible words of wisdom, but in demonstration of the Spirit and of power, so that your faith might not rest in the wisdom of men but in the power of God.
> 1 Cor 2:1-5

So that your faith may not rest in the wisdom of men but in the power of God.

To be specific, the self-sins are these: self-righteousness, self-pity, self-confidence, self-sufficiency, self-admiration, self-love and a host of others like them. They dwell too deep within us are too much a part of our natures to come to our attention till the light of God is focused upon them. The grosser manifestation of these sins, egotism, exhibitionism, self-promotion, are strangely tolerated in Christian leaders, even in circles of impeccable orthodoxy. They are so much in evidence as actually, for many people, to become identified with the gospel. I trust it is not a cynical observation to say that they appear these days to be requisite for popularity in some sections of the Church visible. Promoting self under the guise of promoting Christ is currently so common as to excite little notice.[89]

I have a friend who is not a practicing believer that had occasion in his business to visit large churches in places like southern California, Texas, Atlanta, and Charlotte. He shared with me his conclusions from his visits: The foremost message of the churches he visited was self-marketing, and their popular leaders were "masters of self-promotion."

Paul, on the other hand, ministered out of weakness, fear, and much trembling, and did not proclaim the testimony of God with lofty speech or wisdom. Paul explains that out of his weakness came a demonstration of the Spirit and of power. He pointed only to Jesus Christ and Him crucified. Why? So that the faith of the hearer would not depend on men (including Paul), but on the power of God.

Long ago, for each occasion at which I spoke or in which I participated, I began asking the question of whether the Presence of God was there. A godly leader should ask two basic questions of each ministry event (or program):

1. Does the event encourage the Presence of God to come and dwell among

---

[89] *The Pursuit of God*, p. 29.

the saints in fullness and in power?

2. Does the event point to Jesus Christ and His Cross alone, and not to any man?

> **Meditation:** Spend time with the questions in this devotion above. With these questions in mind, review events or programs which you lead or in which you participate. Write down your thoughts in your journal.

☦ ☦ ☦ ☦ ☦ ☦ ☦

NOTES:_____

IV. Week Six, Day 4 (Date:)   **LEADERSHIP**

> Likewise, you who are younger, be subject to the elders. Clothe yourselves, all of you, with humility toward one another, for "God opposes the proud but gives grace to the humble." Humble yourselves, therefore, under the mighty hand of God so that at the proper time he may exalt you, casting all your anxieties on him, because he cares for you.
> Be sober-minded; be watchful. Your adversary the devil prowls around like a roaring lion, seeking someone to devour. Resist him, firm in your faith, knowing that the same kinds of suffering are being experienced by your brotherhood throughout the world. **1 Pet 5:5-9**

Clothe yourselves, all of you, with humility toward one another.

Barnabas is a wonderful coworker. Sometimes a leader with charisma attends a ministry event. He has a glowing personality, and his bearing shouts "Follow me, people!" That leader acts, talks and walks in a way that causes people to flock to him. Soon, crowds gather around that leader. But Barnabas is not that type of leader. He doesn't display "flash" or stand out in a crowd.

To the contrary, at a large ministry event Barnabas is likely to be working "behind the scenes." Barnabas is a server. If there is a task that needs doing, Barnabas does it. If there is a role that is essential to run the event, Barnabas fills that role. Barnabas rarely speaks at large events. Yet on Sundays he met with a group of refugees from an Asian country and led them in a Bible study. We are hopeful of cultivating leadership from the group for an ethnic church.

Barnabas is an encourager. One of the first times that I met Barnabas, he asked me "Are you encouraged?" I thought "What an odd question!" But Barnabas is serious. He desires that the saints be edified. If you see Barnabas at a ministry event, he later sends you an e-mail that describes a spiritual gift he saw you exercise. If Barnabas visits your home, he sends a "thank you" card expressing his appreciation for your hospitality. Encouragement is important to Barnabas. That is why I call him Barnabas (not his real name) – the "son of encouragement."

Barnabas is faithful – in big and small things. If Barnabas commits to attend a meeting, he will be there. Barnabas recently ministered to a needy family that he met. He helped them move to a better place to live. He assisted the young men in their studies. Barnabas is consistent and steady.

Barnabas is rarely the man "up top." He doesn't strive to be the man "out front." But as I have watched Barnabas operate in the gifts and wisdom that the Lord has given him, I

have decided this: Barnabas is a leader, and probably a leader of the best type.[90]

Leaders fall into two categories – particularly leaders that have a senior position or "top dog" status. One type of leader sees himself as above other people. He is the person on top and has exalted himself into that role.

The other type of leader sees himself (or herself) as below other people. He is self aware enough to view himself as the chief of sinners. He lives to serve other people as Christ did.

When you talk with a leader, you can quickly discern where that person is coming from. The first type of leader approaches you from a position of superiority. In his mind, while he is talking to you, he is above you. His bearing and speech communicate his presumed superiority.

The second leader approaches you from a position of servanthood. He is not above you, but in fact genuinely desires to serve you and your needs.

One test for these two categories is the leader's expectation for ministry. The first leader expects other persons to participate in *his* ministry. Although it may be couched in different terms, that leader expects participants in his organization to devote their efforts to his organization and to align themselves with *his* call. He is further threatened by other persons who (heaven forbid!) may be more gifted in any area than he is.

The second leader is interested in the call of the Lord on the lives of others. He supports, cultivates, and encourages those calls even if it is not remotely related to his call or to his organization.

<u>Leadership is developing close relationships with others, particularly with those persons for whom you have responsibility, and then, with intention, enabling them to flourish in the gifts that God has given them so that they may fulfill the call that God has ordained for them, and as a result, both you and they experience the joy and glory of the Lord.</u>

Meditation: *"Love is not arrogant."* Consider the two categories of leaders. What experiences have you had with both types of leaders? What traits did each one exhibit? How did each one operate? What lessons did you learn from your experiences? Then ask the Holy Spirit to help you become a godly servant.

☦ ☦ ☦ ☦ ☦ ☦ ☦

> Remember the devotional theme as you go through your day. Many devotions have very practical applications.

---

[90] *The Call: Book Three – Fruitful (Transforming Your Community)*, p. 167.

IV. Week Six, Day 5 (Date:)   **LEADERSHIP**

> I have written something to the church, but Diotrephes, who likes to put himself first, does not acknowledge our authority. So if I come, I will bring up what he is doing, talking wicked nonsense against us. And not content with that, he refuses to welcome the brothers, and also stops those who want to and puts them out of the church.
> Beloved, do not imitate evil but imitate good. Whoever does good is from God; whoever does evil has not seen God.
> Demetrius has received a good testimony from everyone, and from the truth itself. We also add our testimony, and you know that our testimony is true. **3 Jn 1:9-12**

Talking wicked nonsense against us.

"Toxic leaders" are easy to find, and their influence has become increasingly pervasive in our culture, perhaps most evident in politics. Toxic leadership has become something of a presumption in the political sphere, but that is certainly not the only realm in which it resides. Leadership of any kind will always be alluring to unhealthy, domineering, and narcissistic individuals. The church is not immune to this, because the church can provide a context for power. A toxic leader is someone who maintains power and significance by manipulating followers through their own fundamental drive to be powerful and significant. Toxic leaders dominate and control. Toxic leaders wield their personalities to cement their power, relegating their followers to a position of dependence on them rather than on Christ. Toxic leaders subvert the systems designed to hold them accountable and quickly establish scapegoats when they fail. Toxic leaders do not develop other leaders, because they pose a threat to their own power. Toxic leaders create an unhealthy symbiosis between themselves and the organizations which they lead, such that their absence would equal the collapse of the organization.[91]

Diotrephes or Demetrius - there are telltale signs of each leader.

1. The first sign is true accountability. A good leader practices mutual submission which puts checks on his power and balances his ministry life. Toxic power, on the other hand, does not like limits. It always seeks more power. Accountability puts limits on power. A leader who likes to be strong does not like to disclose his weaknesses. So he distances himself not just from any true accountability but also from close relationships generally.

2. The second sign is the truth and how it is treated. A good leader adheres to the truth even if it exposes his misdeeds and puts him in a bad light. Toxic power twists the truth. A loss of integrity occurs when the truth is slanted,

---

[91] *The Way of the Dragon or the Way of the Lamb*, pp. 146-147.

spun, or twisted to achieve a political end. The apostle, John, speaks of how Diotrephes used slander and false allegations even against John himself. Toxic power believes that the end justifies the means so truth is manipulated both from the pulpit and in private.

3. The third sign is control of people. Toxic power uses intimidation and domination. In essential terms, a toxic leader is a bully. It is actually a defiance of God and His authority. In order to maintain his power, Diotrephes refused to welcome the brethren and even put them out of the church.

The bottom line is this: A person can not possess and exercise spiritual authority unless that same person operates in true subjection to proper spiritual authority.

> **Meditation:** *"Love is not rude."* Consider the leadership in the circles in which you walk. Look at each of these areas in your life. How are you doing in these areas? Do you need to make any changes? Write down your thoughts in your journal.

☩ ☩ ☩ ☩ ☩ ☩ ☩

NOTES:_____

IV. Week Six, Day 6 (Date:) **LEADERSHIP**

> Now when they saw the boldness of Peter and John, and perceived that they were uneducated, common men, they were astonished. And they recognized that they had been with Jesus. But seeing the man who was healed standing beside them, they had nothing to say in opposition. **Acts 4:13-14**

And they recognized that they had been with Jesus.

Almost daily I would ask my wife, "What are we doing with this man as our pastor?" Yet because there were so many young people just like us, we continued attending. I was very critical of Pastor Ed. He couldn't preach; he stumbled daily with his words, and he rarely prayed. Yet week by week I could see him changing. At first he'd boast that he prayed fifteen minutes each day. My wife and I looked at each other and thought, "Fifteen minutes?" We took fifteen minutes to bless our food! The next week he mentioned he was up to a half hour a day in prayer; the week after that he said he was spending an hour a day before the Lord...

You see, it is not hard to recognize one who has spent an extended time at the newsstand: his conversation overflows with the drama of current affairs. It is also not hard to discern when a person has been to a sporting event, as their expression reveals the outcome of the game. Likewise, people can tell when an individual has spent time seeking God. And imperturbable calm guards their heart and their countenance is radiant with light. The leaders we need must be people who, though flawed, spend time with God. It should be clear that their goal is to be conformed to Jesus Christ.[92]

There is a difference between positional authority and spiritual authority. Positional authority exists because someone has an office, a title, or a commission.

Spiritual authority exists when a person walks in the Spirit with an attitude of humility and service. The person displays the fruit of the Spirit and the power of the word.

A person can have positional authority with little spiritual authority; or a person can have spiritual authority without occupying any position. The Jewish council did not recognize the authority of the positions that Peter and John held as apostles. But they discerned the authority with which they acted and spoke. It can be confusing when a leader in a ministry position functions from a fleshly nature. And it can likewise be confusing when a person with great spiritual authority functions without an office or a title.

We should always have an attitude of submission to authority. Even if a

---

[92] Francis Frangipane, *Spiritual Discernment and the Mind of Christ* p. 155 (Arrow 2013).

person has positional authority without much spiritual authority, the positional authority should be respected. But spiritual authority should be respected as well – even if the person with it does not hold a position or have a title after his or her name.

> **Meditation:** Spend time discerning your vision of leadership. What are the traits of a good leader in a church or in a ministry? Write down these traits. Look at your heart and discern why you think these traits make a good leader.

☦ ☦ ☦ ☦ ☦ ☦ ☦

NOTES:_____

_____

_____

_____

_____

_____

_____

_____

_____

> A time of quiet with the Lord just listening is a good discipline. Practice listening often in your time dedicated to the Lord. Childlike simplicity in attitude and in approach prepares us to hear.

IV. Week Six, Day 7 (Date:)   **LEADERSHIP**

Today is a day of review. Read back over your journal for the last week.

> **Meditation:** Today is a day of silent contemplation. Set aside a block of time to be in silence before the Lord. Eliminate distractions and quiet your mind. Begin with repentance and confession of sins to the Lord. Then spend time in silence before Him as He moves within your heart and soul. If you need a focus, you can keep telling the Lord "I submit myself to You and to Your established authority."

☦ ☦ ☦ ☦ ☦ ☦ ☦

NOTES:_____

SECTION IV – POWER AND GLORY: WEEK SEVEN

IV.Week Seven, Day 1 (Date:)   **FEAR OF MAN**

> But the thing displeased Samuel when they said, "Give us a king to judge us." And Samuel prayed to the LORD. And the LORD said to Samuel, "Obey the voice of the people in all that they say to you, for they have not rejected you, but they have rejected me from being king over them. **1 Sam 8:6-8**
>
> "And in that day you will cry out because of your king, whom you have chosen for yourselves, but the LORD will not answer you in that day." But the people refused to obey the voice of Samuel. And they said, "No! But there shall be a king over us, that we also may be like all the nations, and that our king may judge us and go out before us and fight our battles." **1 Sam 8:18-20**

People want a king.

There is a certain "fear" that foreigners have in going to a place where they are not like all the other inhabitants. We should also have a fear of fitting in with the inhabitants and becoming more and more like them, for the city we are living in is "the City of Destruction" (*Pilgrim's Progress*). When we become so accustomed, acclimated, and used to the foreign land that we no longer have a fear of the King (Jesus) of the land we belong to, we are in desperate shape.

This so much describes much of the church in the USA. God help us. God help me, to not have the goal of "fitting in" with the inhabitants of this land, but to have the goal of witnessing to these inhabitants so they can become "fit" for the Kingdom of God.

I need You, O, I need You!! Every hour I need You!

Come, O fount of every blessing, tune my heart again to sing Your grace, praise, glory, righteousness, goodness. (How often my flesh wants to sing of me, my glory, my greatness, my goodness—and many other non-existent things!) Help me to sing only of You, of Your truth, mercy, grace, greatness, power, love, and acceptance!

Why would I ever crave the "well done" of people here, when the only one worth having, the only one I can count on—is Yours? Help me to quit seeking it from my wife or anyone else.

Yours is all that I can count on, that comes with mercy and grace, with no strings attached, that is steady, and is based on who and what You are!!

O Jesus, thank You for making it so that I can hear "well done" based on Your salvation and redemption in my life!   –Pastor Daniel Martin, 7/5/13

People want a king for security. They want a king to keep order and to fight their battles for them. People look to authority for comfort and protection – to government, to politicians, to parents, and to pastors. There are appropriate times to seek comfort from others, including from persons in spiritual authority. But dependence solely upon persons, instead of dependence on the Lord, is harmful and is a source of false comfort.

The people of Israel wanted tangible security. They were tired of depending on the covering of the Lord which required faith.

But the people of Israel were also tired of their uniqueness. They wanted to be like other nations more than they wanted to be the chosen people of God. The felt approval of "fitting in" was important to them.

The judgment and disapproval of other people causes fear of man. The people of Israel craved approval of men rather than the covenant of God which is why God told Samuel *"They have not rejected you, but they have rejected Me from being King over them."*

Meditation: Think of occasions when disapproval or judgment by other people hurt you. Explore with the Lord how that made you feel. What did you do in response?

Then spend time considering the fear of man in your life. In what ways does a need to "fit in" influence your thoughts and actions? Write down your thoughts in your journal.

☩ ☩ ☩ ☩ ☩ ☩ ☩

NOTES:_____

IV. Week Seven, Day 2 (Date:)   FEAR OF MAN

> You hypocrites! Well did Isaiah prophesy of you, when he said: "'This people honors me with their lips, but their heart is far from me; in vain do they worship me, teaching as doctrines the commandments of men.'" **Matt 15:7-9**

Teaching as doctrines the commandments of men.

Similarly, often political powers, economic ideologies, or scientific methods disrupt doctrine – as they frequently do in denominational assemblies and in the methods of our scholarship...To let ideologies control our theological work is to be subverted by powers other than God...

For example, are our churches' goals set by slogans of the culture around us or by biblical texts? Do our congregational programs find their source in the sociology definitions of the present "needs" of the consumer...or from the Scriptures? What decides the doctrinal content of the worship service – one who is theologically trained or the results of a survey asking people what they want?

[T]he gospel is quickly reduced when confronted with questions of institutional power, wealth, and influence.[93]

The gospel and Biblical doctrine find their source in scripture inspired by the Spirit of God. The ideology of humans can have a destructive effect on the gospel because ideologies of humans are based on the desires of humans. Political ideologies are particularly dangerous because political ideologies are based on human desire for power, not on the cross of Jesus Christ.

Yet many church leaders desire to be relevant to their cultures and to be approved by worldly leaders. Fear of man is a source of this desire. So it is not unusual for political, sociological, or economic ideologies to be proclaimed from the pulpit and by religious leaders. Often there is more concern with the standing of the church in the world than before God.

The discernment that Marva Dawn encourages is critical in order to prevent fallen powers from subverting the gospel through corruption of the gospel with ideologies of man. Church leaders should recognize this danger (and its divisiveness) and use extreme caution when promoting any political ideology.

> **Meditation:** Meditate on the tension between relevance of the church, and adherence to the gospel and to sound doctrine. What temptations does a church face in order to be relevant to the culture around it? How much should a church compromise its message and its doctrine to be relevant to the world? Write down your thoughts in your journal.

---

[93] *Powers, Weakness, and the Tabernacling of God*, pp. 81, 83-84 (quoting, in part, Darrell L. Gruder).

IV. Week Seven, Day 3 (Date:)   **FEAR OF MAN**

> Whoever confesses that Jesus is the Son of God, God abides in him, and he in God. So we have come to know and to believe the love that God has for us. God is love, and whoever abides in love abides in God, and God abides in him. By this is love perfected with us, so that we may have confidence for the day of judgment, because as he is so also are we in this world.
> There is no fear in love, but perfect love casts out fear. For fear has to do with punishment, and whoever fears has not been perfected in love. We love because he first loved us. 1 Jn 4:15-19

There is no fear in love.

I previously wrote about the story of my friend, Keith, and his journey to brokenness and then a return to the Lord with restoration and healing (See II.Week Six, Day 4). Keith writes:

When I came out as gay, I had a "release" which was the freedom I felt from having to live in fear of others' opinions and to put on a front for their benefit. 1 John 4:18 tells us that fear is connected to punishment (although I like the KJV translation that "fear hath torment"). When we live in fear of other people's judgments, we are indeed in torment. The dog my wife and I have now was mistreated at an early stage in her life, and whenever we make sudden movements toward her, she cowers. (She is getting much better, I'm happy to report!) She has been punished brutally and, probably, often without knowing why. She is in fear of punishment; she is in torment, not being able to freely enjoy her existence.

When I came to believe that being homosexual was an innate part of who I was, and I chose to embrace that regardless of others' opinions, it was like a huge weight had been thrown off my shoulders. For the first time in my remembrance, I felt free of the torment I had experienced. This is why I embraced the whole experience as coming from God and continued to move deeper into the gay community, coming out to my family, my employer, and, gradually, the entire community when I became an activist.

I have often reflected on this experience as a journey that I had to go on in order to throw off "fear of man." Generally speaking, the church is not a good place for this as we often enforce, in a variety of spoken and unspoken ways, a form of works-righteousness. Our leaders, who should be demonstrating the freedom available through Christ, are perhaps most wrapped up in this fear. Therefore, instead of leading their people out of it, they reinforce it. I have commented to some in the past that God actually led me into the gay community to find this freedom and bring it back to the church. Of course, most of them correct my theology and tell me that God "allowed" me to do this, and that He would never lead me to such a place. I'm always a bit taken aback when someone who doesn't really know me considers themselves more qualified to understand my reality than I am. (You mean the God who led someone into slavery

and prison in order to make him head over Egypt? Or the God who would raise up a man to be king who ended up committing adultery and killing the woman's husband, and would still call the Messiah after that King's name? That God wouldn't do such a thing? No, of course not.)

Keith's story speaks for itself. But here are two comments on it.

First, note Keith's use of the word "torment." He lived in fear of man but that fear and his actions in response to it placed him in torment. Many people experience torment, but God can use it to prompt restoration and healing.

Second, Keith lived a lifestyle of sexual promiscuity, drug abuse, and homelessness. But this lifestyle was not Keith's core issue. The core issue (or "root cause") was fear of man. Keith did not realize that for many years, but the Lord led him to a place where he could recognize and deal with this root cause. When the core issue was identified, Keith had the key to journey from fear and torment to freedom and love.

In order to gain freedom in my life, I not only need to know the surface issues and symptoms, but I need to ask the Lord for insight into the core issues in my life. Often, root cause(s) must be addressed before healing and freedom can occur.[94]

> **Meditation:** What was your reaction as you read through Keith's story? Did you feel judgment, apprehension, compassion, or maybe even longing? Explore your feelings about it. Those feelings may be helpful to understand the workings of your own heart. Write about it in your journal.

╬   ╬   ╬   ╬   ╬   ╬   ╬

> Set aside time to look back through your journal. Our lives have patterns – ups and downs, and ebbs and flows. The content of your journal is instructive as to the rhythms of your spiritual journey.

---

[94] One tool to look inside our hearts is the Enneagram personality test. This test has ancient roots and explores basic motivations of the heart. There are many good Enneagram tools online. Richard Rohr and Andreas Ebert, among others, have some valuable Enneagram materials from a Christian perspective.

NOTES:

IV. Week Seven, Day 4 (Date:)   **FEAR OF MAN**

> The fear of man lays a snare, but whoever trusts in the LORD is safe. **Prov 29:25**

The fear of man lays a snare.

My friend, Keith, continues his story:

After I repented and returned to the Lord, the "coming out" to the Christian community was very real and intense for six or seven years after prison. I even wrote about it in the Christian newspaper I published. I participated in ministry to help persons struggling with sexual issues. The benefit for me was a deeper work of throwing off "fear of man." I stopped doing it not because I was concerned with people's opinions, but because it became a hindrance as the ministry into which God called me.

In my experience working with people who have same-sex attraction, nearly all of them live in great fear that people will find out about their struggles. Yet, fear of man is often at the root of the issues they face. So they will not find freedom until they gather the courage to share their story with others. But they can't come out to others because of their great fear of man. It is as Proverbs says, *"Fear of man is a snare."*

The solution? Fear of God needs to replace fear of man.

Fear of man is the root cause of issues for many people. Those issues are manifested in many ways. Sexual sin is only one of them. Fear of man is not the only root cause, but it is a common one. Ironically, the judgment which other persons exercised toward Keith can likewise arise from fear of man.

Note Keith's yearning for freedom in his life. He desired freedom from the negative impact and consequences of his sin. But he also needed freedom from fear of man which he realized was the root cause of his issues. *"Whoever trusts in the Lord is safe."* The keys which Keith found in his restoration were God's love, trust, and fear of God.

> **Meditation:** Focus on how much you yearn for freedom in your life, and whether you identify with that desire. Ask the Lord to help you discern the keys to that freedom. Consider the areas of love of God, of trust in Him, and of fear of God in your life. How have you grown in each of those areas? Journal about those areas or other areas of growth that need to occur in your life to experience greater freedom.

☩ ☩ ☩ ☩ ☩ ☩ ☩

IV. Week Seven, Day 5 (Date:)　　　　　　　　　　**FEAR OF MAN**

> For all who are led by the Spirit of God are sons of God.
> For you did not receive the spirit of slavery to fall back into fear, but you have received the Spirit of adoption as sons, by whom we cry, "Abba! Father!"
> The Spirit himself bears witness with our spirit that we are children of God, and if children, then heirs—heirs of God and fellow heirs with Christ, provided we suffer with him in order that we may also be glorified with him. For I consider that the sufferings of this present time are not worth comparing with the glory that is to be revealed to us. **Rom 8:14-17**

For you did not receive the spirit of slavery to fall back into fear.

My friend, Keith, reflects on lessons learned:

I was struck by a quote that suggested that if a person's life is full of trials and battles that they may be "displeasing (God) in some way." Granted, there can be consequences to wrong choices, actions, beliefs, etc. which can cause challenges in our world. This is simple cause and effect, and it is indeed wise to seek God's counsel as to whether there are changes we can make that would be beneficial. But seeing God as "displeased" with us doesn't promote a love-based relationship.

Many people feel guilt and shame because of their perception of divine displeasure, reactions which can keep them from approaching God at all. After all, how many of us want to hang out with someone who is upset with us? This distorted view can also lead one to deny that there is anything amiss at all to avoid painful feelings of shame.

We desperately need to draw near to God in times of battle. What can promote this is an accurate picture of God's nature and character. He is a loving Father who is excited about helping us find solutions to challenges and providing comfort in the midst of our torment. The divine relationship that can spring forth from a healthy and accurate view of God is a key factor in developing resiliency.

Recognizing the nature of God is vital. But recognizing that bad choices have bad consequences is also vital. I believe this is the proper understanding of the "fear of God." Shifting to a place where we are more concerned with the consequences of not following God's directions will allow us to move out of the place of fear of man. Unfortunately, people have not been taught how to properly process negative consequences, so God is limited in His ability to use them to move people forward.

God is a loving Father. When a parent loves his child, the parent uses both positive reinforcement and negative reinforcement to correct, to admonish, to train, and to help the child grow in character, skill, and self care. Fear of God encompasses both His love and a respect for God's character and authority.

At times, when a child experiences negative consequences from a parent, a statement from the child such as "you don't really love me" or "if you cared for me, you wouldn't punish me" is not unusual. But the parent may use or allow negative consequences to teach and to mature the child, and may do so out of love. After all, experience is often the best teacher.

As the Lord works in my life, He teaches me to overcome fear of man through His deep and rich love for me. As my realization of a Father's love for His child grows, fear of man subsides.

But fear of the consequences of not following God's directions is also a part of the fear of God which diminishes the fear of man. The witness of the Spirit bears witness with (and strengthens) my spirit, provided that I suffer with Him in order that I may also be glorified with Him.

> **Meditation:** *"Love does not rejoice at wrongdoing."* Consider parenting and the ways in which a good and loving parent functions. How does a parent that truly loves the child teach, correct, and admonish? Spend time considering if you will allow the Father to be your perfect Father. Repeat "Abba! Father!" during this time as you are led.

☩ ☩ ☩ ☩ ☩ ☩ ☩

NOTES:_____

_____

_____

_____

_____

_____

_____

IV. Week Seven, Day 6 (Date:)   **FEAR OF MAN**

> And calling the crowd to him with his disciples, he said to them, "If anyone would come after me, let him deny himself and take up his cross and follow me. For whoever would save his life will lose it, but whoever loses his life for my sake and the gospel's will save it. For what does it profit a man to gain the whole world and forfeit his soul? For what can a man give in return for his soul? For whoever is ashamed of me and of my words in this adulterous and sinful generation, of him will the Son of Man also be ashamed when he comes in the glory of his Father with the holy angels." **Mark 8:34-38**

Whoever is ashamed of Me and of My words in this adulterous and sinful generation.

O God, this child/sheep needs great boldness!!
- **Boldness to break out of all fear of man!**
- **Boldness to shine into the darkness!**
- **Boldness to go against the grain of society!**
- **Boldness to go against the grain of his own flesh!**
- **Boldness to Trust You!**
- **Boldness to obey You!**

Boldness to let go of everything, and allow You to have full control over all his possessions, time, life, reputation, choices, etc. O Give me more and more BOLDNESS, O Lamb of God!!

Boldness is the antithesis of FEAR OF MAN!!   -Pastor Daniel Martin, 9/1/14

We have previously explored how feelings of shame arise from feelings of worthlessness, feelings of inadequacy, or feelings of isolation (See III.Week Ten, Day 2). These feelings change when a person gains a sense of worth, value, and belonging.

If the source of worth, value, and belonging is from other people, then fear of rejection from man leads to shame of Jesus and of His words. If the source of worth, value, and belonging rests in Jesus, then there is not shame of Jesus and His words. There will be boldness to identify with Jesus and to proclaim Him.

> **Meditation:** Explore the source of your feelings of worth, value, and belonging. How are you validated as a person? Then come before the Lord and ask Him to show you your worth and value to Him.

IV. Week Seven, Day 7 (Date:)　　　　　　　　　**FEAR OF MAN**

Today is a day of review. Read back over your journal in the past week.

> **Meditation:** Seek the Lord for a vision of what freedom in Him looks like in your life. Imagine this freedom. What do you see? Ask the Holy Spirit to show you this freedom and what it looks like to live in it. Exercise faith and trust for freedom and seek the surrender in your life to gain it.

☦　　☦　　☦　　☦　　☦　　☦　　☦

NOTES:_____

_____

_____

_____

_____

_____

_____

_____

_____

_____

_____

SECTION IV – POWER AND GLORY: WEEK EIGHT

IV.Week Eight, Day 1 (Date:)   **THE CAVE**

> And the hand of the LORD was on Elijah, and he gathered up his garment and ran before Ahab to the entrance of Jezreel.
> Ahab told Jezebel all that Elijah had done, and how he had killed all the prophets with the sword. Then Jezebel sent a messenger to Elijah, saying, "So may the gods do to me and more also, if I do not make your life as the life of one of them by this time tomorrow."
> Then he was afraid, and he arose and ran for his life and came to Beersheba, which belongs to Judah, and left his servant there.
> But he himself went a day's journey into the wilderness and came and sat down under a broom tree. And he asked that he might die, saying, "It is enough; now, O LORD, take away my life, for I am no better than my fathers." **1 Kings 18:46-19:4**

Lord, take away my life, for I am no better than my fathers.

1 Kings 19 describes what I call "Elijah's meltdown." Elijah is afraid, he flees to another country, and he prays to the Lord to die. Meltdowns are common, but how a man with the spirit and power of Elijah got there amazes me.

- Elijah raised the widow of Zarephath's son from the dead – the *first* instance recorded in the Bible of a person being raised from the dead.
- Elijah has just confronted and prevailed against King Ahab and 450 false prophets on Mount Carmel – showing no fear of man.
- Elijah has just called fire down from heaven to consume his sacrifice and then prayed for rain that ended a 3 year drought and famine.

"The hand of the Lord was on Elijah." Yet here Elijah sits in hopelessness and despair. He is despondent and he asks to die. What happened?

Even after I have experienced the Lord and walked with him, even after I have ministered with word and with great power, even after I have overcome fear of man, I can have unfulfilled expectations. Elijah expected revival after Mount Carmel. He expected the king and the people of Israel to return to the Lord in dramatic fashion. Instead, though, the queen threatens his life.

Elijah perceives himself as a failure. He has allowed himself to become a victim, and he is now swallowed by a victim mentality.

> **Meditation:** Identify occasions in your life that you felt like a failure – or had fear of failure. What feelings did you experience? How did those feelings impact you? How did you respond?

IV. Week Eight, Day 2 (Date:)   **THE CAVE**

> There he came to a cave and lodged in it. And behold, the word of the LORD came to him, and he said to him, "What are you doing here, Elijah?"
> He said, "I have been very jealous for the LORD, the God of hosts. For the people of Israel have forsaken your covenant, thrown down your altars, and killed your prophets with the sword, and I, even I only, am left, and they seek my life, to take it away." **1 Kings 19:9-10**

Woundedness connects to the original offense and to any offenses that follow after it.

O help me to not fear man and give in to him! Help me to proclaim You and Your Truth to this new generation, and not be afraid of their faces, threats, thoughts, actions, rejection, or any other thing. I don't want to trapped, snared by what man thinks, etc. I want to be freed by Your "well done" being all I am seeking!

Help me to be healed from the root problem — caring more about what man thinks or may do, than I care about what You think or may do! Help me to be less and less like Zedekiah, and more and more like Paul in Acts 20:24! (Being like Zedekiah—fearing what the Jews might do—always leads to loss of sight. He had his eyes put out.)

Fear of man leads to a blindness that is much more subtle and deadly! O God, deliver me!! This child needs more care to avoid all snares.   –Pastor Daniel Martin, 11/11/14

This scripture is Elijah's complaint. It is one that he repeats to the Lord twice. Yet it is clearly untrue. In the prior chapter, Obadiah tells Elijah that he has saved the lives of 100 prophets of the Lord. But in his woundedness, Elijah can't see that others have been faithful to the Lord. He is blinded by his own pain. He feels rejected and he feels alone.

Abuse is a pernicious evil, particularly when inflicted on children. For many years, it seemed strange to me that persons abused as children by alcoholics became alcoholics as adults, that those that suffered physical abuse became physical abusers, and that children subjected to sexual abuse became sexual abusers. I felt that the pain suffered would keep an abused person from inflicting the same pain on another person.

But abuse is pernicious. Abuse robs the child of will in such a way that it erases boundaries and destroys resistance. The abused person seems powerless to fight the temptation to abuse. Abuse inflicts pain, but even more, it also imposes a sense of helplessness. The sense of helplessness and incapacity feeds an identity of worthlessness. The child feels as if he or she has no value. The child is a victim.

For the person that has suffered the evils of abuse, the fear of further abuse, rejection, and worthlessness is debilitating and blinding. The existing woundedness connects to the original offense and to any offenses that follow after it. The wounded and fearful person is unable to see God clearly, and is unable to see himself or herself clearly.

Elijah has experienced much rejection in his ministry. Now he has locked onto those feelings of rejection. He has become a victim and he feels the torment of a victim. He is "in the cave."

> **Meditation:** Identify connections that you have in your life to woundedness. In what ways do you feel like a victim? Write them down as you identify each one.
>
> Then seek to understand the emotional responses and the behaviors that arise from your woundedness. Present each one to the Lord and pray for healing and that you may see Him and see yourself clearly.

☦ ☦ ☦ ☦ ☦ ☦ ☦

NOTES:_____

_____

_____

_____

_____

_____

_____

_____

_____

_____

_____

IV. Week Eight, Day 3 (Date:)   THE CAVE

> O LORD, you have deceived me, and I was deceived; you are stronger than I, and you have prevailed. I have become a laughingstock all the day; everyone mocks me. For whenever I speak, I cry out, I shout, "Violence and destruction!" For the word of the LORD has become for me a reproach and derision all day long.
> If I say, "I will not mention him, or speak any more in his name," there is in my heart as it were a burning fire shut up in my bones, and I am weary with holding it in, and I cannot. For I hear many whispering. Terror is on every side! "Denounce him! Let us denounce him!" say all my close friends, watching for my fall. "Perhaps he will be deceived; then we can overcome him and take our revenge on him."
> But the LORD is with me as a dread warrior; therefore my persecutors will stumble; they will not overcome me. They will be greatly shamed, for they will not succeed. Their eternal dishonor will never be forgotten. **Jer 20:7-11**

O LORD, You have deceived me.

[God] wants them to learn to walk and must therefore take away His hand; and if only the will to walk is really there He is pleased even with their stumbles. Do not be deceived, Wormwood. Our cause is never more in danger than when a human, no longer desiring, but still intending, to do our Enemy's [God's] will, looks round upon a universe from which every trace of Him seems to have vanished, and asks why he has been forsaken, and still obeys. - *C. S. Lewis*[95]

Elijah was a great servant of the Lord. But he has reached the "end of his rope" and he can no longer see the hand of God leading him.

In this scripture passage, Jeremiah has a complaint as well. It may be expressed in different ways, but fundamentally it is not just a complaint against other people. It is a complaint against the Lord. I can reach the point that I have an offense against the Lord. Unfulfilled expectations, chronic pain, piercing grief, or unending burdens can lead to this offense.

The cave is a defining moment in Elijah's life. He is unable to see it, but in his story and in the story of his successor, Elisha, it is a time of momentous change. God is working in the middle of this crushing circumstance.

Offense against God causes some to turn their back on Him. But there is only one holy response: Let go and trust Him. You can tell Him your complaint. He

---

[95] C. S. Lewis, *The Screwtape Letters,* p. 40 (HarperOne 1996).

already knows your thoughts. But He is the Lord and you are not. Release control and fall into Him.

> **Meditation:** Has there been a time or an occasion when you felt offense against God? Write about it in your journal. Then present it to the Lord. Ask Him for His perspective on the offense. Try to release control and let yourself fall into Him.

☫ ☫ ☫ ☫ ☫ ☫ ☫

NOTES:_____

_____

_____

_____

_____

_____

_____

_____

_____

> Friends tell friends how they feel and how they hurt. Jesus called His disciples "friends" (Jn 15:15). Your time dedicated to the Lord is also time with a friend.

IV. Week Eight, Day 4 (Date:)   THE CAVE

> And he said, "Go out and stand on the mount before the LORD." And behold, the LORD passed by, and a great and strong wind tore the mountains and broke in pieces the rocks before the LORD, but the LORD was not in the wind. And after the wind an earthquake, but the LORD was not in the earthquake.
> And after the earthquake a fire, but the LORD was not in the fire. And after the fire the sound of a low whisper. And when Elijah heard it, he wrapped his face in his cloak and went out and stood at the entrance of the cave. And behold, there came a voice to him and said, "What are you doing here, Elijah?"
> He said, "I have been very jealous for the LORD, the God of hosts. For the people of Israel have forsaken your covenant, thrown down your altars, and killed your prophets with the sword, and I, even I only, am left, and they seek my life, to take it away."
> **1 Kings 19:11-14**

No man so feels as he who suffers.

Dispose and order all things according to your will and judgment, and you shall find that you must always suffer somewhat, either willingly or against your will, and so you shall ever find the cross. For either you shall feel pain in the body, or suffer tribulation of spirit in the soul. Sometimes you shall be forsaken of God, sometimes you shall be troubled by your neighbor; and, what is more, oftentimes you shall be wearisome to your own self. Neither can you be delivered or eased by any remedy or comfort; but so long as it pleases God you ought to bear it. For God will have you learn to suffer tribulation without comfort; and by tribulation become more humble. No man so feels in his heart the passion of Christ as he who suffers.[96]

There are occasions, or even seasons, in life when it seems that the Lord withdraws Himself from a believer. These times have been called silence, felt abandonment, or even darkness. It is said that Mother Teresa went through a "spiritual desert" for over 40 years in which she struggled to sense the presence of God. She felt darkness.[97]

In Elijah's meltdown, the Lord brings Elijah back to his prophetic calling. He calls Elijah, who wraps his face in his mantle, to discern which force contains the Presence of the Lord. The Lord is reminding Elijah that he is a prophet of

---

[96] *The Imitation of Christ,* p. 87.

[97] Rick Coronado, *Mother Teresa: A Dark Spiritual Life and Love for the Poor* (from www.benedictine.edu).

the Lord. Only in Him does Elijah's identity, and indeed Elijah's life, exist. God is calling Elijah "back to his core."

The Lord is still at work in times of "the cave," although it may not feel that way. The Lord is cultivating greater yieldedness. He is bringing the saint to a place of deeper surrender. The Lord is bringing His child to the realization and place that, in the words of Job, *"Though He slay me, yet will I trust in Him"* (Job 13:15a) (KJV).

> **Meditation:** How do you relate to "the cave?" Describe times in your life that you felt alone, in darkness, or depressed. What did you learn from those times?

☩ ☩ ☩ ☩ ☩ ☩ ☩

NOTES:_____

_____

_____

_____

_____

_____

_____

_____

_____

_____

_____

IV. Week Eight, Day 5 (Date:)   THE CAVE

> "I tell you, my friends, do not fear those who kill the body, and after that have nothing more that they can do. But I will warn you whom to fear: fear him who, after he has killed, has authority to cast into hell. Yes, I tell you, fear him!" **Luke 12:4-5**

I will be the most proud man in that prison!

I remember the day like it was yesterday, Nik. My father put his arms around me and my sister and my brother and guided us into the kitchen to sit around the table where he could talk with us. My Mama was crying, so I knew that something was wrong. Papa didn't look at her because he was talking directly to us. He said, "Children, you know that I am the pastor of our church. That's what God called me to do - to tell others about Him. I have learned that the communist authorities will come tomorrow to arrest me. They will put me in prison because they want me to stop preaching about Jesus. But I cannot stop because I must obey God. I will miss you very much, but I will trust God to watch over you while I am gone."

He hugged each of us. Then he said: "All around this part of the country, the authorities are rounding up followers of Jesus and demanding that they deny their faith. Sometimes, when they refuse, the authorities will line up whole families and hang them by the neck until they are dead. I don't want that to happen to our family, so I am praying that once they put me in prison, they will leave you and your mother alone."

"However," and here he paused and made eye contact with us, "if I am in prison and I hear that my wife and my children have been hung to death rather than to deny Jesus, I will be the most proud man in that prison!"[98]

Our faith has a floor – a baseline. Deep within us, when everything else is stripped away, that faith either exists or it doesn't. But if it exists, it is as hard as concrete. We can stand on that faith firmly.

Jesus taught clearly on many occasions that the value of your soul is worth far more than the value of your life on this earth. There is a huge difference between physical death and spiritual death. The line between the two is drawn by our faith. The times when we are "in the cave" are when that faith is tested and revealed, and we learn how strong that faith is for future use in our walk.

When Adam and Eve felt abandoned by God, they fled and hid. They did not have a knowledge of God that trusted Him in their "abandonment."

Jesus, the second Adam, was also forsaken on the cross. He cried *"My God, my God, why have you forsaken me?"* And some of the bystanders hearing it

---

[98] *The Insanity of God,* pp. 176-177.

said, "Behold, he is calling Elijah" (Mark 15:34b-35).

But in His abandonment, Jesus still had faith and He had trust. In the next moment, as He expired, Jesus cried *"Father, into your hands I commit my spirit!" And having said this he breathed his last* (Luke 23:46).

> **Meditation:** *"Love never ends."* Spend time in silence before the Lord. Eliminate distractions and take time to quiet your mind. Now try to find the floor – the baseline of your faith. Ask the Holy Spirit to move within you and to show you the basis – the foundation of your faith. Give the Holy Spirit permission to search your heart, your will, and your soul. Write what He shows you in your journal.

☦ ☦ ☦ ☦ ☦ ☦ ☦

NOTES:_____

_____

_____

_____

_____

_____

_____

_____

_____

_____

IV. Week Eight, Day 6 (Date:)　　　　　　　　　　**THE CAVE**

> In the days of his flesh, Jesus offered up prayers and supplications, with loud cries and tears, to him who was able to save him from death, and he was heard because of his reverence. Although he was a son, he learned obedience through what he suffered. **Heb 5:7-8**

Although He was a Son, He learned obedience through what He suffered.

Although it has been many years since I coached soccer, I still have a relationship with some of the young men that I coached. Jorge, who is now 30, is one of those young men.

Jorge says "Coach, the thing that I hated most about soccer practice was the 'suicides.'" Suicides are conditioning drills where the team sprints a distance and walks back. Then the team runs again and again – over and over – pushed to the limit. Jorge continues, "Yes, I hated suicides, but, looking back, I know that we needed them in order to get into good enough shape to last 90 minutes in a game."

Most of my players were refugees from foreign countries that learned to play soccer in the streets and in refugee camps. The instincts they learned were personal skills that displayed individual talent. Unfortunately, many of those skills were not conducive to effective team play. What I quickly realized was that, no matter the instruction in practice, players played by instinct in a game. So every season I spent much of the time retraining instinct. I had to break one set of instincts in order to instill a new set of instincts that enhanced team play.

We all have spiritual instincts. These instincts are habits, feelings, and responses that we are born with or that have developed in our life journey. An instinct is ingrained with us so that it is our immediate response.

I have found that my instincts were not very Christlike. My instincts included:

- Following the desires of my flesh.
- Spending my time pleasing my will.
- Reacting based on the fear of man.

"The cave" is one way in which the Lord, in His mercy, trains (disciplines) me and retools my spiritual instincts. Maybe a "suicide" isn't the worst name for the training because it involves death of my flesh and a cross. The Lord is changing my instinctive response so that I:

- Act in love unselfishly rather than out of my flesh.
- Spend time pleasing Him doing His will instead of pleasing myself.
- React based on fear of God rather than fear of man.

I am still in training. But, like Jesus, I am learning obedience through what I suffer.

Don't be surprised if "the cave" happens to you. In fact, it can happen more than once. Accept it with trust and thanksgiving, and learn obedience.

> **Meditation:** Spend time with the idea of spiritual instinct. What are some holy instincts that you have? What instincts need to change? Write your thoughts in your journal. Ask the Holy Spirit to help you grow in godly instincts. Give Him permission to change instincts that are not holy.

☨ ☨ ☨ ☨ ☨ ☨ ☨

NOTES:_____

_____

_____

_____

_____

_____

_____

_____

_____

> Ups and downs in your devotional life are normal. Your experiences and your feelings will vary. Meeting with your mentor or spiritual director can give you a mature perspective and help you interpret these fluctuations.

IV. Week Eight, Day 7 (Date:)　　　　　　　　　　　　**THE CAVE**

Today is a day of review. Look back over the devotions and over your journal for the past two weeks.

> **Meditation:** Today is a day to express your feelings from the past two weeks. Use artistic or physical expression to tell the Lord your feelings. Sometimes it is good to draw a picture of what you are feeling but paint, draw, compose, dance, express or create. Do something to express your feelings and offer them to the Lord.

☦ ☦ ☦ ☦ ☦ ☦ ☦

NOTES:_____

SECTION IV – POWER AND GLORY: WEEK NINE

IV.Week Nine, Day 1 (Date:)　　　　　**GENERATIONAL THINKING**

> He said, "I have been very jealous for the LORD, the God of hosts. For the people of Israel have forsaken your covenant, thrown down your altars, and killed your prophets with the sword, and I, even I only, am left, and they seek my life, to take it away."
> And the LORD said to him, "Go, return on your way to the wilderness of Damascus. And when you arrive, you shall anoint Hazael to be king over Syria. And Jehu the son of Nimshi you shall anoint to be king over Israel, and Elisha the son of Shaphat of Abel-meholah you shall anoint to be prophet in your place. And the one who escapes from the sword of Hazael shall Jehu put to death, and the one who escapes from the sword of Jehu shall Elisha put to death. Yet I will leave seven thousand in Israel, all the knees that have not bowed to Baal, and every mouth that has not kissed him."
> **1 Kings 19:14-18**

Elisha the son of Shaphat of Abel-meholah you shall anoint to be prophet in your place.

After God calls Elijah back to Himself and to Elijah's spiritual identity as a prophet, God gives Elijah a prophetic word with direction for the future. It is a word of hope. The names involved are relevant. Elisha ("God his salvation") the son of Shaphat ("judge") of Abel-meholah ("the meadow of dancing") you shall anoint to be prophet in your place.[99]

It is as if God is saying "Elijah, I am still in control and I still have a plan for the future, even after you are gone." After God restored Elijah's identity, God restores Elijah's future. It is a restoration of hope.

The fulfillment of this word was generational. We know that Elijah called Elisha to be prophet in his place. But we don't read that Elijah anointed Jehu or Hazael. In fact, *Elisha* sent a messenger who anointed Jehu (2 Kings 9:1-16). *Elisha* prophesied to Hazael about his royal destiny (2 Kings 8:8-15). But Elijah saw these events prophetically through the word of God. Although Elijah did not anoint Jehu or Hazael, those acts were done in the power and spirit of Elijah, which rested on Elisha.

Finally, only after God had lovingly restored Elijah's identity, and had given Elijah a word of hope, did God correct Elijah's meltdown. Elijah, in his frustration, had somehow missed 7000 other believers who would not

---

[99] Source: *Smith's Bible Dictionary*.

worship Baal or kiss that false god. Those faithful worshippers of the Lord would continue the worship of the Lord in Israel.

God is a patient God.

> **Meditation:** Explore your thoughts and feelings about the next generation of believers in the kingdom of God. What hopes, dreams, fears, or concerns do you have about the next generation? Write your thoughts in your journal.

☦ ☦ ☦ ☦ ☦ ☦ ☦

NOTES:_____

IV. Week Nine, Day 2 (Date:)   **GENERATIONAL THINKING**

> So he departed from there and found Elisha the son of Shaphat, who was plowing with twelve yoke of oxen in front of him, and he was with the twelfth. Elijah passed by him and cast his cloak upon him.
> And he left the oxen and ran after Elijah and said, "Let me kiss my father and my mother, and then I will follow you." And he said to him, "Go back again, for what have I done to you?"
> And he returned from following him and took the yoke of oxen and sacrificed them and boiled their flesh with the yokes of the oxen and gave it to the people, and they ate. Then he arose and went after Elijah and assisted him. **1 Kings 19:19-21**

Elijah passed by him and cast his cloak upon him.

I need to surrender CONTROL. O This One! This one which is so often the killer! The killer is the right term! If I hold on to what I should not, my rebellion kills the potential of what You have in store for me!

If I do surrender, Your control will cause many things in me to die, thus becoming a killer. But when what needs to die is killed, real Life follows and takes over! This is what I want! Please take over completely. Every time I yield anything at all, please step in and take charge!   -Pastor Daniel Martin, 3/23/20

This exchange is the calling of Elisha by Elijah in response to the word which God gave Elijah in the cave. The cloak is the symbol of a prophet so placing it on Elisha signified calling Elisha into the role of the prophet. This calling follows the Biblical pattern for spiritual succession. The older, anointed believer selects and calls the younger one. Moses called Joshua (Num 27:18), David called Solomon, and Jesus called His disciples.

This call by Elijah signified momentous changes for both men. Elisha was a farmer. Based on the number of oxen, he was wealthy. But without hesitation he left his family and his livelihood to live the life of a prophet. For Elisha to sacrifice the oxen and their yoke with them was a remarkable commitment.

Elijah was used to being "the man" in control. He was a loner who functioned as the focal point of the ministry. When he appeared, he brought miracles, famine, or fire raining down from the sky. Now, Elijah is being called to function in tandem with Elisha. He has to relinquish his absolute control.

And these are very different men. Elijah is "the show" and inhabits wilderness areas. Elisha is urbane. He doesn't even appear for many of his prophetic acts but sends messengers to convey the word of the Lord. It indeed was a strange pairing but God knew to whom the spirit of Elijah should pass to bless the next generation.

> **Meditation:** Process the idea that anointing passes by the dynamic of the older believer selecting and calling the younger believer. In what ways have you experienced or seen this dynamic? How is it applicable to your own life?

☦ ☦ ☦ ☦ ☦ ☦ ☦

NOTES:_____

_____

_____

_____

_____

_____

_____

_____

_____

_____

_____

_____

_____

_____

IV. Week Nine, Day 3 (Date:)　　　　**GENERATIONAL THINKING**

> Then the king of Israel said, "Alas! The LORD has called these three kings to give them into the hand of Moab." And Jehoshaphat said, "Is there no prophet of the LORD here, through whom we may inquire of the LORD?" Then one of the king of Israel's servants answered, "Elisha the son of Shaphat is here, who poured water on the hands of Elijah." **2 Kings 3:10-11**

Elisha, the son of Shaphat is here, who poured water on the hands of Elijah.

This scripture passage illustrates the biblical model for ministry training. After response to call, the younger believer serves the older believer while they are doing ministry together. Moses and Joshua, Barnabas and Paul, Paul and Timothy...all illustrate this model. The younger believer assists and supports the older believer in ministry while the older believer trains the younger believer in function, in gifts, and in life.

Every generation should plant seeds and sow into the lives of following generations. These seeds are a key to fulfillment of destiny for the younger believer. Regrettably, many persons will not realize their destiny in the Lord because (1) the seeds are not planted or (2) they do not grow. The generations need to connect meaningfully for the seeds to be planted. This connection requires sacrifice by both the older and the younger generation. There is an intentionality to it along with care not to abuse the relationship.

Then, after the seed has been sown, a dying to the flesh must occur for the seeds to grow and to be fruitful (John 12:24-26). As a result, destinies in the Lord are realized.

> **Meditation:** Focus on the idea of the planting of seeds by one generation to another. Think of the ways in which this planting occurs. What seeds have been planted in your life? Write down the ways in which those seeds have been planted and the ways in which they have come to fruition.

☨　☨　☨　☨　☨　☨　☨

> Remember grace as you search your heart. The Lord gives grace through His love. Set aside time to bask in His love often. Grace, love, and peace.

IV. Week Nine, Day 4 (Date:)   GENERATIONAL THINKING

> When they had crossed, Elijah said to Elisha, "Ask what I shall do for you, before I am taken from you." And Elisha said, "Please let there be a double portion of your spirit on me." And he said, "You have asked a hard thing; yet, if you see me as I am being taken from you, it shall be so for you, but if you do not see me, it shall not be so."
> 2 Kings 2:9-10

Our ceiling is their floor.

O God, make me more and more into a "Caleb"! I want to be one who proclaims Your power to this new generation—not just in words of yesterday, but in the release of power today!

I want to see new "resurrection" stories being released daily from my life with Your power, into the world around me! O God, come and help me to take the "mountains," the "Hebrons," the giants of this day! Come and make me such a wholehearted seeker of You, that Your eyes are on me and that You show Yourself strong on my behalf, for Your name's sake!

O God, come and change me more and more into what You are wanting me to be now, in this day, in this time, in this hour!

- Make me a leader among your people, despite my start in life. Num 13:1
- Make me willing to stand for truth, even when outnumbered. Num 13-14
- Grant me a courageous confidence in You and Your promises. Num 13:40
- Help me to refuse to see life through the eyes of men. Num 14:30-33
- Cause me to grieve over the sins of my followers—and to intercede for them. Num 14:5-6
- Teach me to know Your presence, which brings boldness and direction. Num 14:5-10
- Place within me a different spirit. Num 14:24
- Keep me from being fearful of the giants in my way. Josh 14:1-12
- Cultivate within me a fresher and fresher faith as I grow older. Josh 14
- Give me the guts to pray:
    - "Give me the land" Num 13:30
    - "Give me the high ground" Josh 14:11-12

O God, I want to be a Kingdom seeker, a lowly one who seeks Your greatness to be delivered into the earth through an unworthy vessel! Come and flow to and through me into my "world" around me today! I need to see the goodness of the Lord in the land of the living!   -Pastor Daniel Martin, 4/21/15

Another reason that the biblical model for training - a younger believer serving an older minister - isn't very popular in our culture is that abuses can occur. The older saint must be careful to exercise authority properly – in an attitude of humility, love, and submission. He must act wisely in a manner that nurtures the next generation. A local training ministry in Charlotte has this theme: "Our ceiling is their floor."

But Elisha did not just serve Elijah for the training; he affirmatively sought his anointing – the spirit and power of Elijah. An anointing is passed to another person through intentional submission. The younger believer submits to and serves the older believer until the anointing passes.

And Elisha didn't just seek Elijah's anointing; Elisha sought a double portion of it. Elisha's request was granted, but he had to serve Elijah until the end for it to be fulfilled.

In Elisha's subsequent ministry, he parted waters, healed illnesses, and orchestrated the defeat of Israel's enemies. He raised the Shunammite's son from the dead which is the second time the Bible records a person being raised from the dead (2 Kings 4:32-37). But these miracles were all performed in the anointing passed to him from Elijah.

A powerful passing of an anointing is a sign of healthy generational succession. A successful Christian leader works himself out of a job by raising up leaders in the next generation that can continue the work. A *double* portion of the anointing is icing on the cake with a cherry on top.

Meditation: Spend time again with the idea of an anointing in ministry. What does an anointing mean to you? How have you experienced it? Write it down in your journal. Ask the Holy Spirit if there is an anointing you seek or you can pass to another generation.

☨ ☨ ☨ ☨ ☨ ☨ ☨

NOTES:_____

_____

_____

_____

_____

_____

IV. Week Nine, Day 5 (Date:) **GENERATIONAL THINKING**

> Then the people of Judah came to Joshua at Gilgal. And Caleb the son of Jephunneh the Kenizzite said to him, "You know what the LORD said to Moses the man of God in Kadesh-barnea concerning you and me. I was forty years old when Moses the servant of the LORD sent me from Kadesh-barnea to spy out the land, and I brought him word again as it was in my heart. But my brothers who went up with me made the heart of the people melt; yet I wholly followed the LORD my God. And Moses swore on that day, saying, 'Surely the land on which your foot has trodden shall be an inheritance for you and your children forever, because you have wholly followed the LORD my God.' And now, behold, the LORD has kept me alive, just as he said, these forty-five years since the time that the LORD spoke this word to Moses, while Israel walked in the wilderness. And now, behold, I am this day eighty-five years old. I am still as strong today as I was in the day that Moses sent me; my strength now is as my strength was then, for war and for going and coming. So now give me this hill country of which the LORD spoke on that day, for you heard on that day how the Anakim were there, with great fortified cities. It may be that the LORD will be with me, and I shall drive them out just as the LORD said."
> Then Joshua blessed him, and he gave Hebron to Caleb the son of Jephunneh for an inheritance. Therefore Hebron became the inheritance of Caleb the son of Jephunneh the Kenizzite to this day, because he wholly followed the LORD, the God of Israel.
> **Josh 14:6-14**

Surely the land on which your foot has trodden shall be

an inheritance for you and your children forever.

O Father, do the work in me that needs to be done to change me into a Caleb and Joshua, instead of those other 10 spies whose names almost no one knows.

Transform me into one who is so connected to You, who is so focused on Your promise instead of the impossibilities around me, that I am proclaiming You instead of the problems in every issue and detail of my world around me.

Help me to not be a proclaimer of problems, of what "is", but a proclaimer of Your truth, Your promise, Your greatness, and Your WAYS!!

O God, help me in this!

Help me to faithfully proclaim and demonstrate Your power to this generation that is so lost and floundering in the sea of all the enemy's lies! Come and let Your truth and existence be made known—through me, through Your church in powerful ways!! Come, Lion of the tribe of Judah—make Yourself known!! -Pastor Daniel Martin, 12/16/14

Just as dysfunction can be passed from generation to generation, blessing can also be passed from generation to generation as Caleb did. Rich spiritual heritage can be passed down from family to family and from minister to minister. Sowing seeds into the next generation grows this heritage. Some of the most powerful seeds are sown by example and by sacrifice in the areas of giving, service, and humility (not necessarily riches, position, or pride).

Words of life are also very important. Speaking words of blessing, words of encouragement, words of correction, and words of insight lift the younger believer. An older saint can often see things that younger ones cannot. Being diligent to speak into the lives of other believers is a blessing to them!

> **Meditation:** Focus on your vision for generational blessing. Consider how you want to bless the next generation. What are some of the ways that you can bless those who come after you? Write them down in your journal.

☩ ☩ ☩ ☩ ☩ ☩ ☩

NOTES:_____

_____

_____

_____

_____

_____

_____

_____

IV. Week Nine, Day 6 (Date:)   **GENERATIONAL THINKING**

> So Elisha died, and they buried him. Now bands of Moabites used to invade the land in the spring of the year. And as a man was being buried, behold, a marauding band was seen and the man was thrown into the grave of Elisha, and as soon as the man touched the bones of Elisha, he revived and stood on his feet. **2 Kings 13:20-21**

Did not my heart go with you?

This vignette after the death of Elisha tells of the third and last person in the Old Testament to rise from the dead. This story is miraculous and yet it hurts my heart to read it.

During his ministry, Elisha also had an assistant who served him. His name was Gehazi which means "valley of vision" – a good name for a prophet in training. Gehazi worked closely with Elisha in his ministry. He was in the house when Elisha raised the Shunammite's son from the dead.

Elisha also sent Gehazi to deliver words of the Lord to people. One of those people was Naaman the Syrian general. After Naaman was healed from his leprosy, he returned to thank Elisha and urged Elisha to accept great gifts as a token of gratitude. Elisha refused. But Gehazi coveted Naaman's money. He ran after Naaman to ask for silver and clothes and got *two sets* of each. He secretly returned with the goods, except that it is hard to hide misdeeds from a prophet. When Gehazi returned, Elisha asked where he had been.

Gehazi said nowhere.

Then Elisha said this *"Did not my heart go with you when the man turned from his chariot to meet you? Is it a time to receive money and to receive clothes and olive groves and vineyards and sheep and oxen and male and female servants? Therefore the leprosy of Naaman shall cling to you and to your descendants forever"* (2 Kings 5:26-27a). So Gehazi went out from his presence a leper as white as snow.

Gehazi craved silver and nice clothing. He should have coveted his master's anointing (a double portion) instead of silver, and the mantle of Elijah that his master possessed instead of the latest Syrian fashions.

This story is so sad. It grieves me. The spirit of Elijah should have passed on from Elisha to Gehazi! What we realize from the scripture above is that Elisha took the power and spirit of Elijah to the grave with him which is why it resurrected a dead man. It should have passed to Gehazi, but Gehazi forfeited his spiritual inheritance through his greed. So the prophetic anointing did not pass on.

Yet God is a God of redemption.

Meditation: Consider the seeds which were planted in Elisha by Elijah and how they came to fruition. Now consider the seeds planted in Gehazi by Elisha and how they did not mature to fulfill Gehazi's destiny. Seek the Lord about seeds that have been planted in you and how they can come to full maturity. Write in your journal about it.

☩ ☩ ☩ ☩ ☩ ☩ ☩

NOTES:_____

_____

_____

_____

_____

_____

_____

_____

_____

_____

> Be encouraged that God is working in your heart and mind as you dedicate time to Him. He desires that you fulfill the destiny and call that He has for your life, and He will complete it in His perfect time.

IV. Week Nine, Day 7 (Date:) **GENERATIONAL THINKING**

Today is a day of review. Look back over your journal for this week.

> **Meditation:** Spend your time in prayer today for the next generation. Present to the Lord your hopes and fears for the next generation. *"Love hopes all things."* Focus on your ministry and efforts to cultivate the generations after you. Then seek the Lord for them and for direction for you. Write about it in your journal.

☦ ☦ ☦ ☦ ☦ ☦ ☦

NOTES:_____

_____

_____

_____

_____

_____

_____

_____

_____

SECTION IV – POWER AND GLORY: WEEK TEN

IV.Week Ten, Day 1 (Date:)   **RESTORATION**

> "Remember the law of my servant Moses, the statutes and rules that I commanded him at Horeb for all Israel. Behold, I will send you Elijah the prophet before the great and awesome day of the LORD comes. And he will turn the hearts of fathers to their children and the hearts of children to their fathers, lest I come and strike the land with a decree of utter destruction." **Mal 4:4-6**

Behold, I will send you Elijah the prophet.

These are the last 3 verses of the Book of Malachi. They hold a promise about Elijah the prophet. The spirit of Elijah may have gone to the grave with Elisha. Gehazi's greed seemingly ended that anointing. But God is a God of redemption and of restoration.

Centuries later, when the angel appeared to John the Baptist's father, the angel said *"And he will turn many of the children of Israel to the Lord their God, and he will go before him in the spirit and power of Elijah, to turn the hearts of the fathers to the children, and the disobedient to the wisdom of the just, to make ready for the Lord a people prepared"* (Luke 1:17). The spirit and power of Elijah was at work again!

How did John the Baptist operate in the spirit and power of Elijah? The connection seems almost strange. Elijah did many signs and wonders, including raising the widow's son from the dead. John the Baptist, on the other hand, did no miracles or signs (John 10:41).

But both Elijah and John the Baptist preached to a lost and fallen people. The essence of their message was reconciliation. Reconciliation of the people to the Lord their God; and reconciliation of generations to one another. *"Answer me, O LORD, answer me, that this people may know that you, O LORD, are God, and that you have turned their hearts back"* (1 Kings 18:37).

Then, at the Transfiguration, both Moses and Elijah appeared to show that their work found fulfillment in the person of Jesus.

God takes the catastrophe and turns it to salvation. He takes the disaster and makes it glorious. God is a God of redemption and restoration.

> **Meditation:** Identify areas of your life or areas around you that need redemption and restoration. These areas can be relationships, emotions, dysfunctions, or even anointing. List them in your journal. Then seek God for restoration. Ask Him what needs to occur for restoration to happen.

IV. Week Ten, Day 2 (Date:) **RESTORATION**

> When Joseph's brothers saw that their father was dead, they said, "It may be that Joseph will hate us and pay us back for all the evil that we did to him."
> So they sent a message to Joseph, saying, "Your father gave this command before he died: 'Say to Joseph, "Please forgive the transgression of your brothers and their sin, because they did evil to you."' And now, please forgive the transgression of the servants of the God of your father." Joseph wept when they spoke to him.
> His brothers also came and fell down before him and said, "Behold, we are your servants."
> But Joseph said to them, "Do not fear, for am I in the place of God? As for you, you meant evil against me, but God meant it for good, to bring it about that many people should be kept alive, as they are today. So do not fear; I will provide for you and your little ones." Thus he comforted them and spoke kindly to them. **Gen 50:15-21**

Thus he comforted them and spoke kindly to him.

God never ends anything on a negative; God always ends on a positive. –Edwin Louis Cole[100]

These men are Joseph's persecutors. They caused him a world of hurt. But Joseph understood God's divine plan. He trusted in God without regard to whether his own brothers treated him well or treated him poorly. He did not resent, repay, or retaliate for the wrong done to him, even when it was within his power to do so. Joseph only had to say the word and his brothers would have been imprisoned or enslaved as they did to him. That sentence would have been just.

But Joseph refused to retain the offense because his confidence in the Lord and his trust in His redemptive nature.

God is working in times of pain, loss, disaster, or darkness in my life. I might look around me and ask "How can God be mixed up in this mess?"

But God has a divine plan that is bigger, better, and more loving than I can imagine. God uses the evils in my life and turns them to good. My trust in Him prevails over any circumstance that I may face – even if that circumstance is in the form of a grievous offense.

---

[100] Quoted from *www.wiseoldsayings.com*.

Meditation: *"Love believes all things."* What virtues did Joseph employ to enable him to see the perspective of God's divine plan rather than to focus on his brothers' offense against him? How can you rise above the seemingly negative circumstances in your life in such a way that they do not control your reactions and your emotions?

☦ ☦ ☦ ☦ ☦ ☦ ☦

NOTES:

IV. Week Ten, Day 3 (Date:) **RESTORATION**

> Thus says the LORD: "A voice is heard in Ramah, lamentation and bitter weeping. Rachel is weeping for her children; she refuses to be comforted for her children, because they are no more."
> Thus says the LORD: "Keep your voice from weeping, and your eyes from tears, for there is a reward for your work, declares the LORD, and they shall come back from the land of the enemy.
> There is hope for your future, declares the LORD, and your children shall come back to their own country." **Jer 31:15-17**

Keep your voice from weeping and your eyes from tears, for there is a reward for your work.

O God, come and deliver. You reminded me of the message I have preached about "Chapters." That many people around us may be living in a chapter of their lives that are very horrible, but this chapter is not necessarily the end of the book. There are more chapters still to be written and we have a role to play in what will be written in those chapters!! There are "GLORY" chapters still to be written in the books/lives of those around us, and as we pray, believe, love, care, minister, and follow You, Your pen starts going to work writing beautiful chapters of redemption, love, grace, and salvation!
      –Pastor Daniel Martin, 6/17/12

When he recounts the killing of the innocents in Bethlehem in his gospel, Matthew quotes from this passage in Jeremiah. In fact, the tragic slaughter of babies by a despicable tyrant for purposes of political power occurs more than once in scripture.

Pharaoh ordered the Hebrew midwives to kill all male Hebrew babies born in Egypt. Pharaoh was concerned that his slave labor force was growing too large. His power was threatened. So he ordered this gruesome form of population control (Exodus 1).

Herod had a similar fear when he heard of the birth of the king of the Jews (Matthew 2). To counter this perceived threat to his power, he ordered the slaughter of all male babies in Bethlehem. Fallen powers were at work.

But God is a God of redemption and restoration! He brought a great deliverance out of these occasions of mourning and lament. God freed His people from physical bondage and death through Moses, and then from all spiritual bondage and death through Jesus.

God is a God of redemption and restoration. The horror of these slaughters was great. The salvation which God wrought through them was greater. God turns evil and darkness into great salvation.

Meditation: Explore your feelings as you read about the killing of the innocents. What do these stories make you feel? Then compare the babies that were killed with martyrs – persons who were killed because of their faith. The babies were killed because of their identity among the people of God and, in a sense, their deaths placated the tormented passion of tyrants so that Moses and Jesus could survive and deliver the people of God. Journal about your thoughts and feelings.

NOTES:_____

IV.Week Ten, Day 4 (Date:)   **RESTORATION**

> And the LORD blessed the latter days of Job more than his beginning. And he had 14,000 sheep, 6,000 camels, 1,000 yoke of oxen, and 1,000 female donkeys.
> He had also seven sons and three daughters. And he called the name of the first daughter Jemimah, and the name of the second Keziah, and the name of the third Keren-happuch. And in all the land there were no women so beautiful as Job's daughters. And their father gave them an inheritance among their brothers.
> And after this Job lived 140 years, and saw his sons, and his sons' sons, four generations. And Job died, an old man, and full of days.
> **Job 42:12-17**

Full of days.

We have already explored how the church makes known the manifold wisdom of God to powers and principalities, and calls them into submission to Christ's Lordship (See IV.Week Three, Day 3). Job had this same call on his life. God called Job to witness to Satan of faith in God and its reality in the middle of crushing loss and despair. God took the evil that Satan inflicted on Job and, through Job, converted the evil for His glory.

But God also restored Job as described in this passage. His goods, his family, and his heritage were all restored to him after his season in "the cave." Note the unusual heritage that Job left. Job not only gave an inheritance to his sons as was the custom in his day, but he gave an inheritance to his daughters. We know *their* names. What a remarkable and meaningful endowment that foreshadowed the kingdom of God!

The book of Job emphasizes a meaningful principle: *The glory of God is more important than this life.* The purpose of creation is to proclaim the glory of God. Every created thing was made for His glory. The glory of God is more important than my possessions, my health, my power, my security, my glory, and yes, even this life.

> **Meditation:** How do you feel about the treasure of your own earthly life and the value of the glory of God? Which do you hold as more precious? Then consider the connection between trials, restoration, and the glory of God. Write your feelings in your journal. You may want to write an honest letter to God about your life and about His glory.

☩ ☩ ☩ ☩ ☩ ☩ ☩

IV. Week Ten, Day 5 (Date:)   RESTORATION

> Now those who were scattered because of the persecution that arose over Stephen traveled as far as Phoenicia and Cyprus and Antioch, speaking the word to no one except Jews. But there were some of them, men of Cyprus and Cyrene, who on coming to Antioch spoke to the Hellenists also, preaching the Lord Jesus. And the hand of the Lord was with them, and a great number who believed turned to the Lord. The report of this came to the ears of the church in Jerusalem, and they sent Barnabas to Antioch. **Acts 11:19-22**

The hand of the Lord was with them.

The early chapters of the Book of Acts detail great miracles and mass conversions in Jerusalem that followed Pentecost. But the death of Stephen, the first martyr, and the persecution that followed, was a blow to the young church. *Devout men buried Stephen and made great lamentation over him* (Acts 8:2). Believers fled from Jerusalem to escape the wrath of the Pharisees, of the rulers, and of Saul.

But the trials and deaths from the persecution planted seeds in the places to which believers fled. It is almost as if God's people became too comfortable in Jerusalem and God had to "push them out of the nest" in order to spread the good news of His kingdom to other regions.

Some the believers fled to Antioch and nowhere else were the seeds more fruitful than those planted in Antioch. Revival broke out in that place. As a result, the church there engaged in productive fivefold function.[101] The missionary journeys of Paul, Barnabas, and Silas were birthed in Antioch. God used the persecution of the church to save many lives. Antioch became a center of gospel proclamation. *And in Antioch the disciples were first called Christians* (Acts 11:26).

The proclamation of the gospel is more important than your earthly life.

Meditation: Explore the idea that God can work through the evil that men or fallen powers perpetrate. How do you feel about that idea? Is there a part of you that is repulsed by it? If so, why? Bring your thoughts and feelings to the Lord and surrender them to Him. Ask Him to reveal His goodness and glory to you.

☩   ☩   ☩   ☩   ☩   ☩   ☩

---

[101] See *The Call: Book Two – Foundational (Progressive Fivefold Function), Lesson 12* for a description of the effective fivefold function in Antioch.

IV. Week Ten, Day 6 (Date:)   **RESTORATION**

> "You serpents, you brood of vipers, how are you to escape being sentenced to hell? Therefore I send you prophets and wise men and scribes, some of whom you will kill and crucify, and some you will flog in your synagogues and persecute from town to town, so that on you may come all the righteous blood shed on earth, from the blood of righteous Abel to the blood of Zechariah the son of Barachiah, whom you murdered between the sanctuary and the altar." **Matt 23:33-35**

Therefore I send you prophets and wise men and scribes.

A deeper enlightenment and wider experience than mine is necessary to explain the dark night through which a soul journeys toward the divine light of perfect union with God that achieved, insofar as possible in this life, through love. The darknesses and trials, spiritual and temporal, that fortunate souls ordinarily undergo on their way to the high state of perfection are so numerous and profound that human science cannot understand them adequately. Nor does experience of them equip one to explain them. Only those who suffer them will know what this experience is like, but they won't be able to describe it.[102]

This promise of Jesus follows His scathing condemnation of the Pharisees and religious teachers of Jesus' day in Matthew 23. This passage is important, but I don't know that I have ever heard a sermon preached on it.

When I read this scripture, I get the part about the Pharisees and the religious leaders. But I also ask the question: "Lord, what about the poor prophets and wise men and scribes? What about Your followers that You are sending for murder, crucifixion, flogging, and persecution? What about them, Lord?"

St. John of the Cross and other contemplative writers have an interesting perspective on the "dark night" that believers may experience – a dark night of the sensory parts of my soul and even a dark night of the spiritual parts. They teach that the obscurity of the dark night is necessary to remove sensual appetites, idols, fear of man, and every vestige of my will. It can be a difficult purgation, but it is one that paves the way for the work of the Lord.

The night happens for a loving reason. St. John of the Cross calls the souls that experience it "fortunate." The night occurs so that I can experience God and only God. The night occurs so that I can experience the breadth and length and height and depth of God's love. What awaits on the other side is an experience of His love and a revelation of His glory.

After all, we have the testimony of Stephen at the point of his death by

---

[102] *The Ascent of Mount Carmel,* Prologue 1.

stoning. *And he said, "Behold, I see the heavens opened, and the Son of Man standing at the right hand of God"* (Acts 7:56). The experience of the first martyr of the church contains promise for each believer who surrenders everything to God, even the warm feelings of spiritual delight (for a season).

> **Meditation:** Consider the idea that God purges sensual appetites and idols, or even allows a spiritual desert, so the believer can journey into His fullness. How do you relate to this experience? *"Love endures all things."*

☩ ☩ ☩ ☩ ☩ ☩ ☩

NOTES:_____

_____

_____

_____

_____

_____

_____

_____

> One significant reason to keep a journal is to record the times that God touches your life – the "markers." If you experience "darkness" or a time that is confusing, reading about times that God touched you can sustain you and bolster your faith.

IV. Week Ten, Day 7 (Date:) **RESTORATION**

Review your notes over the past week.

> **Meditation:** Today is a day of silence before the Lord. Set aside time to sit before the Lord in silent contemplation. Eliminate distractions and quiet your mind. If you desire a focus, focus on Jesus as the Light of the world. Repeat "You are the Light of the world" slowly as you minister to Him.

☦ ☦ ☦ ☦ ☦ ☦ ☦

NOTES:_____

_____

_____

_____

_____

_____

_____

_____

_____

_____

SECTION IV – POWER AND GLORY: WEEK ELEVEN

IV.Week Eleven, Day 1 (Date:　　　　　　　)　　　　　　　　**GLORY**

> When Jesus had spoken these words, he lifted up his eyes to heaven, and said, "Father, the hour has come; glorify your Son that the Son may glorify you, since you have given him authority over all flesh, to give eternal life to all whom you have given him.
> "And this is eternal life, that they know you the only true God, and Jesus Christ whom you have sent. I glorified you on earth, having accomplished the work that you gave me to do. And now, Father, glorify me in your own presence with the glory that I had with you before the world existed." **John 17:1-5**

Glorify Your Son that the Son may glorify You.

There is a special relationship within the Trinity. It is a relationship of Oneness. But it is also a relationship in which love is exchanged and glory is bestowed. Each Person of the Trinity glorifies the Other Persons. I call it "glory share."

The Father glorifies the Son and the Son glorifies the Father. The Holy Spirit glorifies the Father and the Son and bears witness to them. The love and the glory which is shared is part of the Oneness of the Trinity.

But "glory share" extends beyond the Trinity. In the same prayer, Jesus prays *"The glory that you have given me I have given to them, that they may be one even as we are one, I in them and you in me, that they may become perfectly one, so that the world may know that you sent me and loved them even as you loved me. Father, I desire that they also, whom you have given me, may be with me where I am, to see my glory that you have given me because you loved me before the foundation of the world."* (John 17:22-24).

Jesus shares His glory with His followers. It is part of the plan for all the earth to see His glory. His followers both see His glory and they share in it. The result is that they have the same oneness as the Father, the Son, and the Holy Spirit. The unity and function of the Trinity is a model to seek after.

Meditation: What does it mean to glorify another person? How is that glory bestowed and manifested?

Consider the ways in which Jesus glorified the Father during His life on earth. Make a list of the ways that He gave His Father glory. Consider how you can glorify the Father in the same ways.

IV.Week Eleven, Day 2 (Date:)　　　　　　　　　　**GLORY**

> Has the potter no right over the clay, to make out of the same lump one vessel for honorable use and another for dishonorable use?
> What if God, desiring to show his wrath and to make known his power, has endured with much patience vessels of wrath prepared for destruction, in order to make known the riches of his glory for vessels of mercy, which he has prepared beforehand for glory—even us whom he has called, not from the Jews only but also from the Gentiles?
> **Rom 9:21-24**

Vessels of mercy which He has prepared beforehand for glory.

O come and let my heart overflow with the glory of all You are—it now does overflow in ways my body can hardly contain. I never knew life in You could be so rich and full, so delightful and fulfilling—Here and Now!

O give me more and more of this! Come and take over completely in my life, O my God and King! Have Your way in all I am, do, think, and meditate! Grow and grow in Your glory in my life. Change me and change me and change me! Give me more and more of You! What an awesome God You are!

As I sit here and allow waves of Your glory to flow over me, I am stunned with how You are, with the glory of Your presence, with the joy and ecstasy of Your purity, holiness, righteousness, and cleanliness! O come and take over in me, letting Your purity, Your robes of righteousness wash out all my filth.

I remember the father in Luke 15 commanding that <u>first</u> the robe of sonship be placed on his son, that in effect that robe would remove his need of a good cleansing, soaking bath, that the robe would give him all the cleansing he needed at the moment. What an awesome Father You are! O come and clothe me with those robes of righteousness that wash me clean, that change me not just in my outer flesh, but all the way to the core of being, my entire being, all Daniel Martin is in every sense of the word—flesh, body, soul, heart, spirit, emotions, thoughts, actions, motives, desires—All! Come and cleanse, purify, purge, and make holy—all I am in every way.
　　　-Pastor Daniel Martin, 9/17/13

God desires to put His glory on display. *But truly, as I live, and as all the earth shall be filled with the glory of the LORD* (Num 14:21). The display is so great that all the earth will be filled with the glory of the Lord.

God has chosen to display His glory through His followers – the church. His followers are vessels of mercy and that alone shows the riches of His glory – grace, mercy, forgiveness, and patience. But He has also prepared those vessels for glory. That is part of "glory share." God shares His glory with His followers and, as bearers of His glory, they display His glory to the world.

But there is preparation. The vessel must be prepared to contain and to display His glory. The phrase "beauty of holiness" is appropriate. A person who lives in purity, innocence, and humility displays a beauty that is seen by all. The beauty of holiness, for which Pastor Martin prays, displays the glory of the Lord.

> **Meditation:** Ask the Lord to show His desire to you for revealing His glory in you. Then pray the prayer of Pastor Martin. Seek the Lord about how His glory can be displayed in your life. Write what He shows you in your journal.

☩ ☩ ☩ ☩ ☩ ☩ ☩

NOTES:_____

_____

_____

_____

_____

_____

_____

_____

_____

_____

_____

IV. Week Eleven, Day 3 (Date:)   **GLORY**

> Then God said, "Let us make man in our image, after our likeness. And let them have dominion over the fish of the sea and over the birds of the heavens and over the livestock and over all the earth and over every creeping thing that creeps on the earth."
> So God created man in his own image, in the image of God he created him; male and female he created them. And God blessed them. And God said to them, "Be fruitful and multiply and fill the earth and subdue it, and have dominion over the fish of the sea and over the birds of the heavens and over every living thing that moves on the earth." **Gen 1:26-28**

Let them have dominion.

What is the glory that God reveals in us? What does it mean to be made in God's image and then conformed to the image of Christ (Rom 8:29)? I tend to think of glory in terms of radiance, light, magnificence, and splendor, and "glory" can have that connotation.

Haley Jacob suggests a further and different perspective on glory. After exhaustive research, she writes that a Hebrew word for glory that is often interpreted as "weight" or "heaviness" can also mean "honor." The Greek word for glory that is often interpreted as "light" often means "honor, status, wealth, and possession" as attributed to "power, authority, character, and riches." Ms. Jacob connects Romans 8:29 to the passage in Genesis 1 above.[103]

Humanity's glorified physical status described in the Genesis 1 passage above is-

- we are made in the image of God;
- we are to be fruitful (note that fruitfulness leads to dominion); and
- we have dominion over all other things living on earth.

Time and again, the Old Testament foreshadows the New Testament using a tangible example to foretell a spiritual reality. The believer's glorified spiritual status in Christ is-

- (s)he is transformed into the image of Christ's glory;
- (s)he is fruitful in the kingdom (note that fruitfulness leads to dominion in the parables of the talents and the minas); and
- (s)he is given dominion to rule and reign with Christ in His kingdom.

Scripture tells us that the saints will rule and reign with Christ (Rev 5:10;

---

[103] Haley Goranson Jacob, *Conformed to the Image of His Son* pp.31ff, 82ff (IVP 2018).

22:5). But like the triumph of the Cross (See IV.Week Four, Day 4), it has been set in eternity, but is not yet fully manifested. The revelation of the saints in glory is a work of the Lord in process.

> **Meditation:** Spend time asking the Holy Spirit to reveal aspects of glory to you. You can consider the aspects of glory in this devotion or other aspects. Then ask the Holy Spirit to reveal how the glory of God will be poured out on you.

☩ ☩ ☩ ☩ ☩ ☩ ☩

NOTES:_____

_____

_____

_____

_____

_____

_____

_____

_____

_____

> It is fine to spend more than one day on a single devotion. Allow God to speak to your heart during the devotions. Explore what he reveals thoroughly in order to understand and to apply it fully.

IV. Week Eleven, Day 4 (Date:)   **GLORY**

> Therefore I endure everything for the sake of the elect, that they also may obtain the salvation that is in Christ Jesus with eternal glory. The saying is trustworthy, for: If we have died with him, we will also live with him; if we endure, we will also reign with him; if we deny him, he also will deny us; if we are faithless, he remains faithful— for he cannot deny himself. **2 Tim 2:10-13**

If we endure, we will also reign with Him.

Suffering and glory are inextricably linked in scripture. When Christ told His Father in John 17 that the hour had come to glorify the Son, He was preparing to be arrested, beaten, and crucified. For Christ the cross was necessary. *"O foolish ones, and slow of heart to believe all that the prophets have spoken! Was it not necessary that the Christ should suffer these things and enter into his glory?"* (Luke 24:25b-26). Christ was glorified as a result of His suffering. It was necessary.

But me? Well, I want to go straight to the glory – especially the part about reigning. This stuff about taking up my cross offends me. But my cross is necessary for the glory. The character which the cross works in me reveals the glory of the Father. It is the path that God has ordained.

It isn't that suffering automatically leads to glory. A person can suffer in bitterness, resentment, denial, and despair, and it may lead to little glory. The manner in which we suffer glorifies God. In fact, numerous times in scripture we are exhorted to rejoice in suffering (Rom 5:3, 2 Cor 7:4; James 1:2; 1 Pet 4:13).

The path to glory that God has chosen for His church travels through suffering and weakness. When the church imitates the Lamb of God and His passion, the glory of God is put on display. The way of the Cross is the path to glory – a glory that ultimately includes reigning in His power, not in our own power.

Meditation: Spend time on the concept of suffering well – suffering in a way that displays the glory of God. Consider the importance of glorifying God in the middle of suffering. Why is there an emphasis in scripture on joy in times of trial and tribulation? Write your thoughts in your journal.

☦ ☦ ☦ ☦ ☦ ☦ ☦

IV. Week Eleven, Day 5 (Date:)   **GLORY**

> He will render to each one according to his works: to those who by patience in well-doing seek for glory and honor and immortality, he will give eternal life; but for those who are self-seeking and do not obey the truth, but obey unrighteousness, there will be wrath and fury.
> **Rom 2:6-8**

Dominion and freedom.

My son, you cannot possess perfect liberty unless you wholly renounce yourself (Matt 16:24; 19:21).

Bound in fetters are all they who seek their own interest, and are lovers of themselves – covetous, inquisitive, wandering in a circle, seeking ever soft and delicate things, not the things of Jesus Christ, but oftentimes devising and framing that which will not stand. For it shall perish altogether, whatever is not born of God.

Keep this short and perfect word: Let go all and you shall find all; leave desire and you shall find rest. Weigh this thoroughly in your mind, and when you have fulfilled it you shall understand all things.[104]

Dominion has responsibility. It is a basic principle of authority. In order to be free to rule over nature, I must have dominion over my own flesh and natural appetites (disordered desires). I can have many types of appetites:

- Appetites for possessions and money.
- Appetites for fame and popularity.
- Appetites for illicit sex and titillation.
- Appetites for food.
- Appetites for power and control.
- Appetites for drugs and alcohol.
- Appetites for what excites my will.
- Appetites for prestige and honor.
- Appetites for entertainment.

I cannot exercise dominion over nature outside of me when I do not have dominion over nature inside of me. To many, denying carnal appetites is a form of suffering. Certainly, it is a form of sacrifice or surrender.

When I yield to my fleshly appetites, I am overcome by them and become enslaved to them. Bondage to appetites is a deception of the world today. Society values a "freedom" to pursue worldly appetites rather the true freedom (and dominion) that comes from mastering worldly appetites. The

---

[104] *The Imitation of Christ*, p. 157.

"freedom" that the world offers actually leads to bondage. This passage from Romans describes this dynamic. Using the logical conclusions of evolutionary theory, the world allows nature and animals to dictate behavior to it instead of exercising dominion over its animal instincts.

But God has called me to freedom and to dominion. My freedom results from the character of Christ that God works within me. The freedom of Christ leads to His glory and dominion.

> **Meditation:** Spend time discerning the links between freedom and dominion. How does exercise of your freedom in Christ in obedience to His will and righteousness lead to dominion?

✝ ✝ ✝ ✝ ✝ ✝ ✝

NOTES:

IV. Week Eleven, Day 6 (Date:)   **GLORY**

> Now the Lord is the Spirit, and where the Spirit of the Lord is, there is freedom. And we all, with unveiled face, beholding the glory of the Lord, are being transformed into the same image from one degree of glory to another. For this comes from the Lord who is the Spirit.
> **2 Cor 3:17-18**

Beholding the glory of the Lord.

Transformed by Beholding!

Who but You, Father, could come up with something so rich, so unique, so powerful, and life-giving! What an awesome way to work the needed changes into our lives, while enriching and blessing us at the same time.

What glory there is just in beholding You. But for there to be the added bonus of transformation into Your nature and character at the same time is overwhelming! Help me to make use of this truth today by spending hourly time "beholding," looking to You, meditating on who and how You are!

Come and change me, step by step, more and more into the glory that is You! O how I need You!   -Pastor Daniel Martin, 12/18/13

A. W. Tozer says that faith is the gaze of the heart at God and that the gaze is but the "raising of the inward eyes to meet the all-seeing eyes of God."[105] Both A. W. Tozer and Pastor Martin encourage the believer to spend time to behold the glory of the Lord. This beholding is something that can only come from the Lord through His Spirit.

As I learn to behold, I am transformed and changed by what I see. One area of transformation is compassion. As I see the love in the eyes of the Lord for that person that I don't like, that is repulsive to me, or that has offended me, it changes my heart and my attitude toward that person. I become more compassionate and thus more suitable to exercise authority.

There is glory of the Lord reflected in countenance. That glory can be the radiance (or brightness) which shone on the face of Moses after he spent time with the Lord (Ex 34:29ff). But that glory can also be other attributes reflected in countenance such as authority, honor, compassion, and love.

> **Meditation:** Ask the Holy Spirit to help you behold the glory of the Lord. Set aside time to spend with Him and to behold Him. Record in your journal what you see.

---

[105] *The Pursuit of God*, p.62.

IV. Week Eleven, Day 7 (Date:)   **GLORY**

> And when he had taken the scroll, the four living creatures and the twenty-four elders fell down before the Lamb, each holding a harp, and golden bowls full of incense, which are the prayers of the saints. And they sang a new song, saying, "Worthy are you to take the scroll and to open its seals, for you were slain, and by your blood you ransomed people for God from every tribe and language and people and nation, and you have made them a kingdom and priests to our God, and they shall reign on the earth."
> Then I looked, and I heard around the throne and the living creatures and the elders the voice of many angels, numbering myriads of myriads and thousands of thousands, saying with a loud voice, "Worthy is the Lamb who was slain, to receive power and wealth and wisdom and might and honor and glory and blessing!"
> And I heard every creature in heaven and on earth and under the earth and in the sea, and all that is in them, saying, "To him who sits on the throne and to the Lamb be blessing and honor and glory and might forever and ever!"
> And the four living creatures said, "Amen!" and the elders fell down and worshiped. **Rev 5:8-14**

Meditation: Review your notes for this week. Then spend time with this passage. Use this passage as a catalyst to join in the heavenly praise which it describes.

☩ ☩ ☩ ☩ ☩ ☩ ☩

NOTES:_____

_____

_____

_____

_____

SECTION IV – POWER AND GLORY: WEEK TWELVE

IV.Week Twelve, Day 1 (Date:)   **THE BRIDE**

> Husbands, love your wives, as Christ loved the church and gave himself up for her, that he might sanctify her, having cleansed her by the washing of water with the word, so that he might present the church to himself in splendor, without spot or wrinkle or any such thing, that she might be holy and without blemish. **Eph 5:25-27**

So that He might present the church to Himself in splendor.

The Bride is radiant. The church will be presented as a bride to Christ in splendor. In her splendor, the church will be holy and without blemish – pure, clean, and radiant. The church will have no spot or wrinkle.

But this passage about the church is a passage for faith. This passage does not describe the church that I now see. Realistically, it doesn't describe my church because I belong to it. There are times when I observe the assembly of believers and ask "How can God be involved in this mess?" I need His eyes to see the splendor and perfection of the church.

But the point is not that the church accomplishes this radiance. Christ performs the sanctification and cleansing by the washing of water with the word. He has the power and authority to bestow this splendor. We are only grateful recipients of His gracious desire for an unblemished Bride.

> **Meditation:** This week focuses on the destiny of the church as the bride of Christ. During this week, ask God to give you a vision for the glorification of the church in this role. Spend time envisioning a holy, perfect, and unblemished people of God presented in splendor to Christ. How do you see yourself as part of this bride? Write your thoughts in your journal.

☩   ☩   ☩   ☩   ☩   ☩   ☩

> This section on the Bride is a good time to experience the perfect love of Christ. Allow yourself time to give and receive Christ's love as you meditate on the spiritual union between Christ and His Bride.

IV. Week Twelve, Day 2 (Date:) **THE BRIDE**

> Then I heard what seemed to be the voice of a great multitude, like the roar of many waters and like the sound of mighty peals of thunder, crying out, "Hallelujah! For the Lord our God the Almighty reigns. Let us rejoice and exult and give him the glory, for the marriage of the Lamb has come, and his Bride has made herself ready; it was granted her to clothe herself with fine linen, bright and pure"— for the fine linen is the righteous deeds of the saints.
> And the angel said to me, "Write this: Blessed are those who are invited to the marriage supper of the Lamb." And he said to me, "These are the true words of God." **Rev 19:6-9**

For the fine linen is the righteous deeds of the saints.

I have attended many weddings under many circumstances. I have seen brides of many shapes, sizes, races, and ages. But there is one constant: The bride is always beautiful.

A number of years ago, a family member became engaged to a young lady. I met her and she did not seem real pretty. I thought "Oh my, I hope he loves her. She is not very attractive!"

But at the wedding I was amazed. She was beautiful! I even asked myself "How is it possible for her to look so beautiful?" But she did!

The Bride is beautiful. In this passage, the Bride is adorned with fine linen, bright and pure.[106] The writer explains that the fine linen is the righteous deeds of the saints.

Note that the beauty of the bride is not just internal virtue. The beauty of the bride emanates from action – righteous deeds. Righteous deeds include acts of service, acts of sacrifice, acts of mercy, acts of kindness, kingdom proclamation, giving, obedience, and worship. The list is voluminous.

Everyone sees the bridal gown. It is a centerpiece of the wedding. The guests comment on it. Likewise, righteous deeds of the church are evident to all the world. Those deeds are put on display as proof of the glory of God which has been given to the church.

But the bride does not make herself beautiful for the guests. The bride makes herself beautiful for the Groom. Her adornment is not displayed for the guests. Her righteous deeds are performed out of love for, and out of devotion for, her Beloved.

---

[106] Rev 21:2 identifies the bride as "new Jerusalem" but from the context of this passage, it includes and probably refers to the saints, presumably as inhabitants of that city.

Meditation: Consider beauty in the form of virtue and purity. How lovely is a person of virtue? Then consider beauty that is seen by acts of service and acts of kindness. What types of beauty do they display? Apply that beauty to the church. What beauty does the church display when it does righteous deeds?

NOTES:

IV. Week Twelve, Day 3 (Date:)   THE BRIDE

> For I feel a divine jealousy for you, since I betrothed you to one husband, to present you as a pure virgin to Christ. But I am afraid that as the serpent deceived Eve by his cunning, your thoughts will be led astray from a sincere and pure devotion to Christ. **2 Cor 11:2-3**

A sincere and pure devotion to Christ.

One thing that I appreciate about my wife is that I have always been able to talk with her comfortably and compatibly. In fact, ease of conversation is one of the first things that attracted me to her. Many times during my marriage we have been on long car trips and talked for 2 or 3 hours straight while on the road.

After we had been married a number of years, my wife and I discussed our wedding. The church was pretty full. I asked her "How did you feel about all the other people at your wedding?"

Her response was "I didn't really care about the other people at the wedding. What I wanted was you!"

The Bride is devoted. She is single-minded in her focus on Christ and in her faithfulness to Christ.

Devotion has been an issue for the people of God. The perfidy of Israel led to all sorts of mayhem. The church historically has struggled in the areas of Trinitarian doctrine, the proclamation of the gospel, the authority of the Word, and cultural corruption. But I need to recognize that the inordinate attachments, disordered desires, search for comfort from people or things, fear of man, and addiction to possessions in my own life are also issues of bridal devotion.

Perhaps the strongest indication of devotion is chastity. Chastity before marriage is a manner in which a bride can be devoted to her husband.[107] My wife's devotion to me arose from her fidelity before marriage – even before she met me. And my confidence in her marital fidelity is strengthened by my knowledge of her chastity before she married me.

The Bride of Christ has a sincere and pure devotion to Him, and to no other.

> **Meditation:** Consider the importance of fidelity and devotion in marriage. Explore the feelings of devotion that you want from a spouse. Then explore your feelings of devotion to Christ. Respond to your feelings as you are moved in repentance, worship, and/or declaration. Ask the Holy Spirit to make you single-minded in your devotion to Christ.

---

[107] As in many areas, the same applies to a husband in marriage but our focus is on the Bride.

IV. Week Twelve, Day 4 (Date:) **THE BRIDE**

> In the same way husbands should love their wives as their own bodies. He who loves his wife loves himself. For no one ever hated his own flesh, but nourishes and cherishes it, just as Christ does the church, because we are members of his body.
> "Therefore a man shall leave his father and mother and hold fast to his wife, and the two shall become one flesh."
> This mystery is profound, and I am saying that it refers to Christ and the church. However, let each one of you love his wife as himself, and let the wife see that she respects her husband. **Eph 5:28-33**

The two shall become one flesh.

This I long for, that I may be wholly united unto Thee, and may withdraw my heart from all created things, and by means of sacred communion, and the frequent partaking thereof, may learn more and more to relish things heavenly and eternal. Ah, Lord God, when shall I be wholly made one with Thee, and lost in Thee, and become altogether forgetful of myself? Thou in Me, and I in Thee (John 15:4); so also grant that we may continue together in one. Verily, Thou art "my beloved...the chiefest among ten thousand" (Song of Sol 5:10), in whom my soul is well pleased to dwell all the days of her life.[108]

This scripture describes spiritual union. The love of the groom and the bride are so great that they become one flesh — one heart, one mind, one body, and one spirit.

The means of spiritual union is love. Through love, Christ and His Bride become one. Love in marriage is given and shared through feeling, action, respect, forgiveness, giving, sacrifice, compassion, service, affirmation, and intimacy.

Meditation: Set aside time for an exchange of love with the Lord. Spend time loving Him and receiving His love. Tell Him that you want to become one with Him in spiritual union. Then seek the Lord about how He desires to be loved by you. Ask Him what you can do to show your love for Him. Record what He shows you in your journal.

╬   ╬   ╬   ╬   ╬   ╬   ╬

---

[108] *The Imitation of Christ*, pp.246-247.

IV. Week Twelve, Day 5 (Date:)   **THE BRIDE**

> For in him dwelleth all the fulness of the Godhead bodily. And ye are complete in him, which is the head of all principality and power. **Col 2:9-10 (KJV)**

Fullness and completion.

My wife and I continued our discussion about our wedding. I asked her "What were you thinking as you were getting married?"

I anticipated a lengthy response about her feelings, fears, and hopes. But I was mistaken. She only had one word. She said "I can sum up my thoughts in one word: FINALLY!"

The Bride is complete. To the bride, marriage represents a culmination. She has spent her life preparing for this union. Now, her longing has been fulfilled. It is the fulfillment of all of her desires and dreams.

The Bride is complete because Christ has shared His fullness with her (Eph 1:22-23). Everything that He is, everything that He has, everything that He desires – He shares it with His Bride.

Not the least of these things is His love. The Bride is fulfilled because she is loved – fully, completely, wholly, and perfectly.

> **Meditation:** Focus on longing today. What longing do you have for Christ and for spiritual union with Him? Spend time telling Him about your longing. Then ask the Holy Spirit to reveal His longing for you. Allow His longing for you to wash over you. Feel His pleasure.

✡ ✡ ✡ ✡ ✡ ✡ ✡

NOTES:_____

_____

_____

_____

_____

IV. Week Twelve, Day 6 (Date:)   **THE BRIDE**

> The nations shall see your righteousness, and all the kings your glory, and you shall be called by a new name that the mouth of the LORD will give. You shall be a crown of beauty in the hand of the LORD, and a royal diadem in the hand of your God.
> You shall no more be termed Forsaken, and your land shall no more be termed Desolate, but you shall be called My Delight Is in Her, and your land Married; for the LORD delights in you, and your land shall be married. For as a young man marries a young woman, so shall your sons marry you, and as the bridegroom rejoices over the bride, so shall your God rejoice over you. **Isa 62:2-5**

You shall be called My Delight Is In Her.

My brother-in-law was the most excited bridegroom I have ever seen. His glee was such that he could barely contain himself. A couple of days before the wedding I rode with him in his car which he had named Arky. We stopped at a stop light and my brother-in-law's leg started bouncing on the floor board. "This is going to be great!" he exclaimed. "I can't believe I am getting married!"

Then he began slapping his leg repeatedly with the back of his hand. "Oh glory!" he shouted. "Glo-o-o-REE!" I just smiled. That guy was a pretty happy groom.

We are the betrothed. The Lord delights in you. Spiritual union is a primary Source of Joy. But the Lord has delight as well. His Bride is a source of deep and lasting joy for Him.

> **Meditation:** Tell the Lord the things that a bride would tell the groom – things like "You are desirable to me," "I give myself wholly to you," "I am Yours forever," "Let's have many (spiritual) children." There are many whisperings from a bride to a groom. Bring joy and delight to the Lord as you minister to Him.

☩   ☩   ☩   ☩   ☩   ☩   ☩

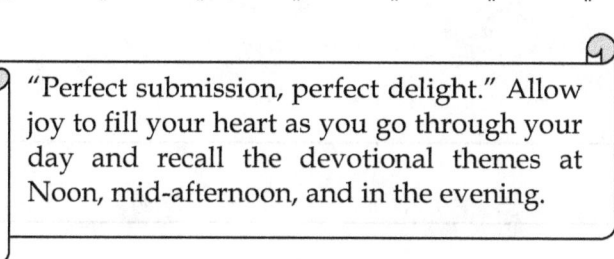

"Perfect submission, perfect delight." Allow joy to fill your heart as you go through your day and recall the devotional themes at Noon, mid-afternoon, and in the evening.

IV. Week Twelve, Day 7 (Date:)   **THE BRIDE**

Today is a day of review. Review your journal notes over the past week.

> **Meditation:** Today is a day of physical or artistic creativity. Use artistic or physical creativity to express the feelings, longings, and completion of the bride and groom. Whatever you do, offer it to the Lord as an expression of your heart and spirit.

☦ ☦ ☦ ☦ ☦ ☦ ☦

NOTES:_____

_____

_____

_____

_____

_____

_____

_____

_____

_____

_____

SECTION IV – POWER AND GLORY: WEEK THIRTEEN

(This final full week of Section IV is a practicum for the people of God. The focus of the devotions will be the word in 2 Chr 7:14. Pastor Martin told me he doesn't think that he has preached a sermon in the last six months without mentioning this scripture. 2 Chr 7:14 contains instructions when disaster strikes. The motivation is to seek forgiveness and healing for God's people and for their land.)

IV.Week Thirteen, Day 1 (Date:) **PRACTICUM: MY PEOPLE**

> Then the LORD appeared to Solomon in the night and said to him: "I have heard your prayer and have chosen this place for myself as a house of sacrifice. When I shut up the heavens so that there is no rain, or command the locust to devour the land, or send pestilence among my people, if my people who are called by my name humble themselves, and pray and seek my face and turn from their wicked ways, then I will hear from heaven and will forgive their sin and heal their land. Now my eyes will be open and my ears attentive to the prayer that is made in this place. For now I have chosen and consecrated this house that my name may be there forever. My eyes and my heart will be there for all time." **2 Chr 7:12-16**

If My people who are called by My name...

The Bride is called by His Name. As a Groom, God gives His Name to His people. A bride entrusts herself to her husband. He becomes her protector. He not only protects her safety; he also protects her heart. It is a blessing for His Bride based on identity.

This scripture passage occurs immediately after the glory of the Lord filled the temple at its dedication (See IV.Week One, Day 2). Then the Lord appeared to Solomon with special instructions for him, for the people, and for the temple. The glory which fell is analogous to the consummation of a marriage, and the words to Solomon are analogous to marriage vows. *"My eyes and My heart will be there for all time."*

God will fulfill His promise. He promises to put His Name on His people (Rev 3:12). As bearers of His Name, His people can call on Him when calamity occurs or when disaster strikes. Note that this scripture concerns the people of God, not just a specific tribe or nation. His name bearers act on His will and His instructions, and He promises to hear and to respond.

Meditation: Consider what it means for the Bride to take the name of her Husband. What is she communicating when she relinquishes her identity to Him? What does it mean to you that God calls you by His name and places it upon you? Are you willing to relinquish your identity to receive His name? Write your thoughts in your journal.

☩ ☩ ☩ ☩ ☩ ☩ ☩

NOTES:_____

_____
_____
_____
_____
_____
_____
_____
_____
_____
_____
_____
_____
_____

IV. Week Thirteen, Day 2 (Date:)   PRACTICUM: MY PEOPLE

> The LORD spoke to Manasseh and to his people, but they paid no attention. Therefore the LORD brought upon them the commanders of the army of the king of Assyria, who captured Manasseh with hooks and bound him with chains of bronze and brought him to Babylon. And when he was in distress, he entreated the favor of the LORD his God and humbled himself greatly before the God of his fathers. He prayed to him, and God was moved by his entreaty and heard his plea and brought him again to Jerusalem into his kingdom. Then Manasseh knew that the LORD was God. **2 Chr 33:10-13**

He humbled himself greatly before the God of his fathers.

What glory follows humility! <u>It's amazing how much our pride buys into the lie that pride will bring us glory!</u> Ugh! Pride is the very thing that leads to rottenness, corruption, and filth! There is no eventual glory in pride. Any "glory" that seems to be connected to our pride quickly becomes stripped, leaving us in a pile of ashes, losses, and filth. Ugh! What lies are always connected to pride! How horrible for me to believe the lies and to trust the webs that pride spins!

Lord, deliver me from pride. Help me to embrace the path of humility, to diligently ward off all the tentacles of pride that try to ensnare my life! O God, I need help here. My flesh and ego are not in agreement with this, but I am! Help me to say no to my flesh and ego and to take the path of humility!

The next afternoon as I was walking from the building to the car, You showed me that the 4 issues in 2 Chr 7:14 are not just like running the four bases—they are also to be compared with the four corner pillars that a house rests on. If any one of them is missing, is weakened enough, the house collapses in that section, leading to the eventual collapse of the whole house if it is not corrected and repaired—repented of and cleansed.

<u>Humility is one of those bases/pillars!</u> O God, show me clearer how important it is that I increasingly:

    1. Humble myself!

    2. Pray!

    3. Seek Your face, presence!

    4. Turn from My wicked ways!

Humility is connected to Forgiveness! How full of pride is all bitterness and unforgiveness! When I am unforgiving, I am failing to see how broken and needy I am—focusing only on the wrongs of others instead of my own—glossing over my wrong, while focusing in on the wrongs of others—what Pride!

O help me to humble myself and forgive—considering others better than myself!
   -Pastor Daniel Martin, 11/7/12

By all accounts, Manasseh was a wicked king. He erected altars to the Baals, made Asheroth, and worshipped all the host of heaven (2 Chr 33:3). The Lord warned him and the people but they paid no attention. So the Lord gave Manasseh into captivity.

But in his distress, Manasseh humbled himself greatly before the Lord and prayed. The Lord is merciful and compassionate and eager to forgive. As great as Manasseh's sins were, the Lord still heard his prayer and restored him to his throne. The heart of the Lord is close to the humble.

> **Meditation:** Today is a day to humble yourself before the Lord. Ask the Holy Spirit to show you any vestige of pride, bitterness or unforgiveness. "Do business" with the Lord in those areas as needed. Then put yourself in a physical position of humility as you bring entreaty and petitions before Him about the land in which you dwell.

☦ ☦ ☦ ☦ ☦ ☦ ☦

NOTES:_____

_____

_____

_____

_____

_____

_____

> Remember to seek the Presence of God in your time dedicated to Him. To the extent you are able, invite the Holy Spirit to move in you and around you during your devotional time.

IV. Week Thirteen, Day 3 (Date:)   **PRACTICUM: MY PEOPLE**

> And they said to me, "The remnant there in the province who had survived the exile is in great trouble and shame. The wall of Jerusalem is broken down, and its gates are destroyed by fire." As soon as I heard these words I sat down and wept and mourned for days, and I continued fasting and praying before the God of heaven. And I said, "O LORD God of heaven, the great and awesome God who keeps covenant and steadfast love with those who love him and keep his commandments, let your ear be attentive and your eyes open, to hear the prayer of your servant that I now pray before you day and night for the people of Israel your servants, confessing the sins of the people of Israel, which we have sinned against you. Even I and my father's house have sinned.
>
> "We have acted very corruptly against you and have not kept the commandments, the statutes, and the rules that you commanded your servant Moses." **Neh 1:3-7**

Hear the prayer of your servant that I now pray before You day and night.

"I...have sinned." "We have acted very corruptly against You." **By all accounts, Nehemiah was a righteous man. He walked closely with God, praying regularly. But consider how he prayed. He took the part of his people in confessing their sins against God.**

Daniel was likewise a righteous man. But when Daniel prayed, he also confessed the sins of Israel as his own. "*[W]e have sinned and done wrong and acted wickedly and rebelled, turning aside from your commandments and rules...To us, O LORD, belongs open shame, to our kings, to our princes, and to our fathers, because we have sinned against you*" (Dan 9:5, 8).

"We...us...we." In their intercession, Daniel and Nehemiah demonstrate two significant principles that are necessary for restoration of a community. The first principle is Corporate Responsibility. Corporate responsibility means that a person who is a part of a body, a community, or even a nation, bears its burdens. If there is guilt in a people, as part of that people, the righteous person assumes responsibility for it. It is not that he personally is guilty. As an intercessor, he "steps in between" and addresses it with the Lord "on behalf of" his people, just as Nehemiah and Daniel did.[109]

Prayer is the second base (or pillar) of 2 Chr 7:14. The prayers of Nehemiah (Nehemiah 1) and Daniel (Daniel 9) occurred when the people of Israel were in distress, shame, and captivity. But these righteous and godly men repented on behalf of their people and entreated God for restoration.

---

[109] *The Call: Book Three – Fruitful (Transforming Your Community)*, pp.32-33.

Corporate responsibility is the first principle – the idea that a person who is part of a body, a community, or a nation, shoulders its sins and transgressions. That person, as an intercessor, repents of them on behalf of his people.

The second principle is Brokenness. The godly person, in intercession, assumes the brokenness of his people. That brokenness is a catalyst for both humility and for prayer.

> **Meditation:** Spend time reading the prayers in Nehemiah 1 or Daniel 9 (or both). Use these prayers as a model of prayer for your people that God lays on your heart – such as your community, your city, or your nation. Pray these models to God and try to be faithful in them day by day until God hears and intervenes.

☦ ☦ ☦ ☦ ☦ ☦ ☦

NOTES:_____

_____

_____

_____

_____

_____

_____

_____

_____

_____

IV. Week Thirteen, Day 4 (Date:)   PRACTICUM: MY PEOPLE

> Then the king said to the wise men who knew the times (for this was the king's procedure toward all who were versed in law and judgment, the men next to him being Carshena, Shethar, Admatha, Tarshish, Meres, Marsena, and Memucan, the seven princes of Persia and Media, who saw the king's face, and sat first in the kingdom).
> **Esther 1:13-14**

Seek My face.

I will seek You in the morning! O Bring me back to this truth of my deep need of seeking You – First, Hourly, Intensely. Help me to it right now!

5:44-5:52 AM on my knees. What You showed me during that time:

There are two basic areas to seek You about:

I. You and my relationship with You.

- **Knowing You. Philippians 3:10 (AMP), 2 Peter 3:18**
- **Becoming more like You. 2 Corinthians 3:18**
- **Holiness and purity. Psalm 139:23-24, Psalm 51:6, 10-13**

II. What You have to say about my world and how I am to respond to it today.

- **The events and concerns that I now know about this day.**
- **The events that I know nothing about at this point—need for Guidance, for power, anointing, grace, peace, etc. Isaiah 33:6, Jeremiah 10:23-24, Proverbs 3:5, Psalm 25:3-4, etc.**

O God! You have opened up a door of understanding and of deep need in my life with the revelation that came to me in just 8 minutes of seeking You, waiting on You this morning! Let this grow in me! Cause me to respond to You in this and not just "have more info" that I do nothing about!

Plow deeper in my life and heart in this matter. Come and show me my deep need of this Hourly! Help me to Hourly apply the things You have shown me here! Let this be a real turn around for me in areas I know nothing about right now—as well as areas I do know about!

I must grow in this matter of SEEKING You!   –Pastor Daniel Martin, 8/13/15

"Seek My face" is Pastor Martin's third base (or pillar) of 2 Chr 7:14. Seeking God is an expectation that God has of His people, and it is frequently commanded and exemplified in scripture (Psa 27:8; Hos 5:15).

But why does God instruct His people to seek His face instead of just to seek Him? To see the face of a person is an indication of intimacy. When I look into the face of my wife, there is an immediate connection. In her face, I can see her beauty, her emotions, and her reactions. Many times, I believe I can see her heart.

In the context of royalty, the persons who see the face of the King are in a position of privilege. As the scripture above says, they "sat first" in the kingdom.

So seeking countenance is also seeking favor. "Lifting up of countenance" is looking on a person with favor. Those princes who saw the face of the King were able to do so because they had favor with Him.

The exhortation to seek God's face is an exhortation to seek His favor to hear, to forgive, and to heal.

> **Meditation:** Spend time seeking God's face. Ask Him to look upon you and upon your community, city, tribe, or land. As you ask Him for favor, be open for a word, a nudge, or movement from Him. Make a commitment to continue to seek His face in the coming days.

✝ ✝ ✝ ✝ ✝ ✝ ✝

NOTES:_____

_____

_____

_____

_____

_____

_____

_____

IV. Week Thirteen, Day 5 (Date:)   PRACTICUM: MY PEOPLE

> As it is, I rejoice, not because you were grieved, but because you were grieved into repenting. For you felt a godly grief, so that you suffered no loss through us.
> For godly grief produces a repentance that leads to salvation without regret, whereas worldly grief produces death. For see what earnestness this godly grief has produced in you, but also what eagerness to clear yourselves, what indignation, what fear, what longing, what zeal, what punishment! At every point you have proved yourselves innocent in the matter. **2 Cor 7:9-11**

And turn from their wicked ways.

According to the above, there is 'sorrow God wants us to have' and there is 'sorrow God wants us to experience.' Worldly sorrow, which lacks repentance, results in spiritual death. Godly sorrow has the power to PRODUCE in me:

- **earnestness and carefulness**—about what sin can do in my life, etc.
- **clearing of ourselves** (from missing the mark)
- **indignation** (about missing the mark in my life)
- **alarm** (about what missing the mark can do in my life, can damage me and others, etc.)
- **fear** (about the above things)
- **zeal, vehement desire** (to be free from missing the mark, to be free from every impurity, everything that is not like You, does not honor You, etc.)
- **readiness to punish wrong** (primarily in myself more than in others!)

O God, give me deep Godly sorrow over the things I have allowed to grow in my life, knowingly and unknowingly. Help me to never excuse the sins in any way.

My flesh wants to minimize them, to gloss over them, but the only thing that will actually deal with them is the blood, repentance, Godly sorrow, and confession of them. O, help me to cling to these "four biggies"—Blood, confession, Godly sorrow, repentance!

I need this in my life today. Help me to hourly allow confession and Godly sorrow over what You have exposed to flow in my meditation!   -Pastor Daniel Martin, 12/21/12

The fourth base (or pillar) is to turn from their wicked ways. The turning not only has to be in desire, in attitude, and in word, but it also has to be in action – in reality.

Information and knowledge in modern times has expanded dramatically and access to information and knowledge has increased exponentially. But that has led to a curse in our times: <u>We think that if we know something, then we control it and we have mastered it.</u> In fact, we know many things that are wrong or harmful but that doesn't mean that we have turned from them and repented of them with Godly sorrow.

The transformation in 2 Chr 7:14 is active. It is a corporate turning as the people of God. We turn away from our wicked ways so that we reject them and put them behind us. In that turning, we turn toward God. We accept His ways, and we walk in them.

Worldly sorrow condemns and thus results in death. Godly sorrow brings life because the grace that is freely given and because of the genuineness of the turning to God in my life.

> **Meditation:** Identify the areas of brokenness and wickedness of your community, nation, tribe, or land. Ask the Holy Spirit to put them on your heart. Write them down in your journal.
>
> Next, discern how these areas impact your own life or your church. Ask God to show you if you need to turn from any of these areas so that you can turn to Him. Seek the Holy Spirit about Godly sorrow for that area, and then turn away from it and turn toward Him.
>
> Finally, use these areas of brokenness or wickedness as an impetus to ask the Lord to hear, to forgive, and to heal your land.

☩ ☩ ☩ ☩ ☩ ☩ ☩

NOTES:_____

_____

_____

_____

_____

_____

_____

_____

IV. Week Thirteen, Day 6 (Date:)　　　　**PRACTICUM: MY PEOPLE**

> "Come, let us return to the LORD; for he has torn us, that he may heal us; he has struck us down, and he will bind us up.
> "After two days he will revive us; on the third day he will raise us up, that we may live before him. Let us know; let us press on to know the LORD; his going out is sure as the dawn; he will come to us as the showers, as the spring rains that water the earth." **Hos 6:1-3**

Let us press on to know the Lord.

In Daniel 9, Daniel grasped God's plan that the "desolations of Jerusalem" would be completed in seventy years as "revealed" by the prophet Jeremiah (Dan 9:2). He immediately began interceding for his people in accordance with God's revealed will.

Revelation of God's intentions for a community leads to effective intercession for it. It is a matter of revelation <u>and</u> timing. If Daniel or Nehemiah had begun intercession for the people of Israel seventy years earlier, that intercession would not have been effective! Seventy years earlier, God told Jeremiah not to intercede for his people. "As for you, do not pray for this people, and do not lift up cry or prayer for them, and do not intercede with Me; for I do not hear you" (Jer 7:16). God's revealed will is the key.[110]

God's people turn to Him in trust, because they know Him and they know His heart.

Part of this trust is trust in His power, in His timing, and in His plan and purpose for His people. His people may not see His kingdom fully manifested at this time. But He will build His kingdom and He will perfect His Bride.

This trust is an impetus to pursue the promises outlined in 2 Chr 7:14 – to humble, to pray, to seek His face, and to turn from their wicked ways.

> **Meditation:** Seek God for His heart for your community, tribe, city, or nation. How is He working and moving in that area now? What is His will for that area? How does He want to work? As God reveals, or moves your heart, intercede to Him and act accordingly.

☦　　☦　　☦　　☦　　☦　　☦　　☦

> Remember to meet with your mentor or devotional partner to share what the Lord shows you about His people and His plans.

---

[110] *The Call: Book Three – Fruitful (Transforming Your Community)*, p. 30.

IV. Week Thirteen, Day 7 (Date:) **PRACTICUM: MY PEOPLE**

> After this I looked, and behold, a great multitude that no one could number, from every nation, from all tribes and peoples and languages, standing before the throne and before the Lamb, clothed in white robes, with palm branches in their hands, and crying out with a loud voice, "Salvation belongs to our God who sits on the throne, and to the Lamb!"
> And all the angels were standing around the throne and around the elders and the four living creatures, and they fell on their faces before the throne and worshiped God, saying, "Amen! Blessing and glory and wisdom and thanksgiving and honor and power and might be to our God forever and ever! Amen." **Rev 7:9-12**

Today is a day of vision. Look back over your journal for the last week.

Meditation: Spend time envisioning what the worship of God around the throne will look like. Ask the Holy Spirit to direct you. See the glory. Hear the sounds.

Next, envision what it looks like for the Lord to bless His people on earth – to hear from heaven, to forgive their sin, and to heal their land. Ask the Holy Spirit to give you vision of this blessing from 2 Chr 7:14. Write down what the Lord shows you.

☦ ☦ ☦ ☦ ☦ ☦ ☦

NOTES:_____

_____

_____

_____

_____

_____

IV. Final Day (Date:)   **LOVE**

> Deep calls to deep at the roar of your waterfalls; all your breakers and your waves have gone over me.
> By day the LORD commands his steadfast love, and at night his song is with me, a prayer to the God of my life. **Psa 42:7-8**

At night His song is with me.

You, and You alone are Worthy of all glory, honor, praise, and surrender! And You are so Worthy of it all! You gave up far more than I could ever dream or imagine for my sake, for me, one so unworthy!

Surely, I, the recipient of so much can return the favor in my feeble, weak, impoverished ways! I feel like a little child who wants to please and bless his mother, so I go out, knowing she likes beautiful flowers, and pick some flowery weed and bring it in to her, thinking she will be ecstatic over my wonderful offering— AND SHE IS!

She is starved to find any measure of love for herself from me, so she is overwhelmed with the offering of mere trash, looking beyond its worthlessness to my heart's attempt to please her. She makes over it as if that is the greatest gift she has ever received, and even views it that way.

O how much You delight over the smallest of gifts, signs of love for You as Your feeble, dirty, nasty sheep make signs of wanting to please, bless, glorify, magnify, and delight You!! O how awesome and powerful Your great love for Your creation is!!

How awesomely patient, kind, and wonderful You are to me in all Your ways! O the glory of Your Presence, of Your great purity and love for us!
    –Pastor Daniel Martin, 6/16/20

Today we sense the pleasure of God. Once I faced a difficult circumstance and could not see any good in it. But I committed to trust God despite what I felt. That evening, as I was spending time in devotion, I sensed how much it pleased God that I trusted Him in that crisis. Such pleasure!

As a loving Parent, God takes pleasure in our love and in our devotion to Him. He loves children even when we fail, mess up, or present flowery weeds to Him. So we end this devotional journey as we began it – with the love of God. Love is our destination. *His song is with me.*

God delights in the love of His people who bear His name. He desires to lavish Himself upon them.

> **Meditation:** Spend time with the Lord and ask Him about His pleasure. Ask Him to show you the pleasure that He feels because of you. Ask Him to place His song in your heart.

FINAL ENCOURAGEMENT

You have reached the end of this book, but you have not reached the end of your devotional journey. Please continue faithful and steadfast in your devotional time which will keep you in times of danger, feed you in times of stress, and preserve you in times of trial. *Joy comes in the morning* (Psa 30:5).

It is often helpful to use a devotional book as a guide for your devotions. There are many good devotional books and writings that can assist you. But also consider repeating *Surrender and Trust* at some point. Now that you have experienced it, maybe you can serve as a mentor or spiritual guide to another believer who wants to go through it.

Second, to build on your devotional life, consider the "daily office." The daily office can take many forms, but essentially, it is a discipline to keep your heart and mind in tune with the Holy Spirit throughout the day. Even if I have engaged in a wonderful devotion at the beginning of the day, the busyness of my work and of my life often lead me away from the Presence and direction of the Holy Spirit. Using the discipline of daily office, a believer has set times of the day that are used to re-orient toward the Lord and renew the focus on Him. Research the daily office and consider adding to your devotional life by incorporating more than one time a day for worship, reading, meditation, and/or prayer. This discipline can enrich your life and increase your ministry to those around you. Even five minute pauses ("resets") can make a difference.

Third, continue to seek God and His call on your life. We are always seeking Him and His face. God has a spiritual path and destiny for you. We find and follow that path through continual prayer and through seeking.

One exercise that can assist in discerning call is a spiritual life history, also called a Life Tapestry or a spiritual autobiography. A prompt for writing a spiritual life history is on the website *www.surrenderandtrust.net*. After you write your spiritual life history, share it with your mentor or spiritual director and discuss it together. That process can help in discernment.

Finally, there is love. Live in love, walk in love, grow in love, and share love. His perfect love is our destination, but He desires for us to experience His love throughout our journey in this life and into eternity.

Amen.

David Thurman

12/25/20

APPENDIX A

DISCERNMENT: A PROCESS FOR MAKING GODLY DECISIONS

"When the Spirit of truth comes, He will guide you into all the truth…" (Jn 16:13a)

A significant part of devotional discipline is seeking the Lord and His will in a matter. Guidance and decision making are difficult areas for many believers. We are faced with large decisions in our walk with the Lord, and we are faced with seemingly small decisions every day that may actually be just as important to our spiritual journey as the "large decisions."

Since every person and every circumstance is different, there is not one correct way to discern a matter and to make a decision. But there are principles and practices that can be helpful. The following summary (Preparation, Principles, and Process) is not exhaustive, but it may contain steps, guidelines, or practices that prove useful.

A. PREPARATION.

(Preparation is a time to discern your heart and to gather information. Effective discernment rarely occurs in a vacuum but in a place of prayer, stillness, and silence and in communion with other trusted persons, so that your voice and thoughts are not the only things you hear. It is helpful to write down answers to the questions and then to refine the answers as more clarity comes.)

1. To the extent you are able, clarify the core issue for which you seek guidance.

2. Discern the attitude of your heart. Empty yourself of fleshly desires, pride, and worldly attachments. Seek the freedom only to desire God's will in the matter and not your own.

-Commit your life to God and give Him control of it.

3. What are the options available? (Note: Many times another trusted person such as a mentor or spiritual director may see options that you do not see).

-Marshal information about the circumstances under which the decision is being made.

4. What will be the impact of each option (on you and on other people)?

-What responsibilities has God entrusted to you (such as family, church, community, workplace)?

5. As you explored the options and their impact, did you have an instinctive reaction regarding the decision (such as an intuition or a "gut feeling")?

6. Which option will increase your hunger for God?

-For each option that you identify, where and how do you see God working in each option?

7. How do you feel about each option based on your desires (personal or spiritual)?

-How will each option affect your identity in God and His call upon your life?

8. What are historical patterns in your life or personal tendencies that may influence your decision?

-Have you experienced deception previously in your life that might be relevant to this decision?

B. <u>PRINCIPLES OF DISCERNMENT</u>.

(Note: These principles should be applied in conjunction with each other and used in balance. Undue focus on one principle to the exclusion of the other principles can be unbalanced and thus dangerous.)

1. Whatever pleases God is the best decision for you.

-A good decision invites the Presence of God.

-A good decision is motivated by love for God.

2. A good decision is consistent with obedience to God.

-A decision should always be in accordance with the commands of Scripture, and not contrary to Scripture.

-A decision should be made with an attitude that desires to submit to every authority as established by God.

3. Be true to yourself and to your identity in God.

-You should desire to fulfill God's call on your life, including the hopes and dreams that He has placed within you.

4. God has placed creativity in us and often desires to unlock and to free our creative spirit.

-God wishes for us to experience joy in Him.

5. Your eternal soul is more important than this earthly life.

-Eternal consequences are more important than the temporal consequences.

6. A good decision will draw you closer to God and will increase your faith, hope, and love.

-A bad decision will lead you further away from God and will decrease your faith, hope, and love.

7. God often gives us past experiences that direct our present path.

-Our hearts and minds are often deceived.

8. Positive feelings that do not have an external cause (such as worldly blessing, honor, or personal affirmation) probably come from God.

-Positive feelings that have an external cause can come from God or from the enemy.

9. *The wisdom from above is first pure, then peaceable, gentle, open to reason, full of mercy and good fruits, impartial and sincere* (James 3:17).

-Feelings that are very strong or that vacillate may not come from God.

-The fruit of the Spirit is evidence of God's work in your life.

10. Sometimes God calls you to be still and to allow Him to act in your situation on your behalf.

-Don't make an important, life changing decision while you are adrift spiritually or feel separated from God by worldly desires.[111]

C. PROCESS.

(The Preparation and Principles above may have already led you to a clear decision. If you engage in the process below, record your impressions and keep notes.)

1. Dedicate time to seek God about your decision and to seek His will in the matter.

-Seek God using spiritual disciplines (such as prayer, worship, fasting, meditation, and contemplation).

2. Spend time listening to God and sensing nudges, promptings, or words.

-Seek and listen to the wisdom and advice of other persons you trust (including church leaders, spiritual directors, and accountability partners).

3. Seek God's perspective on your situation.

–Desire to know the heart of God in the matter. It is critical that you do so without attachment to an outcome or without specific expectations, and in a spirit of freedom to allow the Holy Spirit to direct you.

4. For each option that you identified, write down (a) the factors that support the option; (b) the factors against the option; (c) possible benefits from the option; and (d) possible detriments from the option.

---

[111] Source Material for some Principles: *The Spiritual Exercises of St. Ignatius*.

-Employ the means of discernment through the Holy Spirit that are beneficial (such as intuition (A.5), imagination (A.6), feelings (A.7), memory (A.8), reason (C.4 above), your body, or nature).[112]

5. To the extent that you are able, wait on God in the matter. Seek Him and His timing.

-Is God calling you to do something now or should you wait and do nothing?

6. As you begin to reach a decision, discern if that decision is consistent with a love of God and will increase your faith, hope, and love in its fulfillment.

7. When you reach a decision, seek confirmation by God.

–Are you at peace in the decision and at rest in God as a result of the decision?

8. As you walk out your decision, does the peace of God remain?

-If you realize the decision does not increase your faith, hope, and love, should you change course and try another option?

---

[112] See Elizabeth Liebert, *The Ways of Discernment* (WJK 2008) for exercises for discernment in each of these areas.

APPENDIX B

MEME'S KEYS TO RESTORE WOUNDED SOULS

1. Love the unlovable. Shower the wounded person with love. Demonstrate kindness and care for the person. Establish a foundation of love in the relationship. In order to receive ministry, the person must know that you love her and she must trust you. "People need love the most when they deserve it the least."

2. Listen to the person patiently, especially when the person describes the wounds that person has suffered. Meme had good practice at listening. She lived with Jimmy.

3. When Meme spoke, she spoke from a place of humility and showed respect for the person. Meme had the experience and authority to "speak into" someone's life, or to address them as a superior. But Meme instead came alongside a person and spoke gently as an equal.

4. Serve the person and meet her needs. Wounded souls were beneficiaries of mercy and compassion from Meme, and that cultivated a sense of value and worth in them.

5. Address areas of needed correction without condemnation. From her platform of love, Meme corrected detrimental or dysfunctional actions or thoughts, but did it in a way that was not judgmental or demeaning to the person.

6. Encourage forgiveness by the person toward people that have wounded her. Forgiveness is the gateway to grace.

7. Meme knew the value of work to the person who did the work. Meme expected that anyone in the household would contribute his/her share to it. If training was needed, so be it, she slowed down to give it. However, in her posture of constantly serving, she also realized that everyone ought to "work in order to eat" and do what was needed to keep things running smoothly.

8. Always people over things. This care communicated honor to the person and showed how much Meme valued her. How many times did we see her turn from food preparation at the kitchen counter, or put some sewing handwork down, because she realized that a conversation with another person required her full attention that moment?

When I was a child, Meme would play a game with me while she sewed. We set up the game in front of her sewing station. I don't think Meme cared about the game, but she played the game because she knew it pleased me.

9. Model love, communication and family function. Those souls who visited

the Martin home or who lived in the home saw how Meme and Papa lived. Observing functional family dynamics helps to acquire those dynamics, but also stimulates hope for the forlorn.

10. Find areas of mutual interest. Then do things together with the wounded person in those areas. Working together toward a common goal can create a strong bond.

11. Maintain a good confession and attitude. Monitor what you say or think. Replace negativity with positivity. When the person expressed negative thoughts or expectations, Meme graciously suggested positive alternatives. "I am not going to believe that will happen" or "Let's think that [a good alternative] will happen instead."

12. Identify good traits and gifts in the person. Underscore those traits and gifts. Encourage healthy habits. Find ways that person's gifts can be applied and put into action. Meme specialized in discerning positive characteristics in people, in large part because she looked for them. Helping a person grow in her gifts helps to restore her esteem and increase the sense of worth.

13. Pray for that person - intensely and frequently. No person in the household rose earlier than Meme. She rose well before the sun (normal time was 4:00 AM) in order to spend time in the Word and prayer. Meme kept a prayer notebook filled with names, places, and prayer requests that she prayed through daily. Meme's prayer fueled her daily, and fueled her love and concern for the people around her.

14. Pray with that person. Any concern, crisis, or celebration was a matter for prayer and worship.

"A bruised reed He will not break, and a dimly burning wick He will not snuff out; He will faithfully bring forth justice" (Isa 42:3, quoted in Matt 12:20) (NASB).[113]

---

[113] By the author, with contributions by Sharon Freeman.

APPENDIX C

ENGAGING WITH CHRIST IN EVERYDAY LIFE

A TEMPLATE By Steve Parker

"When something doesn't agree, remember to TTD!"

Our lives are designed to be our classroom. Each day can bring opportunities to hear from God, to learn from Him, and to move forward in our relationship with Him in Christ. Here is a simple template you can apply to any challenging situation you encounter that will cause it to yield beneficial results.

- **THANK** God for the challenge.
- Ask God what He is trying to **TEACH** you from the challenge.
- Ask God what He wants you to **DO** in response to the challenge.

As you can see, the first letter of the key word in each step, "THANK," "TEACH," and "DO" creates the acronym "TTD." Putting that into a simple rhyming phrase creates a valuable mnemonic device that you can draw on when facing a difficult situation: *"When something doesn't agree, remember to TTD!"* But how do I apply it? Read on.

God's desire is that you walk in peace and that you join Him in the perfect union that He has with His son, Jesus. He will gladly take us on a journey to move us in that direction if we allow it. One of the signature hallmarks of this union is a deep abiding rest that is not dependent upon what is going on in the world around you. Whenever something happens that triggers strong negative emotions, and takes away your peace, this feeling is a good indication that something inside you has been activated that does not belong in this united life. Usually this is connected to a part of our life that is not yet sanctified and is not yielded to the Holy Spirit. Therefore, through the experience, you have an opportunity to identify this area and offer it up to God for His healing, cleansing, and an interaction that leads to a greater depth of relationship. You are being offered a chance to go further along the highway to union with God!

The above outline offers three simple steps you can take whenever you encounter a situation or interaction that is taking away your peace. Learning to apply it may take some effort and intentionality at first. But if you begin to implement it and stick with it, you will not only find it becomes easier, you will begin to see really positive results as God uses it to transform you more and more from the inside out and to draw you closer and closer to Him.

The following information is designed to explain the purpose and Scriptural basis of each of the three steps in the template.

I.   **(T) THANK God.**   I Thessalonians 5:18 reads *"Give thanks in all circumstances, for this is the will of God in Christ Jesus for you."* Three important elements here:

A.   In what kind of circumstances are we supposed to give thanks? ALL! Not just those that make us feel good. Not just those where we believe we've received something valuable. Not just those times when we're not having difficulties and life looks okay. No! God says that we are to give thanks even when our life appears to be falling apart. Even when we've just received bad news.   God's will is that we give thanks in EVERY circumstance.   We frequently pray that God's will be done. Well, when we give thanks, we are bringing God's will to fruition.

B.   Note that the passage doesn't say "Give thanks FOR all things." This is not a commandment to thank God for the horrible tragedy that just occurred. But we are to give thanks IN all things. That means that even when a tragedy does strike, instead of lamenting how awful it is, we need to turn our hearts toward heaven and remember that God is with us in the midst of the circumstance. We can be thankful for His presence and for His promise to bring good out of even the worst situation (Romans 8:28).

C.   This is God's will for us "in Christ Jesus." This gratitude is impossible to accomplish on our own. As fallen, human creatures bound to our emotional states, it is challenging to set aside the hurt, pain, and anger we may feel when confronted with a negative situation. But in Christ it is possible because He lives in a state of perpetual rejoicing and gratitude in relationship with His Father. And because He lives in us, we have access to this as well. So we can turn to Him to accomplish this seemingly impossible goal, and through the power of the Holy Spirit, we will receive what we need to do it!

But why is thankfulness the first step in our template for growing in Christ? Because gratitude frees us up to hear from God. When we encounter a challenging situation through which God desires to draw us to Himself, the negative emotions that arise keep us from hearing. Most people have grown accustomed to letting their emotions define their reality. If I'm having positive emotions such as joy or enthusiasm, I usually define the situation as positive. If I'm angry, sad, or in pain, I look at the matter at hand as negative. For us to be able to receive insight from God as to what is actually happening means we have to set aside our emotions and become attuned to the Spirit. Gratitude helps to accomplish this by shifting our emotions from negative to positive.   After all, it's hard to be upset about something if you are experiencing Thanksgiving. Further, you are releasing faith through this act because we are trusting that God is Who He says He is. We are believing that He is good and He is powerful and He is able to redeem our current situation for good. This shift away from emotional turmoil toward gratitude and faith positions us to be able to hear God clearly, which leads us to step two.

II.	**(T)** *Ask God "What are you trying to TEACH me?"* *"If any of you lacks wisdom, let him ask God, who gives generously to all without reproach, and it will be given him…But the wisdom from above is first pure, then peaceable, gentle, open to reason, full of mercy and good fruits, impartial and sincere. And a harvest of righteousness is sown in peace by those who make peace"* (James 1:5, 3:17-18). There are also three major elements here upon which we want to focus.

A.	God's wisdom is available to those who ask. The Apostle Paul exclaims in Romans 11:33, *"Oh, the depth of the riches and wisdom and knowledge of God!"* God is filled with wisdom and longs to make us wise. And all we have to do is ask! So we can turn a challenging situation into a learning opportunity. Call out, "God teach me! What do you want me to learn here?"

B.	Several characteristics of God's wisdom are listed here, but the one upon which we are focused is that it is "peaceable." God's wisdom brings peace. And remember, peace is one of the hallmarks that we are seeking in union with God. This is one of the ways that leads us into God's rest (Heb 4:9-11).

C.	The peace we are entering into leads to righteousness. This process is likened to growing a garden. As we partake in God's wisdom in every situation we encounter, it is as if we are receiving divine seeds into our life. The result is a harvest of righteousness. Our life begins to look more and more like our King as we become closer and closer to Him.

Once we have stilled our inner self by moving into a position of gratefulness, we are able to perceive what God is saying. It is important here to realize that God has MANY things He wants to show us, and we could easily be overcome if we were to receive it all at one time. So we are only interested in what He wants to show us at this time. We don't have to try to figure it out. We just have to ask. And we need to be open to whatever He wants us to see. At any given time, we may be carrying a list of things that we believe we need to do to be a better Christian. But God may not really be concerned about any of those things at the moment. There may be a matter that's completely off our radar that He wants to bring to our attention. So we listen attentively, realizing that we may not see anything right at that moment. It may be the next day or the next week before we see it. But God will give us something. All we have to do is ask and be open.

III.	*Ask God, "What do you want me to DO?"* Often, this question is where we go first when our emotions get stirred. We want to DO something to make things better. And oftentimes we make poor choices and end up doing things that make matters worse or that we often regret. When we are following this template, however, we don't make those mistakes because we are no longer being moved by our emotions. We have moved from a place of turmoil to gratitude and peace, and now we can use the wisdom that God gives us to make wise choices concerning courses of action. Ephesians 2:10 says, *"For we are his workmanship, created in Christ Jesus for good works, which God prepared beforehand, that we should walk in them."* From this scripture we can see that:

A. God has works for us to do. We are designed to do things. We have been given power and energy to impact the people and world around us. We are meant to make a difference.

B. He has determined beforehand what those works are. He does not expect us to figure out what we are to do in a situation all on our own. In fact, that's often the question that plagues people who face difficult circumstances: "What am I going to do?" Someone once said that they felt like there were demons sent from hell to sit on our shoulder and just say, over and over, "What are you going to do? What are you going to do?" Well, the good news is, God knows what you need to do. He has a course of action for you!

C. We walk with Christ in the works that we do. We have been reborn into His eternal life, and the power to do what he wants comes as we walk with Him in that life. The more closely we walk with Him, the greater the power we have to do the works He asks us to do. This is a further indication of the power of applying this template to our lives. This template is designed to lead us into closer communion with the Lord, transforming us into His image which empowers us to live Godly lives. We find that we are no longer struggling to do the right thing. Instead, we are living a life of right choices that flows out of our relationship with Christ.

There is one thing we need to bear in mind as we put this third step in place. Even though we are created to DO, sometimes (or many times), the Lord may want us to DO… NOTHING! That's right. He may just want us to focus on what He is teaching us and wait for the Holy Spirit to move in our situation. This waiting is often hard for us because, as I said earlier, we often feel like we NEED to do SOMETHING! However, our "doing" often gets in the way of God working to accomplish His purposes in a situation. Sometimes he just needs us to step aside and wait for Him to act. During these times, our character is being formed. We are learning to be still, to wait patiently, and to trust God. These are often the times that are most effective at drawing us into a greater union with God. And from this place of peace, if there comes a time for us to act, we will know with certainty what it is. And then, instead of getting in God's way, we will be partnering with Him to further His work in the matter.

Examples of Practical Application:

The Lord wants to use all of the elements of our life to draw us closer to Him. Many times, people feel that it is only in the major experiences of their life that they really receive wisdom from God. But God wants to use all things, both big and small, to help us on our journey toward becoming more like Him. Here are some of my personal examples of how this template can be applied to every aspect of life.

1. My life with Bill.

Part of my testimony is how God changed my life while I was in prison on drug-related offenses. I was locked up for a little over a year, and the whole experience was like a custom-designed school of the Spirit. God taught me SO much during that year. A lot of it is what resulted in understanding the power of applying this template to the events of my life.

One of the experiences that really drove this home for me was a situation I faced with a fellow inmate named Bill. That's not his real name, but he represents a real person. In this prison, I was in what was called a dormitory, but it was really just a huge building with long rows of bunk beds. I had a bunk about half-way down one of those rows, and Bill was in the bunk right next to me. Bill had been in prison about 20 years and had originally been incarcerated for murder. He was also about twice my size. So Bill was a little scary. And Bill didn't care for me at all. He didn't like me; he didn't like my religion. And he let me know this quite frequently.

Bill worked in the laundry, so he was usually up before everybody else. And sometimes he would grab hold of my bunk and just jerk it to wake me up. That gives you an idea of the kind of relationship we had.

This irritation went on for a while, and I got really tired of it. And so I started praying and asking God to do something about it. And being the deeply spiritual person that I was, I asked God if he would just maybe kill Bill. It sounds ridiculous now, but that's a sign of the anger and hurt that I was carrying deep inside of me. I was so angry at Bill that it would have pleased me to see him die. Well, as you might have guessed, God didn't kill him. He did something much better.

You know, most people have things that happen in their life that are stuck in their memory forever because they have such an impact. What I'm getting ready to tell you about is one of those things. One day I was walking from the restroom to my bunk. And I was about half-way there when all of a sudden I heard a voice in my head go, "You know, you could try forgiving and loving Bill!"

I froze in my tracks and it felt like water was rushing all over my body. It was amazing - the power of the moment. And it was as if a switch had been flipped in my brain and I said to myself, "Oh! I'm supposed to be loving Bill!" So from that time on, I changed my attitude toward Bill. It was at this point that I started applying the TTD template.

Step 1: (T) Give God THANKS. I started praying for Bill on a regular basis, and most importantly, I started thanking God for my experience with Bill. I thanked Him for putting me in the bunk next to Bill. I thanked him for Bill's life. As I did this every day, the part of my heart where the hatred and anger towards Bill resided began to change. The darkness that lived there began to be replaced with the light of God. I was now in a position to hear from God what I was supposed to be learning in this situation.

Step 2: (T) Ask God what He's trying to TEACH me. The more thankful I became, the more I could see God's love for Bill. I began to truly understand how God's love for a person was based on God's nature, not on how much I cared for the person! That may sound silly, but I believe it is common for people to ascribe value to others based on their view of that person. I was beginning to see how much God loved everyone, including Bill. I also saw more clearly how God could take the hard things in my life and turn them into a blessing. Before I started praying for Bill, I harbored murderous intent in my heart toward him, all the while professing the name of Jesus. I now saw how limited my understanding of Jesus' character was, and became willing to let Him change me.

Step 3: (D) Ask God what He wants me to DO. As I continued to be thankful for Bill and pray for God's wisdom, I began to ask God if there was anything I needed to do. There was! I was fortunate enough to have family who was sending me money each week, so I was able to buy candy at the prison canteen. Candy is a big deal in prison. A lot of inmates don't have the resources to buy these "luxuries." God showed me to begin offering to share my candy with Bill.

Now at first, he was suspicious, but slowly things began to change between us. I wouldn't say we became friends, but we developed a respect for one another. And he even began asking me to pray for some of the things that were going on in his life.

Now I don't know how Bill was impacted in the long run. I would love to say that he ended up giving his life to Christ, but I don't know. But what I do know is that I was changed! A dark place in my heart that harbored evil was transformed into a place where the spirit of God lived. And I came to know Christ in a much deeper way. And not only that, but the people around me saw that change. They saw the different way I was responding to Bill, and they saw the change in our relationship, and the change in me. God was glorified through this experience. People could see clearly how powerful He is, and how good He is. And all of this happened because I remembered to TTD.

2.   My life with Sadie
A more recent experience in my life demonstrates how God can use all things to draw us closer to him, even a puppy dog. My wife, Susanne, and I recently were given a puppy. We named her Sadie. She was a rescue dog, and we didn't know a lot about

her. But we felt that she was a gift from God. In fact, I had a dream about us getting a dog a couple days before we received her.

At first, she seemed gentle and well-suited for our quiet home life. We were able to housebreak her without too much trouble, and she seemed intelligent and well-behaved. As time went on though, Sadie became more and more energetic. We would be sitting on the sofa and she would come flying into the living room and just leap into the air at high speed and land on one of us. Sometimes this was actually painful, she was moving so fast. Some days, it seemed she forgot all about being housebroken and would just pee where she was. And she developed a desire for attention, and not just part of the time. All of the time! I found myself growing quite frustrated. All of a sudden, our gift from God did not seem like such a great present.

Then, one morning, we had a breakthrough! I remembered the TTD template! My wife and I began to apply it to the situation with Sadie.

Step 1. (T) Give God THANKS. We put the first step into place and thanked God. We not only thanked him for Sadie, we thanked him for the good things that were going to come out of what He would teach us through Sadie being there.

That's when the breakthrough happened. As we were praying and giving thanks to God for our dog, Sadie came over directly in front of us, looked straight at me, and then squatted and peed!

You were probably thinking that the breakthrough was going to be that the dog started behaving, right? Well, not exactly. The breakthrough was that, at the time she started peeing, I didn't get mad or feel frustrated. Instead I stayed in that position of gratitude and felt the peace of God, even as the dog was doing the exact thing I didn't want her to do.

Step 2. (T) Ask God what He's trying to TEACH me. After cleaning up Sadie's mess, I spent some time asking God what He was trying to teach me. I began to see that I had control issues that I had not yet offered up to God. My need to feel safe and at ease in my home environment meant that I wanted everything to be just so. And while that is understandable, God wants us to be willing to give up every element in our life. Was I willing to give up my need to be in control in order to have deeper communion with God, trusting Him to be my source of security as opposed to feeling safe because my home was in order and under control? Of course I was. But the truth is, I would not have realized I needed to look closely at that area of my life without the blessing of Sadie's misbehavior. Now my gratitude moved from a place of obedience to a place of gratitude for what I received.

Step 3. (D) Ask God what He wants me to DO. After reflecting upon this for a while, I went to the next step in the template and asked God what He wanted me to do. I immediately sensed that He desired me to show more patience toward Sadie. After all, she was only six months old! I had an impression that my tone needed to become more gentle and my correction more kind.

At the time of this writing, this experience is only a few days old. We are seeing what appears to be some positive changes in Sadie's behavior. And while that's certainly a good thing, the most important thing is that I am changed. An area in my heart that needed to be in control has now been offered up to God and is being filled with His presence instead. My walk today is closer with the Lord than it was a week ago, thanks to a rambunctious pup named Sadie and a template to use in every situation I encounter, big or small. Whether you're dealing with a murderer in the bunk next to you or a challenging puppy, God has a plan to make it work out for your good. Thank you, God for Sadie, and thank you for your guidance.

When something doesn't agree, remember to TTD!

[Steve Parker is the President and Founder of FOCHUS Ministries (**www.fochus.org**). He can be contacted at steve.parker@fochus.org.]

APPENDIX D
LIST OF IDOLS

Key Thought: An idol is not just something that you worship as god. An idol is not just something that you worship instead of the One True God.

1. An idol is any longing, any thought, or any possession that keeps you from a total surrender to God.

2. An idol is that affection that keeps you from a complete devotion to God.

3. An idol is any source of personal security (a relationship, a nest egg, or even a comfort food) that prevents your full trust in the Lord in all things.

4. An idol is that really special gift or talent that has become your personal trademark instead of the Lord your God's imprint on your life.

5. An idol is a wound in your soul that keeps you in bondage and hinders you from an unfettered pursuit of God.

6. An idol is a fleshly longing that blocks clear direction and guidance from the Lord.

7. An idol is any desire that you have that is lies outside of God's desire for His kingdom. It is a personal need for attention or praise from others that keeps you from being united with God's will for the lives of the brothers and sisters around you – which is His body, the church.

8. An idol is a personal goal (maybe even an achievement) that is not fully aligned with God's desire for your life.

9. An idol is a cultivated bitterness – an offense - that hinders you from experiencing the fullness of Jesus Christ and His loving grace.

10. An idol is a performance-based reputation that focuses others on yourself rather than on Christ in you, the hope of glory (Col 1:27).

11. An idol is a misguided mindset – a wrong belief – that prevents intimate knowledge of the Holy One and His redemption.

12. An idol is a personal habit or routine that hampers you from living a godly lifestyle that pleases the Lord.

13. An idol is that area of worry that regularly renders you anxious or stressed.

14. An idol is that secret pleasure that you cling to – that "precious" in the words of Golem – that has a self-destructive impact on you and blocks your heart from a pure and unadulterated love for the Lord.

APPENDIX E
FULL INDEX OF DEVOTIONS

<u>SECTION III – TRUST</u>

Week One: Contrition

Day 1: *The Lord alone shall be exalted in that day.*

Day 2: *To worship God in truth is to acknowledge Him to be what He is, and to acknowledge ourselves to be what we are.*

Day 3: *Therefore I despise myself, and repent in dust and ashes.*

Day 4: *Fear of You and humility.*

Day 5: *I am the foremost of sinners.*

Day 6: *Associate with the lowly.*

Day 7: *Review – Magnificat of Mary.*

Week Two: Sources of Pride

Day 1: *Adam was not deceived.*

Day 2: *You in your lifetime received your good things.*

Day 3: *Those who walk in pride He is able to humble.*

Day 4: *The foolishness of God is wiser than men.*

Day 5: *He likes to put himself first.*

Day 6: *This story hurts my heart.*

Day 7: *Review – Sources of Pride*

Week Three: The Shema

Day 1: *Hear, O Israel!*

Day 2: *With all of your mind.*

Day 3: *A loud cry in the ears of God.*

Day 4: *The Lord has brought you out with a mighty hand.*

Day 5: *I would have been false to God above.*

Day 6: *For the love of money is a root of all kinds of evils.*

Day 7: *Review – The Shema*

Week Four: Control

Day 1: *I believe in You, O Lord, Maker of the heavens and the earth.*

Day 2: *I too am a man set under authority.*

Day 3: *In the very next second of my life, I am in need of You.*

Day 4: *We take every thought captive to obey Christ.*

Day 5: *Take My yoke upon you.*
Day 6: *The Father Who sent Me has Himself borne witness about Me.*
Day 7: *Review – Control*

Week Five: Submission

Day 1: *God shares His authority with people.*
Day 2: *"The Lord forbid that I should do this thing to my lord, the Lord's anointed."*
Day 3: *"I did not know, brothers."*
Day 4: *Obey your leaders and submit to them.*
Day 5: *In order to make sure I was not running or had not run in vain.*
Day 6: *There is a friend who sticks closer than a brother.*
Day 7: *Review – Submission*

Week Six: Love One Another

Day 1: *You are not far from the kingdom of God.*
Day 2: *This is My commandment, love one another as I have loved you.*
Day 3: *People need love the most when they deserve it the least.*
Day 4: *You go and do likewise.*
Day 5: *We ought to lay down our lives for the brothers.*
Day 6: *Outdo one another in showing honor.*
Day 7: *Review – Day of Gentleness*

Week Seven: Judgment

Day 1: *You who are spiritual…*
Day 2: *For with the judgment you pronounce, you will be judged.*
Day 3: *"Woman, where are they? Has no one condemned you?"*
Day 4: *We tried to stop him..*
Day 5: *"Man, who made Me a judge or arbitrator over you?"*
Day 6: *He did not presume to pronounce a blasphemous judgment.*
Day 7: *Review – Judgment*

Week Eight: Consolation and Desolation

Day 1: *No good thing does He withhold from those who walk uprightly.*
Day 2: *The people of Israel cried out to the Lord.*
Day 3: *The king made silver as common as stone.*
Day 4: *I will make a way in the wilderness and rivers in the desert.*

Day 5: *Constant practice.*
Day 6: *Stay awake at all times, praying that you might have strength.*
Day 7: *Review – Consolation and Desolation*

Week Nine: Offense
Day 1: *See to it...that no root of bitterness springs up and causes trouble.*
Day 2: *He should come and apologize to me!*
Day 3: *What is the purpose of my approach?*
Day 4: *How have I been wrong in the matter?*
Day 5: *How is God working in this situation?*
Day 6: *What rights are You calling me to surrender to You?*
Day 7: *Review – Offense*

Week Ten: Power of Confession
Day 1: *His face fell.*
Day 2: *The man and the wife hid themselves.*
Day 3: *Shame exposed.*
Day 4: *Confess your sins to one another.*
Day 5: *He who does not slander with his tongue and does no evil to his neighbor.*
Day 6: *Father, I have sinned against heaven and before you.*
Day 7: *Review – Power of Confession*

Week Eleven: Power of Forgiveness
Day 1: *So are My ways higher than your ways.*
Day 2: *So also my heavenly Father will do to every one of you if...*
Day 3: *Lord, do not hold this sin against them.*
Day 4: *Come now, let us reason together.*
Day 5: *Do not be overcome by evil, but overcome evil with good.*
Day 6: *As the Lord has forgiven you, so you also must forgive.*
Day 7: *Review – Power of Forgiveness*

Week Twelve: Goodness of God
Day 1: *He treats me in all respects as His favorite son.*
Day 2: *Benefits of the kingdom of God.*
Day 3: *Do I really believe in the goodness of God?*
Day 4: *Blessed is the one who is not offended by Me.*

Day 5: *The truth will set you free.*
Day 6: *Seventy-seven times.*
Day 7: *Review – Goodness of God*

Week Thirteen: Practicum - Stillness
Day 1: *Let all the earth keep silence before Him.*
Day 2: *No one comprehends the thoughts of God except the Spirit of God.*
Day 3: *Today we focus on breath.*
Day 4: *Today is a day to yield pain, wounds of the heart, or discomfort to the Lord.*
Day 5: *His voice was like the roar of many waters.*
Day 6: *A habitual, silent, and secret communion of the soul with God.*
Day 7: *Today is the seventh day, a day of rest.*

SECTION II – POWER AND GLORY

Week One: Power
Day 1: *Serve Him with a whole heart.*
Day 2: *For He is good, for His steadfast love endures forever.*
Day 3: *My wife shall not live in the house of David king of Israel.*
Day 4: *He had 700 wives, who were princesses.*
Day 5: *Did not Solomon king of Israel sin on account of such women?*
Day 6: *They love the place of honor.*
Day 7: *Review – Power*

Week Two: The Cup
Day 1: *Shall I not drink the cup that the Father has given Me?*
Day 2: *Get thee behind Me, Satan!*
Day 3: *The Romans will come and take away both our place and our nation.*
Day 4: *The cup that I drink you will drink.*
Day 5: *Always carrying in the body the death of Jesus.*
Day 6: *He killed James the brother of John with the sword.*
Day 7: *Review – The Cup*

Week Three: Weakness
Day 1: *For the weapons of our warfare…have divine power to destroy strongholds.*
Day 2: *My power is made perfect in weakness.*
Day 3: *That through the church the manifold wisdom of God might now be made known.*

Day 4: *Christ also suffered for you, leaving you an example, so that you might follow in His steps.*
Day 5: *I am sending you out as sheep in the midst of wolves.*
Day 6: *Do they now throw us out secretly? No!*
Day 7: Review – Weakness

Week Four: Triumph

Day 1: *I am filling up what is lacking in Christ's afflictions for the sake of His body, that is, the church.*
Day 2: *Worthy are You to take the scroll and to open its seals for You were slain and by Your blood ransomed people for God.*
Day 3: *This He set aside, nailing it to the cross.*
Day 4: *At present, we do not yet see everything in subjection to Him.*
Day 5: *We are the aroma of Christ to God.*
Day 6: *That you may also rejoice and be glad when His glory is revealed.*
Day 7: Review – Triumph

Week Five: Refiner's Fire

Day 1: *I will put this third into the fire.*
Day 2: *The Lord tests hearts.*
Day 3: *Let those of us who are mature think this way.*
Day 4: *Share in suffering for the gospel by the power of God.*
Day 5: *We went through fire and through water; yet You have brought us out to a place of abundance.*
Day 6: *And the appearance of the fourth is like a son of the gods.*
Day 7: Review – Refiner's Fire

Week Six: Leadership

Day 1: *The Son of Man came not to be served but to serve, and to give His life as a ransom for many.*
Day 2: *None of the rulers of this age understood this.*
Day 3: *So that your faith may not rest in the wisdom of men but in the power of God.*
Day 4: *Clothe yourselves, all of you, with humility toward one another.*
Day 5: *Talking wicked nonsense against us.*
Day 6: *And they recognized that they had been with Jesus.*
Day 7: Review – Leadership

Week Seven: Fear of Man

Day 1: *People want a king.*
Day 2: *Teaching as doctrines the commandments of men.*
Day 3: *There is no fear in love.*
Day 4: *The fear of man lays a snare.*
Day 5: *For you did not receive the spirit of slavery to fall back into fear.*
Day 6: *Whoever is ashamed of Me and of My words in this adulterous and sinful generation.*
Day 7: *Review – Fear of Man*

Week Eight: The Cave

Day 1: *Lord, take away my life, for I am no better than my fathers.*
Day 2: *Woundedness connects to the original offense and to any offenses that follow after it.*
Day 3: *O LORD, You have deceived me.*
Day 4: *No man so feels as he who suffers.*
Day 5: *I will be the most proud man in that prison!*
Day 6: *Although He was a Son, He learned obedience through what He suffered.*
Day 7: *Review – The Cave*

Week Nine: Generational Thinking

Day 1: *Elisha the son of Shaphat of Abel-meholah you shall anoint to be prophet in your place.*
Day 2: *Elijah passed by him and cast his cloak upon him.*
Day 3: *Elisha, the son of Shaphat is here, who poured water on the hands of Elijah.*
Day 4: *Our ceiling is their floor.*
Day 5: *Surely the land on which your foot has trodden shall be an inheritance for you and your children forever.*
Day 6: *Did not my heart go with you?*
Day 7: *Review – Generational Thinking*

Week Ten: Truth – Restoration

Day 1: *Behold, I will send you Elijah the prophet.*
Day 2: *Thus he comforted them and spoke kindly to him.*
Day 3: *Keep your voice from weeping and your eyes from tears, for there is a reward for your work.*
Day 4: *Full of days.*
Day 5: *The hand of the Lord was with them.*
Day 6: *Therefore I send you prophets and wise men and scribes.*
Day 7: *Review – Restoration*

Week Eleven: Glory

Day 1: *Glorify Your Son that the Son may glorify You.*

Day 2: *Vessels of mercy which He has prepared beforehand for glory.*

Day 3: *Let them have dominion.*

Day 4: *If we endure, we will also reign with Him.*

Day 5: *Dominion and freedom.*

Day 6: *Beholding the glory of the Lord.*

Day 7: *Review – Worthy is the Lamb!*

Week Twelve: The Bride

Day 1: *So that He might present the church to Himself in splendor.*

Day 2: *For the fine linen is the righteous deeds of the saints.*

Day 3: *A sincere and pure devotion to Christ.*

Day 4: *The two shall become one flesh.*

Day 5: *Fullness and completion.*

Day 6: *You shall be called My Delight Is In Her.*

Day 7: *Review – The Bride*

Week Thirteen: Practicum: My People

Day 1: *If My people who are called by My name…*

Day 2: *He humbled himself greatly before the God of his fathers.*

Day 3: *Hear the prayer of your servant that I now pray before You day and night.*

Day 4: *Seek My face.*

Day 5: *And turn from their wicked ways.*

Day 6: *Let us press on to know the Lord.*

Day 7: *Review – Practicum: My People.*

Final Day: *At night His song is with me.*

APPENDIX F
INDEX OF SCRIPTURE PASSAGES
(Listed by book of the Bible with devotional page number)

Reference	Page	Reference	Page
Gen 1:26-28	264	2 Kings 2:9-10	244
Gen 3:6-12	106	2 Kings 3:10-11	243
Gen 4:3-10	104	2 Kings 13:20-21	248
Gen 4:23-24	136		
Gen 45:3-8	99	1 Chr 28:6-10	149
Gen 50:15-21	252		
		2 Chr 7:1-3	151
Deut 3:23-27	22	2 Chr 7:12-16	279
Deut 6:4-9	25	2 Chr 8:11-13	152
Deut 7:6-8	30	2 Chr 33:10-13	281
Josh 14:6-14	246	Neh 1:3-7	283
		Neh 13:23-27	156
Jdg 3:7-10	83		
		Esther 1:13-14	285
1 Sam 8:6-8	216		
1 Sam 8:18-20	216	Job 31:24-28	32
1 Sam 24:3-7	49	Job 42:5-6a	6
1 Sam 30:3-4,6	39	Job 42:12-17	256
1 Kings 10:21, 27	85	Psa 15	112
1 Kings 11:1-4	154	Psa 27:13-14	132
1 Kings 18:46-19:4	227	Psa 34:5	116
1 Kings 19:9-10	228	Psa 42:7-8	291
1 Kings 19:11-14	232	Psa 62:5	145
1 Kings 19:14-18	239	Psa 66:8-12	199
1 Kings 19:19-21	241	Psa 84:10-12	81
		Psa 139:23-24	97

Pro 15:33	...	7
Pro 17:3	...	193
Pro 18:24	...	56
Prov 29:25	...	222
Songs 4:16a	...	142
Isa 1:18	...	122
Isa 2:10-17	...	3
Isa 6:5a	...	6
Isa 30:15a	...	146
Isa 41:10	...	143
Isa 42:1-4	...	70
Isa 43:19	...	87
Isa 55:6-9	...	117
Isa 62:2-5	...	277
Jer 9:23-24	...	5
Jer 20:7-11	...	230
Jer 31:15-17	...	254
Eze 1:28b	...	6
Dan 3:16-18, 23-26		201
Dan 4:27-37	...	17
Hos 6:1-3	...	289
Hab 2:20	...	140
Zech 13:8-9	...	192

Mal 4:4-6	...	251
Matt 7:1-5	...	73
Matt 10:16-22	...	177
Matt 11:2-6	...	134
Matt 11:27-29	...	43
Matt 12:20	...	70
Matt 15:7-9	...	218
Matt 16:21-24	...	161
Matt 18:15	...	94
Matt 18:21-35	...	119
Matt 23:1-7	...	157
Matt 23:33-35	...	258
Mark 8:35-37	...	29
Mark 8:34-38	...	225
Mark 9:38-40	...	76
Mark 10:32-40	...	164
Mark 10:41-45	...	203
Mark 12:28-34	...	27, 58
Mark 12:29b-31	...	35
Luke 1:46-55	...	12
Luke 5:8b	...	6
Luke 6:37-38	...	131
Luke 7:2-10	...	37
Luke 10:25-37	...	64
Luke 12:4-5	...	234
Luke 12:13-15	...	77
Luke 15:20-32	...	114
Luke 16:19-31	...	15
Luke 21:36	...	90

Luke 23:33-34a	129
John 5:37-40 ...	44
John 8:2-11 ...	74
John 8:31-36...	135
John 11:45-53..	162
John 15:9-13 ...	60
John 17:1-5 ...	261
John 18:10-12..	159
Acts 4:13-14 ...	213
Acts 7:54-8:1a..	121
Acts 11:19-22 ...	257
Acts 12:1-3 ...	168
Acts 16:34-40..	178
Acts 23:1-5 ...	51
Rom 2:6-8 ...	267
Rom 8:1 ...	80
Rom 8:14-17 ...	223
Rom 9:21-24 ...	262
Rom 12:14-21...	124
Rom 12:16 ...	11
Rom 13:1-2, 5...	47
Rom 15:1-3 ...	62
1 Cor 1:18-25 ...	19
1 Cor 2:1-5 ...	207
1 Cor 2:6-8 ...	205
1 Cor 2:9-11 ...	141
1 Cor 6:5-10 ...	101

2 Cor 2:14-16...	187
2 Cor 3:17-18...	269
2 Cor 4:6-12 ...	166
2 Cor 5:18-21...	96
2 Cor 7:9-11 ...	287
2 Cor 10:3-6 ...	171
2 Cor 10:5-7 ...	41
2 Cor 11:2-3 ...	274
2 Cor 12:5-10...	172
Gal 2:1-2 ...	55
Gal 6:1-7 ...	71
Eph 3:8-12 ...	174
Eph 5:25-27 ...	271
Eph 5:28-33 ...	275
Php 3:7-15 ...	195
Col 1:16-18 ...	36
Col 1:24-29 ...	181
Col 2:9-10 ...	276
Col 2:13-15 ...	184
Col 3:12-14 ...	126
1 Tim 1:15-16 ...	9
1 Tim 2:13-14 ...	13
1 Tim 6:8-12 ...	33
2 Tim 1:8-12 ...	197
2 Tim 2:10-13...	266

Reference	Page
Heb 2:6-10	185
Heb 5:7-8	236
Heb 5:11-14	88
Heb. 12:1-2	108
Heb 12:14-16	92
Heb 13:7, 17	53
James 2:1-9	68
James 5:14-16	110
1 Pet 2:19-23	176
1 Pet 4:12-14	189
1 Pet 5:5-9	209
1 Jn 3:16-18	66
1 Jn 4:15-19	219
3 Jn 1:9	21
3 Jn 1:9-12	211
Jude 1:6-10	78
Rev 1:14-15	144
Rev 1:17a	6
Rev 5:1-10	182
Rev 5:8-14	270
Rev 7:9-12	290
Rev 19:6-9	272

APPENDIX G
BIBLIOGRAPHY

Albert Barnes, *Notes on the Bible* (e-sword.net)

David Benner, *Desiring God's Will* (IVP 2015)

Brené Brown, *The Gifts of Imperfection* (Hazelden 2010)

Oswald Chambers, *My Upmost For His Highest*, Introduction by James Reimann (Discovery House 1992)

Marva Dawn, *Powers, Weakness, and the Tabernacling of God* (Eerdmans 2001)

Richard J. Foster, *Celebration of Discipline*, (Harper One 1998).

Francis Frangipane, *Spiritual Discernment and the Mind of Christ* (Arrow 2013)

Jamin Goggin and Kyie Strobel, *The Way of the Dragon or the Way of the Lamb* (HarperCollins 2017)

St. Ignatius, *The Spiritual Exercises of St. Ignatius* (Translated by Louis J. Puhl, S.J. 1951)

Haley Goranson Jacob, *Conformed to the Image of His Son* (IVP 2018)

Philip D. Jamieson, *The Face of Forgiveness* (IVP 2016)

Robert Jamieson, A. R. Fausset, and David Brown, *A Commentary on the Old and New Testaments* (e-sword.net)

St. John of the Cross, *The Ascent of Mount Carmel* (From *The Collected Works of St. John of the Cross*, Kavanaugh and Rodriguez (ICS Publications 1991))

St. John of the Cross, *The Dark Night* (From *The Collected Works of St. John of the Cross*, Kavanaugh and Rodriguez (ICS Publications 1991))

St. John of the Cross, *The Sayings of Light and Love* (From *The Collected Works of St. John of the Cross*, Kavanaugh and Rodriguez (ICS Publications 1991))

St. John of the Cross, *The Spiritual Canticle* (From *The Collected Works of St. John of the Cross*, Kavanaugh and Rodriguez (ICS Publications 1991))

Keil & Delitzsch, *Commentary on the Old Testament* (Hendrickson 1989)

Pope John Paul II, *Salvifici Doloris (On the Christian Meaning of Human Suffering)* (1984)

Thomas a Kempis, *The Imitation of Christ* (Moody 1958)

Brother Lawrence, *The Practice of the Presence of God* (Translated by Marshall Davis 2013)

C. S. Lewis, *Screwtape Letters: The Annotated Edition* (HarperOne 2013)

Elizabeth Liebert, *The Way of Discernment: Spiritual Practices for Decision Making* (WJK 2008)

Scot McKnight, *The Jesus Creed* (Paraclete Press 2009)

Eric Metaxas, *Bonhoeffer* (Thomas Nelson 2010)

Nik Ripken, *The Insanity of God* (B&H 2013)

Corrie Ten Boom and Elizabeth and John Sherrill, *The Hiding Place* (Chosen 2006)

Mother Teresa, *Total Surrender* (Servant 1985)

Curt Thompson, MD, The Soul of Shame (IVP 2015)

David Thurman, *Dod Knows* (KDP 2006)

David Thurman, *The Call: Book One – Functional (Keys to Effective Discipleship)* (KDP 2007)

David Thurman, *The Call: Book Two – Foundational (Progressive Fivefold Function)* (KDP 2009)

David Thurman, *The Call: Book Three – Fruitful (Transforming Your Community)* (KDP 2017)

A. W. Tozer, *The Knowledge of the Holy* (Harper One 1961)

A. W. Tozer, *Prayer: Communing with God in Everything* (Moody 2016) (Compiled by W.L. Seaver)

A. W. Tozer, *The Pursuit of God* (N/P 1948)

Merrill F. Unger, *Unger's Bible Dictionary* (Moody Press 1978)

Brian Zahnd, *Unconditional? The Call of Jesus to Radical Forgiveness* (Charisma House 2010)

ACKNOWLEDGEMENTS

Pastor Daniel Martin is my uncle but he is also my friend and brother. The impact of His walk with the Lord on me and on many other people is huge.

I have a friend and accountability partner who was intentional to visit with me consistently during my extended illness and to minister to me. His help and input in *Surrender and Trust* have been invaluable.

The de facto editor of *Surrender and Trust* is a person to whom I feel so close that I love her like a sister.

Many extended family members have influenced my life significantly. One has provided spiritual direction to me humbly, gently, and hospitably.

I see my closest friend almost every day. His insights have been crucial, and he sacrificially facilitated time for me to work on *Surrender and Trust*.

Another friend served as proofreader for *Surrender and Trust*. Thank you for finding my many mistakes!

I have been privileged to work together in ministry and in vocation with wonderful and godly men and women for many years. Thank you for such rich experiences in ministry together that have refined and shaped me!

E-sword is a Bible research tool that I used for many years (*www.e-sword.net*).

I have a coworker in the Residency ministry training program who is a brilliant person. Thank you for enhancing the vision for training in ministry.

I am grateful for a friend whose strong prophetic gift has impacted my life and my understanding.

I have met in Bible study with a group of younger men for over 15 years. Thank you for sharing such rich times and such rich meals together!

My accountability partners speak into my life regularly. I appreciate the time you each have invested in me and the love shown to me.

A ministry coworker exemplifies walking in love without attachments to the world. Thank you for that example.

Many saints wiser and more devout than I are quoted in *Surrender and Trust*. We all have persons that have gone before us. I have many people that have poured into my life at different ages and seasons.

I love my family dearly.

My wife, Mary Beth, is a part of everything that I do. This book does not exist without her.

TO GOD ALONE BE GLORY, HONOR, AND PRAISE!

OTHER BOOKS BY THE AUTHOR
(Available on Amazon.com and other online booksellers)

THE CALL series will help you identify God's call in your life and equip you to fulfill that call. God calls His people to live under His kingship and to participate in His work. God's call is His imprint on you and on your life. You need to understand God's special purpose for your life.

Formatted as work books for use in ministry training programs, THE CALL series is written in a progression. This first book, *THE CALL (Book One – Functional)*, describes a discipleship progression designed for maximum impact. In Book One, you will learn how to:
- ✓ Create a model for exponential spiritual reproduction
- ✓ Operate ministry with lasting results
- ✓ Share truth in a manner that hits home
- ✓ Equip others for ministry through shared experience
- ✓ Help other disciples realize and fulfill their call

Endorsements of THE CALL series:

"THE CALL series is steeped in powerful Biblical truth, profound insights derived from decades of personal ministry experiences, and is directly applicable in your personal life and ministry environments. David's brilliant mind, heart for making disciples, and intimacy with God are earthed in these pages. We at Missionary Athletes International have utilized this great work for years as a cornerstone for our curriculum in our one-year Residency Training Program. THE CALL is essential to our success and will catalyze yours as well."
DAVID SANFORD
US Director, Missionary Athletes International

"THE CALL books have been very influential for myself and our staff with I AM 24/7. After personally going through David's books a number of years back, I remember having the thought that if I ever was responsible for leading a church or ministry that I would use them as a part of training staff and include the revelatory teachings on the "Cycle of Discipleship" as part of our core values for training up Godly leaders. When my wife and I co-founded an urban ministry in Charlotte, NC, David was one of my first calls. We took our young staff through the books and David met with them weekly during a summer Residency program during our first 2 years of operation. THE CALL books and his teachings helped solidify a solid foundation of Biblical understanding on effective discipleship ministry, operating under authority, understanding spiritual gifts, and defining individual call for each of the young men in our program. Ephesians 4:12 declares the duty of the church is to "equip the saints for works of ministry." In light of the lack of equipping of disciples of Christ in the American church today, I pray that the Lord would continue to use THE CALL books as a voice in the desert, calling the body of Christ to a new level of power and influence one disciple at a time. I am forever grateful for my good friend, David Thurman, and his humble devotion to his own call and the role his example and legacy left in the pages of these books has played in my personal walk with the Lord and the ministry I serve."
BEN PAGE
President and Co-founder, I AM 24/7 Ministries

"THE CALL series provides experience-based practices and Christ-centered teaching to equip the urban missionary who seeks to advance the Kingdom of God in their unique setting. I have personally partnered with the author, David Thurman, in applying this material while working within the refugee community of Charlotte, NC. It is effective and life-changing."
STEVE PARKER
President and Founder, FOCHUS Ministries

OTHER BOOKS BY THE AUTHOR
(Available on Amazon.com and other online booksellers)

THE CALL series is written in a progression. The first book, *THE CALL (Book One – Functional)*, described important discipleship principles. This second book, *THE CALL (Book Two – Foundational)*, shows how the fivefold gifts operate in a progression to train, equip and mature the Body of Christ. In Book Two, you will learn how to:
- ✓ Apply key principles of God's authority to your life and ministry
- ✓ Identify God's call on your life
- ✓ Function in the context of the fivefold gifts in the way that God intended
- ✓ Discern and replicate the Cycle of Discipleship to maturity
- ✓ Operate effectively in a body context to maximize the potential of its members

OTHER BOOKS BY THE AUTHOR
(Available on Amazon.com and other online booksellers)

THE CALL series is written to train workers in the kingdom. The second book, *THE CALL (Book Two – Foundational)*, showed how the fivefold gifts operate within the Cycle of Discipleship to train, equip and mature the Body of Christ. This third book, *THE CALL (Book Three – Fruitful)*, explores God's call in a corporate context. In Book Three, you will learn how to:
- ✓ Discern the heart of God for the world around you
- ✓ Survey your community for needs and resources
- ✓ Change the culture of the people around you
- ✓ Cast a vision to your church or ministry for transformational action
- ✓ Implement a plan to bring the kingdom of God to your area

OTHER BOOKS BY THE AUTHOR

(Available on Amazon.com and other online booksellers)

DOD KNOWS chronicles the story of Jimmy Stuckey, an undisciplined five year old boy with Down's Syndrome, who was taken into the Martin home because no one else wanted him. What started as temporary foster care for a few days turned into fifty years of fun, laughter, and unpredictability.

DOD KNOWS details the trials and challenges of raising a strong willed but tenderhearted Down's Syndrome child in a large family, and the joys and misadventures of a fun-seeking and oh so competitive young man. Jimmy was raised as the author's uncle and as the brother of Pastor Daniel Martin. What the family did not realize is the huge impact and the marvelous blessing that Jimmy would bring to the Martin family and to every other person that came into contact with him!

"DOD KNOWS" was one of Jimmy's many sayings. When something happened that Jimmy did not understand or that confused him, Jimmy simply held up his hands, shrugged his shoulders, and said "Dod knows" (God knows). And, as in many things, Jimmy was right!

For more information on these books, go to: **www.surrenderandtrust.net** (Note: .net).

www.ingramcontent.com/pod-product-compliance
Lightning Source LLC
Chambersburg PA
CBHW060454090426
42735CB00011B/1978